# A Flick,
## of the
# Tale

# Aknowledgements

Way back in the 1600's some smart arse poet sat down, licked his quill, and penned those immortal words

'No man is an Island' and never have truer words been written.

I, for one, certainly do not thrive on isolation and I need the people around me that I count as real friends.

As an angler I love solitude but, as a human being, I am gregarious and crave the company of like minded souls.

I look at my personal life as if it were a bank, you make deposits freely, and you can withdraw favours as and when you wish, safe in the knowledge that nobody is keeping an eye on the balance.

Only true friends let you slide unnoticed into the red, and only true friends will go unnoticed if they themselves overdraw.

It is these lousy bankers that I now wish to thank for helping me make this book a reality, for turning a dream found only in the late night, smoke filled bars and cobwebs of my sometimes addled mind, into the tangible and tactile piece of reality that now lays open before you, begging to be indulged.

So thank you all.

Thank you to Keith for being, as ever, at the top of the list, god knows how much I owe his bank but I know I'll never receive a snotty letter or have my card cancelled. Apart from being my best mate and confidant, he has suffered my interminable questions throughout the writing of both of my books, he is my portable memory, my phone a friend, the guy who fills in all the gaps, weights, dates, names and, of course, punctuation without a single complaint.

For the others found within the pages, without whom these stories would pale into insignificance and become chapters of fact, without humour, character or life. These people are many and each and every one has their own story to tell and I hope, I really do, that I have played as big a part in their stories as they have in mine, and left memories even half as vivid.

Nobody with an ounce of soul can spend time with people like Reg Bampton, Chrissy Pearson, Mr F, Jacko, Chilly, Clive, and the host of other colourful eccentrics I have met along the way, without being effected by their combined madness. It really has been a white knuckle ride!

My Mum, of course, not only for launching me into this mad world but for her literary critique and reality check, I haven't seen so much red pen on a sheet of paper since I was at school!

And, more recently, in the actual formulation of these pages I have needed help, not only in the actual written word but also in the mind, and much more importantly in the belly!

Living now in the wilds of Suffolk my life has changed dramatically and so have the people involved in it. Just when you think you have everything planned and mapped out before you, just when you think the cogs are oiled and the wheels of your world are turning in unison, fate, or destiny, throws a bloody great oily spanner in the works.

Luckily for me there have been people there to help sort out the various bits and pieces for me, people into whose accounts I have made precious little in the way of previous deposits but who care not, either way.

Foremost of these, I would like to doff my cap to Lindsey and Jenny who have befriended, fed, watered and occasionally poisoned me, but always welcomed me into their home, never once mentioning the fact that I always turn up exactly ten minutes before dinner time!

More recently they have both helped with the proofing of this book and poor Jenny actually worked on corrections for two days with conjunctivitis, and as she put it, until her eyes bled!

Even more recently I would like to thank Dee, who has stepped in at the eleventh hour and made sense of many things.

Not only has she supplied a constant flow of bacon sandwiches and tea but she has read the entire book, re-laid chapters, proofed and corrected page after page, and even chauffeured me to and from the publishers when I broke my foot on the sofa while pacing up and down the lounge searching for inspiration.

To all the above I am truly grateful and in your debt, so I'll see you all at the bar!

---

*I dedicate this book to two very special people who grow even more so with the passing of each day.*

*My wonderful children, Amy and Conor.*
*Thank you both for making my life complete.*

# Contents

# *Foreword*

I find it somewhat comforting how the Wheel of Fortune can spin and, eventually, everyone gets the good, and bad, spin of the wheel.

For so many years I had to endure Laney calling me at work, whilst he was at the lake, telling me of yet another carp in the bottom of his landing net. The big, wide world of 'work' seemed to be a mythical place to him; one that he rarely, if ever, visited, and then it was only a fleeting visit in order to fund his next fishing expedition.

Much as I knew he wasn't a 'Time Bandit', and that his frequent successes came, ironically, from hard work, I still envied him his time at the lake, and would have loved just a little of that flexibility.

But then, suddenly, along came a family, and his infrequent visits to the land of work had to become much more frequent in order support the extra mouths and the roof they lived under.

Oh, how I laughed!

He would now call me from somewhere that wasn't a lake and bemoan his great misfortune, as 'they must be down the far end in this wind!' My mirth was rarely very well concealed and soon he, like Chilly, gave up trying to wring any sympathy from me.

Then, irony upon irony, he got employed by JRC as a full time consultant/designer; a job in fishing, what could be better? Well, quite a lot if you needed some free time to go fishing because, after all these years, he had at last joined the ranks of the nine to fivers, and his fishing time was condensed down to the same as the majority of us had had to suffer over all these years – two days a week.

Now we were on a level playing field, I thought, but I'd forgotten one rather important fact – he's Dave Lane!

What is remarkable about the exploits detailed in this book is that they weren't achieved by a full time/anytime angler who simply had to wait until his target fish waddled past and slurped up his hookbait. No, this is a book about a guy like you and me, with the same constraints on his angling time as any of us with a family to support and a mortgage to pay every month. But that's the only way we are similar because, when it comes to determination and will power in the pursuit of his goal, Dave is far from your everyday bloke. Just look at how he caught Two–Tone; I certainly wouldn't have been up in the middle of the night to see it jump a hundred yards out, nor would the majority of anglers.

He and I don't get to fish together much nowadays, what with him disappearing to the wilds of Suffolk, but then that makes me feel a little better about my own fishing because, when Laney's around, you tend to realise how stationary you are!

There are many very good anglers around, anglers who can catch a fish out of a flooded washing-up bowl, but the difference is that Dave catches monsters – from anywhere.

And now he does it whilst holding down a full-time job – bugger!

This is a very good book (I should know, I proofed the bloody thing), but don't be intimidated by what you read in here, take inspiration from it, because it shows that hard work is rewarded in any walk of life, and the rewards, in carp fishing terms, are simply mind blowing.

I'm off to have a little doze, now. That's one thing I can get away with now that I'm not fishing with Laney so much.

Oh, and my liver is gradually recovering, too!

Keith Jenkins

# Copyright

ISBN NUMBER 978-0-956093-5-0

Further copies are available from:
www.calmproductions.com
or on:
0845 408 2606
or at
Calm Productions
89 Warren Road
Orpington
Kent BR6 6JE

Published by,

Unit 4, Ashton Gate, Harold Hill, Romford, RM3 8UF

# Chapter 1

# Blood Sweat and Guinness

"*The smoke lay suspended like a low-presure rain cloud, five feet from the floor of the public bar of the Perseverance pub in Wraysbury village. Although only late afternoon, the colourful array of 'good old boys' from the local houses*

*were already propping up the bar and trying to out-lie each other, as they had been doing for years*".

The floorboards were permanently sticky from the spilt beer of ages and, on a normal day, sat in the dark corner by the fire, I would have gone totally unnoticed.

Today, however, I warranted a few furtive glances, even from the usually self-obsessed 'fat bloke' on his own stool at the bar, a glance in the mirror behind the bar as I had been served had shown a sorry looking reflection.

As I sat there I was aware of another warm trickle of blood leaking from a gash on my forehead, working its way down my cheek. I wiped it away with a torn sleeve and took another sip of my Guinness.

I had spent the last ten minutes trying to extract a particularly stubborn splinter from the back of my hand.

It held fast, imbedded between the criss-cross lines of crimson rips that had been inflicted by the inhospitable bramble and dog rose bushes in which I had, so recently, been entwined.

My clothes were shredded and bits of nettle leaf and various dead bugs were still stuck to the sweat at the back of my neck.

My hands and face buzzed with a thousand small welts inflicted by a veritable sea of stinging nettles but my mind burned with a new and bright light, for I had just walked, limped, and crawled my first circuit of the 'Secret Mere'.

From finishing my time at the famous Wraysbury Lake, where I was fortunate enough to catch 'Mary' the equally famous 50lb carp, I had been searching for a new quest.

Lakes that offered the level of freedom, and that magical sense of the great and wild outdoors that I had become accustomed to over the previous three years, were few and far between.

Wraysbury had ignited a spark within my soul that burned brightly now, with a hunger for something more than just another 'big carp'.

The whole situation at Wraysbury had enthralled me, not only the actual fish but also the lifestyle that went with it. It's not so much the fish themselves but the catching of them that makes the story complete.

Things like floating around in a boat with a glass-bottomed bucket, exploring the depths in intricate detail.

Witnessing wild nature at close quarters and becoming one with your surroundings.

The lack of other anglers and, especially, the lack of bailiffs!

The overriding feeling that we were, to some extent, pioneering, and the mystery of fishing for the unknown.

Although some of the fish that lived within the waters of Wraysbury had been extremely well known, there were an equal amount of carp that seldom, if ever, graced the banks and, having been fortunate enough to capture one or two of these myself, I was hungering for more of the same.

The Secret Mere was a similar proposition in as much as it had one very large carp in there, that I knew definitely existed, and a few otherlesser known leviathans, swimming around in its mysterious depths.

There had always been talk of a massive common that had been happily avoiding capture for years, but then there always is isn't there?

Whatever the stock really comprised of, the main thing, as far as I was concerned, was that nobody knew for sure and equally importantly, hardly anybody ever fished for them.

The 'Mere' is only 40 acres in size and a very basic 'tapering rectangular' shape but it still takes about 2 hours of sheer jungle warfare tactics to get even once around its perimeter. The first bank, being a public footpath, is comparatively easy but only when compared, that is, to the back bank. Five hundred yards of solid bramble and dog rose bushes that reach out and hold hands across the path, becoming so entwined together they form an almost impenetrable barrier to all but the smallest of creatures.

Every step I took on that first fateful visit was met with grabbing, tearing and ripping from the brutal surroundings, but I was determined to make it right around the lake.

The back bank was sealed to such a degree that the last 200 yards were passable only by laying flat on my face and shuffling along on my elbows.

A one-foot high tunnel that, in bygone days, constituted the path was the only access left and even my passage along this 'crawl space' had to be punctuated every few yards by double-jointed contortionism to free my hair from the relentless clawing of thorn and bramble.

After eventually reaching the end of the back bank, or 'suicide alley' as I soon named it, I reached a small clearing in the south west corner of the lake.

The next wall of undergrowth lay a few yards ahead, beckoning me, daring me to take up its challenge, but I needed a rest first.

If I climbed down the bank I could see part of the lake from here, which was novel as I hadn't seen water for an age, either to fish in or to drink.

I'd been warned by my good friend Phil Thompson, who'd fished here in the past, never to drink the 'Mere' water no matter how thirsty you are, so I settled for stripping down to my pants and splashing it all over me in an attempt to cool down.

The humidity within the confines of the bushes had to be felt to be believed and I was soaked in sweat which, unfortunately for me, only served as an attractor for the formidable army of mosquitoes and gnats that existed in that 'near tropical' environment.

Fresh warm blood was a rare commodity within the 'Mere' insect kingdom and, with the sudden arrival of a ready supply, they wasted no time collecting as much as they could carry.

Standing there, half naked, in the margins I was a target that they just couldn't miss so I hurriedly struggled into my freshly tattered and torn kit, whilst swatting maniacally at anything within range.

Once dressed, I set off along the 'path' once more, shuffling on my belly and pushing my small pack before me. I had set out with a 'stalking bag' containing a few bits of tackle; a bag of crisps, one very inadequate bottle of fizzy drink and a cheese roll. A rod, reel and net had all been crammed in a padded rod sleeve but, to be honest, its main purpose up until now had been as a stinging nettle beater!

Fifty yards further along the way I came to another, smaller, clearing that was situated right in the middle of the bottom bank and, as such, it gave me an unexpected view of about ninety percent of the pit.

I sat on the bank with my feet dangling over the edge and laid out my pathetic picnic on my lap. I'd hardly taken two bites from the dried up cheese roll before a large golden Common carp leapt skywards from the rippled surface of the lake in front of me. He was only thirty or forty yards out from where I sat and I saw every scale as he caught the sunlight along his flanks.

The roll was instantly forgotten as I scrambled around, desperately trying to put together the rod and net as quickly as possible.

Already baited with a couple of dried up tiger nuts and a bit of cork from a previous session elsewhere, the rig sailed out to land in the vicinity of the showing fish and suddenly the whole scene took on a totally different perspective.

Sitting there on the grass, picking splinters out of my hands and arms, bitten, stung, and parched with thirst, I couldn't help but feel incredibly confident.

It had only started out as a brief reconnaissance mission but already I was hooked. I loved the place; wild, inhospitable and overgrown and oh so definitely the place for me!

I sat there in hope for an hour or so but I knew there was no rush to catch one of these special fish, I would be back, and next time I'd be better equipped for it, with thick gardening gloves for a start.

Eventually I gave in to the allure of the pub and wound in from the weedy depths, suitably encouraged by my first sighting, but definitely in need of some stronger clothes.

It wasn't until I caught sight of myself in that pub mirror that I realised how badly I'd suffered. I looked like Wurzle Gummidge on a Monday when all his good clothes are in the wash, I even had various leaves and twigs poking out at all angles, no wonder I was drawing so many strange looks.

Luckily though, I had still been served and I sat in my little corner with my Guinness, replaying the 'jumping fish scene' in my head, ignoring the furtive glances. After all, if I had stood up and explained myself would I have appeared any the saner for it?

# Chapter 2

# The Voyage of Discovery

"*I couldn't wait to get back down to the Mere for a crack at those elusive beasts. I'd phoned Phil and punished him for hours until he'd imparted every bit of information he knew*  *about the place, after all, he had actually caught one from there years earlier*".

Nothing I could do, however, would persuade him to join me in my new quest; he said he'd rather give up fishing than go back there.

He assured me that I'd understand after a while and, to be honest, just that first walk around had left me in no doubt about the severity of the place.

I'd decided to start by making a few short stalking trips and, each visit, I would leave as much spare and well camouflaged tackle hidden away as I could.

The plan was to kit out the bushes with everything that I'd need for the season, that way I wouldn't have to keep dragging it all on and off the lake.

Back in Phil's day, fishing the lake had been allowed through Amy Road Stone angling but since then the lake had been left to go wild, officially a no fishing area but, due to the wild nature of the place, it was viewed more as a case of who dares wins!

It was never going to be left totally alone, as it was home to one of the most impressive carp in the country, only ever captured once in its life, the highly desirable Black Mirror!

The Black Mirror had become the ultimate prize and, if legend was correct, there were other jewels in the Mere's crown that shone almost as brightly.

There was a linear mirror of around forty pounds and the long, mid-thirty pound, mirror that Phil had captured a few years previously. Not to mention the mythical big common that no lake would be complete without, and the documented handful of ex-Redmire commons that had been caught by the lucky few.

I knew that it would be hard going, probably my biggest challenge yet, but I was more than ready for it.

I wouldn't be totally alone as I knew that Terry, after his capture of Mary from Wraysbury, had already moved onto the Mere, eager to add this prize to his growing tally.

Also, I knew of three other anglers who would be testing their mettle on the harshness of the Colne Valley's finest battleground that season, so it wasn't just the fish I would be up against.

My first trip down coincided with a burst of warm weather and, therefore, it was no real surprise to find a couple of fish cruising just under the surface in a secluded corner near a lush reed bed.

Terry was already perched up the tree watching, and he assured me that the carp had shown a total disdain for any kind of floating baits, but I couldn't help but think that they looked right up for it.

There were about five fish there in all; four commons and a short dumpy mirror playing follow the leader around the area in front of the reeds. The aspect of the fish as they circled around, and the way their mouths moved as they rose nearer the surface, convinced me they were 'tasting' the water, looking for anything of interest.

As it happened I had just the thing they wanted sitting in my small shoulder bag only a few yards away.

First I had to persuade Sam, my faithful carp dog, to give up her non-stop vigil of praying to the smell of chum mixers emanating from the tackle bag.

Once I'd prised her nose out of the way I sent a single catapult pouch full of the dog biscuits to settle lightly just upwind of the fish. The breeze was perfect, the line of approach dead on and the result totally predictable.

As soon as the first mixer rippled into the zone it was taken, followed quickly by the next one. As we watched, the line of carp almost queued up to take their turn, all except the mirror and he seemed a bit more wary.

I managed to just watch for all of about two minutes; Terry didn't seem in any hurry to have a go for some reason, which was strange seeing as how he had yet to catch a carp from the Mere.

Alan, who was down there chatting to Terry, had no tackle anyway so it looked like it was down to me then, so be it!

I had a rod propped up behind the bushes and in double quick time it was set up with a small controller and a single chum mixer. The next batch of bait was systematically being destroyed and the slurps and gulps of the feeding carp did little to calm my nerves as I lined up for that all-important first cast.

Terry had suddenly decided he was missing out and he'd scurried off up the bank to retrieve a rod from its hidey hole but I knew he'd be too late, it was straight away or not at all in these situations.

The cast landed perfectly on the back of the group and the breeze brought it slowly back into the zone. Alan was up the tree commentating in a whisper but I wasn't listening, I could see it all unfolding clearly from the elevated bank where I stood.

The group had sunk slightly for another circuit and as they came up, nose to tail, the little dog biscuit hookbait was reflected in the eyes of the lead fish.

Unbelievably, he shied away at the last moment, next up was the mirror and he did the same, as did the following two commons, but the last fish had no such reservations. With a fixed focus and perfect accuracy he slid straight up under the bait and I saw his lips part as the mixer winked out of sight with an audible plop.

At first he didn't seem to understand what was happening, as I swept the rod up and set the hook, but he soon cottoned on, surging out of the corner towards open water, he wasn't a happy carp.

As far as we knew there hadn't been a carp caught from the Mere for at least a couple of years and this knowledge sat on my shoulders like a boulder while I tried to coax the fish back towards the margins.

Playing a fish on light floater fishing hooklinks is always tense and this was no exception but, thankfully, everything held firm and he was soon wallowing in front of the reeds. It was only now I realised that I was a good eight feet above him with no gaps in the reeds to actually land him through. I slid straight down the bank into the back of the reeds while Terry took the net and made a small slot to poke the net through.

With Alans help on the high bank behind, the three of us manhandled the fish up and around to a small clearing by the waters edge in the corner of the lake, where we all gazed in wonder at our first Mere capture.

At twenty-two pounds it was almost definitely the smallest of the group but it was just the tonic that I needed, the Mere's spell was broken and they were all just carp again and I couldn't wait to get amongst them!

If I'd thought that my capture of that twenty-two pound common had somehow cracked the code that held the secrets of the Mere safe, then boy was I in for a shock.

I was soon to find out that the Mere was like no other water I had ever, ever fished. Not just the undergrowth, or overgrowth, and not only the surreptitious and clandestine nature of the fishing itself, always hiding and looking for spies. Of course, all of this would have been enough to make it a veritable nightmare but the fish themselves took it to a different level altogether.

My early success with a floater rod was just the golden hook by which I was snared; the reality of the place could now pour down upon me, safe in the knowledge that I was too deeply hooked to get away.

It was, however, a complete voyage of discovery and every trip opened a new Pandora's Box of secrets, possibilities, problems and solutions.

During one of these early trips I was secreted away on a small point on the East bank, watching the odd fish drift up towards the middle of lake, when I heard a ringing noise.

Being a newcomer to the wonders of modern mobile phone technology it took a while for me to realise that it was my rucksack that was ringing!

After rummaging through the various bits and bobs to find it, I answered the call from Keith. I could tell straight away, from the tone in his voice, that something was wrong.

"Bad news from Horton mate, Jack and a couple of others have been found dead, they floated up this morning apparently"

I couldn't believe my ears, or didn't want to, more likely, I didn't want to face the reality that those wonderful old warriors had slipped away, and

*Keith with one of Hortons finest*

the fact that there was more than one fatality meant that there would almost certainly be others to follow!

The phone was red hot over the next few hours and the general consensus among the lads seemed to be that the fish may have picked up an infection from a batch of stock fish that had 'inadvertently' escaped into the lake two weeks previously!

How the hell fish can just escape into a lake like Horton I couldn't imagine but apparently a batch of stock fish, that had been in a tank in the fish house for at least a year that I could remember, had been put into a holding net in the corner of Horton Church lake for some sort of holiday or something!

Needless to say, but the holding net failed its only task in life and the fish all escaped into the lake.

Nobody knew for sure if this was the cause of the deaths but the effect was worsening by the day.

The losses over the next few weeks were catastrophic and some of the finest carp in the land perished in the waters of Horton that fateful spring. Sixteen of the best we will ever see, all gone.

The final and official prognosis was that a rare gill disease had

*Heart Tail, gone but not forgotton*

mysteriously appeared and wiped them out but I have yet to find anyone who actually believes this theory, there were a couple of strange stocking decisions around this time as well as the 'escapees' and these sort of disasters are almost always associated with introductions of new fish.

Whatever label the disease finally had stuck on it, it still carried the same death sentence! Of the big old A-team members of Horton only two survived, The Parrot lived on and by some freak of luck my old favourite carp, Shoulders, managed to elude death with the same ease that he had eluded me with for so long, back in the 'good old days'.

It was hard to stay motivated for a while after such a tragedy, but my heart really went out to the friends I had who were still fishing the lake at the time.

Obviously, you cannot devote your entire fishing life to tracking down these wonderful old beasts and not be profoundly affected by their passing, but what do you do when your entire fishing plans for the foreseeable future are suddenly taken away from you as well?

There were anglers wandering around the 'Colne valley' in a trance, half looking for somewhere new to fish but not really interested in finding anything at all!

Some have never really got to grips with anything since and still mourn the loss of 'the good old days' and the incredible sights that we used to witness over at Horton in its prime.

I have a video at home, one that Keith and I put together during our time on the lake, and it's heartbreaking now, to see all those wonderful old carp on film again and know that they no longer cruise through the crystal waters or leap skywards for the sheer hell of the feeling.

Sad times indeed!

The Mere, however, was on fine form and the water quality was outstanding, at least before the algae started to raise it head it was, anyway.

I had seen a few fish up close and they all looked fantastic but my first proper look at the Black Mirror came a few weeks into the season and occurred in the mouth of a small bay formed by the reedy point on the East Bank. I called this area the South Westerly, purely because that is the direction of the wind that pushes into there.

I was hanging out of a small spindly looking tree at the waters edge. Like a lot of the trees around the margins it was a willow and, as such, ready to drop its branches, and me, straight into the lake at the slightest provocation.

As I peered down through the rippled surface I saw a fish drift in from my right and I froze, stock still, desperately trying to make myself turn into a branch so as not to spook this long, dark fish away before I'd had a good look at him.

As he pulled up level with my gaze he slowed and circled around, showing me two different elevations. Then, as if on a fashion catwalk, he pirouetted some more, turning first one way and then another until I'd seen every part of his near perfect form.

Extremely dark across the back and chestnut red on his flanks, he sat there with the sunlight reflecting from a row of four mirror scales along his lateral line near the tail. The tail itself had a flattened top lobe, and it was this anomaly that acted like a flag confirming that I was looking at the most desirable carp in the land.

One capture was the only black mark in this carps copy book, one single slip up in all those years of growing to such a colossal size, a very impressive record indeed and now, there he was sitting only a few feet away from me.

If I'd known then just how much effort it would take to narrow that gap, to cross the final few feet, then maybe things would have panned out differently or, then again, maybe not as I've always liked a bit of a challenge!

That first year on the lake was such an exciting time and I spent a lot of it digging out little secluded swims in the bushes, camouflaging up all my tackle and generally reliving my childhood again.

We were like big kids playing war over the woods, only this time there were real adversaries. On one side we had the carp; old, wily and cunning, and on the other side the bailiffs and the self appointed guardians of the Mere. The official bailiff at that time was actually a really nice bloke and he didn't seem to mind us being there at all. Even with all the camouflage and subterfuge everybody got seen at one time or another but he'd often turn his head and just walk off, as if he hadn't noticed a bush just stand up and take a leak up against another bush!

He knew full well that we were not there to cause any grief or damage to anything or anybody, just a handful of carp obsessed lads keeping ourselves to ourselves.

There were, however, two other people to contend with, both of which thought they had reason to protect the Mere from our presence.

Strange things would occur and nobody was ever seen to be doing them, hidden swims were suddenly thrown open, paths were mysteriously hacked through the thick undergrowth at night. The odd bits of tackle that were hidden deep in the bushes would disappear without trace.

The swims we had made at the lake were totally hidden from view, there were no paths in or out, no bushes were chopped away for access and everything was done to keep the appearance of the lake the same and unaltered.

As far as fishermen were concerned, we were probably the most unobtrusive and inconspicuous group of lads ever to wield rods.

Most of our movements were by boat or via a treacherous method of wading along the deep margins, under the overhanging brambles and nettles until we reached our secreted little swims. It would appear, however, that we were being watched.

Behind the swims, on the main paths or on little points where anglers could have reached, had they wished, piles of dog poo kept appearing.

It was quite all right for a dog walker to let this happen I suppose, inconsiderate, but hardly our concern. The bizarre thing, though, was the pink toilet roll that nestled on top of each pile.

It was blatantly not what it was made to look like, no angler would dream of it and, unless the dogs in that area were particularly hygienic and also incredibly dexterous, then it was an obvious ploy to attract the wrong sort of attention to our being there.

Many other strange little eccentricities occurred and all without trace or reason, at times it was all like a bizarre game of chess.

One day, on a small point at the narrow end of the lake, a pile of chalky dog poo appeared in the middle of the swim, the strange thing was that there was enough for a weeks supply, no matter how big the dog. Are there really people in existence who would be sad enough to save it all up and put it there as a deterrent?

It did help us name the swim though, and forever afterwards it was called 'Turds Point'.

One of the main suspects was an angler who we knew had fished there for some years and we suspected he begrudged our being there, on 'his' territory.

The other was a local dog walker, who I remembered from my days at Wraysbury, he was a renowned 'busy-body' and infamous for causing trouble with fisherman whenever he could.

The angler, who we used to call Tom, was one of the original anglers at the Mere and he had been fishing there at the same time as Phil, in fact I knew him fairly well from Horton and, although secretive, deceptive and cunning (all good traits for a carp angler) he truly loved the place.

Therefore, I don't think that half of the things he was blamed for, at the time, were actually anything to do with him at all.

He was an angler and a conservationist and I don't think stunts like this were really his cup of tea at all. I truly believe that he just loved the place so much that he came, in time, to covet it to the extent of believing it was somehow his own private place. I can understand this totally, as I found myself always putting others off and treating with suspicion anybody I hadn't seen there before.

Any person who spent any amount of time around the Mere would either grow to love the place or end up hating it.

This is the nature of the lake itself, it's unlike any other place I've ever been to, before or since.

It has its own unique atmosphere that hangs in the air, practically tangible, it gives a strange feeling that the place is alive somehow; that the sheer density of the plant-life has banded together as a single, living entity that watches your every move.

In a strange way, and despite everything that it throws in your path, you can't help but respect the place for defending itself so diligently.

Maybe some people who read this may think 'wow, this bloke's really lost the plot' and it's just a lake but, believe me, anybody who has fished there for any length of time will instantly know what I mean.

The other guardian of the mere, the bane of our lives, was definitely not an angler at all and I got the impression he had some of hatred of all anglers no matter where they fished.

He was infamous for minding everybody's business but his own and, I may be wrong, but I personally believe that most of the bizarre occurrences that happened over the years, especially those that put anglers in a poor light, came from his direction.

Over the course of our time at the Mere others also became convinced of this fact, so at least we knew who to look out for.

Even though I was trying to keep a low profile, the weed was necessitating more and more use of the little carp boat that we kept stashed in the bushes. It was a small 'sportyak' that Terry had originally brought over and the two of us has painted it up with some army paint I found in my shed, so it blended into the undergrowth; apparently the paint was even radar proof, so we were covered from all angles.

Each day that I fished I would take to the water at some stage, either to check spots using a glass-bottomed bucket or to drop baits, especially as most swims were too enclosed to actually cast out from. What I used to see on the bottom, on the days when water clarity would allow, was never that encouraging.

Clear areas were few and far between and the bait that Terry and I had introduced was often still lying there weeks afterwards, totally untouched and rotten.

It seemed as if the fish did not need or require any supplement to their natural food source whatsoever, nothing seemed to interest them at all.

Most days I would end up 'on the fish' and I'd think nothing of packing all the gear up into the boat and relocating as many times a day as it took to stay in contact with them. I had two or three main encampments that I had made, with the intention of baiting and fishing them almost exclusively, but the uneaten bait and the nomadic nature of the fish did not really give me any confidence in that style of fishing.

The problem I had was actually setting up on the fish, but keeping a low profile as far as everything else was concerned, One of the camps I'd made was pure genius and it actually sat right next to the main path along side the lake, this is the route that anyone mad enough to walk around the lake in the first place would have to take.

I'd found a bed of Bulrushes on the waters edge that had a tangled mass of fallen tree and brambles growing from the path right up to the rushes. The old stump of the tree had uprooted to the left of the rushes and formed a perfect wall for one side of the swim and the rushes bent round to the right hand side, concealing me from view. Unfortunately, the back of the swim which butted up to the path was a bit thin, as the brambles had strangled all the greenery, and only thistle, thorn and dead branches remained. But I quickly bolstered this up with a camo net and as much

*The Long Run*

loose green stuff and old branches that I could find in the wilderness section that lay up against the railway line a short distance away.

The rail workers regularly cleared their bit of track and dumped all the left overs behind the wire fence, into the woods, so there was plenty of material to work with. After carefully sewing everything together, I soon had a small secluded swim that was about ten feet wide and six feet deep, not big but big enough for a bedchair and the rods and that was all I needed, really. The clever part, though, came floating across the lake one day and settled in a nearby tree, it was a bright metallic blue, discarded helium balloon from a recent party somewhere nearby.

It only had a little bit of gas left in it anyway, so I punctured it and hung it in a tree dead opposite the tiny entrance to the swim, this naturally caught the eye of any passers by and it looked so out of place in an all green environment that no-one would be able to not turn there head at the precise moment they walked by the swim, genius if I say so myself!

I was tucked away in this Bulrush swim one day and Terry was just a bit further along in the Reeds swim. If I recall correctly we were seeing fish along this margin quite regularly and there was a bank of weed that extended from the shallower water in front of Terry and ran along the front of my swim, making an ideal route for the carp.

Unfortunately, the bottom of the lake in the Bulrush was very silty and good spots were hard to come by, but it was the best I could do at the time as the rest of the path side was too open to fish anytime apart from after dark.

During the afternoon we were sitting drinking tea in Tel's swim when the inevitable happened and we ran out of water; this was an ongoing problem as it was big, bulky and heavy to carry onto the lake.

It was at this moment that Terry produced the solution from out of his rucksack, an army style water filter pump, apparently capable of turning a boggy mangrove swamp into a glass of Evian with just a few cranks of the handle. We'd all been paranoid about drinking the lake water in the past, especially after Phil Thompson's dire warnings "never, ever drink the Mere."

*Canopy Tree Hideaway*

I must admit that the resulting brew actually tasted quite good, and I was even thinking of purchasing one myself when I got back to civilisation, that was until later that night of course!

About midnight I was sitting on my bedchair and feeling a bit weird. I was sweating a lot for no particular reason and my guts were gurgling like an Irish stew on the back burner. Five minutes later all hell broke loose in there, my mouth filled up with saliva and I had contractions that could have given birth to an Elephant.

I charged straight through the rushes into the lake and projectile vomited like that girl in the film The Exorcist, it was horrendous and as soon as I stopped I started again until there was nothing left but a well ground-baited margin.

Any thoughts of buying a water pump went straight out the window and the next day I limped off home feeling like a shadow of my former self, Phil had been right!

My favourite camp, though, was the very first one that I'd made and it was near to the area I'd caught the common from on my first day. It was almost a natural bivvy, set under the vast canopy of a massive Beech tree.

Access was by boat or wading only and, although very tricky to fish from, it was totally secluded and safe. It was one of the few hidden swims that you could actually stand up and move around in, and the tree was so huge that I often stashed my entire kit within its branches when I left.

It always put me in mind of a book by Enid Blyton called 'The Far Away Tree', where strange folk lived in the very bole of the giant tree and magical lands appeared at the top of the branches, the difference in this case being that the magical land was definitely at the bottom!

At this time I was still dragging Sam, my poor old faithful carp dog, around with me and, although the Mere was hardly the place for a lady of her advancing years, I couldn't bear the thought of leaving her behind.

I spent many a night under the canopy tree, picking dirty great big burrs and brambles out from her matted tail, but she never seemed to mind too much. She'd spent so many years trekking around lakes and sleeping out under the stars that she really knew nothing else. Even at home, she'd often go out into the garden and have a kip on the back path, regardless of the weather, and many a time I'd have to drag her back in from the rain, soaking wet but contented.

We had two dogs at home at this stage, Sam and Joey. Sam had been brought up as a carp dog but Joey had been Sue's dog when I'd met her and he was a bit more accustomed to the finer things in life, like a roof and central heating, also I'm convinced he was a bit scared of the dark as well!

I did take him occasionally, but I'm not sure that he actually enjoyed it and usually he was waiting by the van when it came to the time to pack up. Sam, however, at least pretended that she enjoyed the Mere, although the boat seemed to be her favourite mode of transport by far. I can't really fault her there either; the boat was becoming more and more useful and it cut out all the associated agro of trying to relocate your gear through the bushes. I can't count the hand wheels and extending legs I'd lost from my bedchair, the brambles stealing them as I dragged the bed through behind me. I used to spend most of the time with the head end propped up with sticks.

My next chance of a fish came in the middle of a hot spell when the weed was well under way to taking over the centre section of the lake; strangely enough, this was one of the shallower areas. The weed always flourished out in the middle, where the bottom rose from fifteen to about twelve feet in depth, and sand and gravel mixed in with the clay to form an ideal area for the vast beds of Canadian pondweed and milfoil to grow.

Every morning, from upon the high bank, you could see fish rolling in this area but access was near impossible due to the brambles and nettles.

There was actually one swim already made on this section of bank and it was known as the 'Rat hole' because of its cramped and dark confines.

It was dug into the bank under an overhanging bush and was completely hidden from view.

The nature of the swim, though, meant that you could barely stand up straight in it, let alone walk about. I hated it in there and, consequently, I ended up making a new swim about fifty yards further along the bank, bang in the middle of the 'murder mile' bank.

I picked an obscure route into the area that involved clambering through the undergrowth into an old and abandoned swim from years gone by. From here, I had to wade along a steep margin, carefully manoeuvring around a protruding bush that neatly concealed a set of three steps I'd cut up into a solid thicket of brambles. Within this thicket, I had cut a zigzag path that led back to a warren-like area in the middle of the bramble and nettle forest, where I'd covered an old oval brolly in army netting.

From here, I could fish three rods out into the middle, secreting them away on the water line beneath bushes and netting, and relax quite comfortably in my little camp in the bushes.

Unlike most of the hides on the lake, this one had no bushes or brambles overhead so I could actually stand up and move about and, as such, it became a bit of a favourite area for me.

On this particular occasion, I had rowed out the baits, placing them on the small clear spots using the glass-bottomed bucket for viewing. Two rods were fishing tigers and hemp and on the other one I'd decided to try boilies.

A scattering of 10mm grange baits stared up at me through the glass, looking ever so conspicuous on the bottom of the Mere, usually it would have filled me with confidence but these fish were extremely picky in their diet and I wasn't sure if they ever ate boilies at all.

Everything had been set by mid morning and settled in nicely. I'd decided to get up before dawn the next day and spend some time sat out by the water, looking for signs of fish.

I'd obtained a load of army rations from Chilly and I'd been living on these, which was ideal, really, as they come in little silver foil bags that pop in your kettle. You can still drink the water in tea and there is neither washing up, nor rubbish to take home and the food is massively high in carbohydrates to keep you going for long periods on little intake.

I sat down by the rods, sipping tea and tucking into a bag of sausages and beans, as the sun started its ascent over the embankment of the nearby reservoir and I took in the magical ambience of the lake as it woke to a new day. Out in the middle of the lake, to my left, about twenty yards from the little film canister that I'd tethered out there weeks before to

mark my spot, the water erupted as a big old carp frolicked in the first rays of the sun. Unlike most other mornings, he was not joined by his mates and a very quiet period of two hours crept by, during which only one other fish showed and that one was twenty yards to the right of my swim so, eventually, tired and cramped, I retired to the brolly to catch up on a bit of kip.

Unusually for the Mere, there were actually three other people fishing that morning, which practically constituted a full house.

Apparently the run came about an hour later, I say apparently because I was the only person who didn't actually hear it!

Unknown to me, the steep bank at the front of the swim and the added brambles acted like a sound barrier for my usually loud alarms and all the sound was projected forwards across the lake while I, like a Pratt, slept on oblivious.

The first thing I knew about it was when I awoke an hour or so later and went down to the water to tip a bucket full over my head in an attempt to shake off the affects of sleeping in the sunlight and humidity of an airless swim.

One of the tiger rods was obviously not as I'd last seen it, the bobbin had been pulled into the alarm and loads of line was missing from the spool. I wound down as tightly as I could and heaved into a solid resistance as masses of bubbles rose to the surface out in the big weed bed to the right of where I had been fishing. I could see Nick, who was fishing opposite me, looking across from his hidey-hole in the reeds intrigued by what was going on.

The big problem I had now was that Terry had taken the boat back to the other side, where he was fishing in the bulrush swim, and no amount of waving and whistling could get his attention, so I had to run all the way around there.

Running anywhere on the Mere is a joke to start with, but right around the lake while you've got a fish on the end nearly bloody killed me.

I was stumbling about all over the place and at one stage I was so entangled in brambles it was like running in slow motion, as they tore at my clothes and face.

Eventually I got to Terrys swim and we set off in the boat across the lake. It transpired that everyone else had heard a screaming take and couldn't figure out why I didn't appear; I think, eventually, they had decided it must have been something else that just sounded like a buzzer.

Nick said later that he saw a huge fish crash angrily out of the water right in-between the two of us as the run had stopped!

Taking the rod and net, we followed the taut line out to the weed where I found it wrapped twice around a huge clump of Canadian, the lead was nestled on top but the hooklink was out of sight within the centre of the clump. I gingerly prised it all apart with the net handle but all I got back was half a hooklink, snapped clean with the power of an angry Mere carp.

On the way back to the swim we passed the little film canister on the surface and I stopped to peer down at my spots to try and make sense of it all. The tiger and hemp spot had been stripped bald, and where a small hole in the weed had been it was now a big glowing patch of sand. The boilie spot, however, had been left completely untouched and the way the baits had now swelled, and been coated in settled silt from the nearby feeding, they looked huge and ridiculously conspicuous.

I was devastated by that loss and I was sure it was a big fish, as was Nick who assured me the fish that thrashed out of the water over the spot was massive. Forever after, this swim became known as 'The Long Run', for obvious reasons!

It was a short time after this that a strange turn of events happened at the Mere and it was to totally alter the way we fished and led, in quite short order, to a rare burst of captures.

Nick had been in the reed swim again and, having seen a fish jump, he'd decided to chuck a yellow pop-up at it. Not an earth shattering decision by any account, but we had such a low opinion of the carps reaction to boilies that I must admit I wouldn't have been happy doing it at that time.

The fish responded instantly, though, and before long Nick had also captured the same 'twisted mouth common' that I'd had off the surface, what seemed like a lifetime beforehand.

Shortly after this, another common was lost at the net on a boilie, I think this may have been Nick again, or maybe his mate Dan, I can't be sure now but it was becoming obvious that the carp were willing to pick up a single pop-up if it was presented in the right place at the right time.

This created an entirely different situation, whereby the boat may be no longer necessary for dropping rigs and a jumping fish was an instant target for single baits.

Obviously the amount of weed prevented most casts from landing anywhere near the bottom, but at least if you did, you would be in with a chance, which was novel, to say the least.

I was still unconvinced, though, that those ultra cautious mirrors would eat bait, although quite why, I don't know, and I still kick myself now when I look back and think how stupid I was.

I think that Terry, Steve and I had convinced each other that we knew far more about the Mere carp than we actually did and somehow, somewhere along the way, we forgot everything we'd all learnt over our many years of angling; carp love boilies!

I was soon to learn the error of my ways, the clock was ticking and pretty soon the secrets would be unlocked but, for now, my last non-boilie session started on a damp and dismal Wednesday morning.

For some reason I thought that it would be a good idea to take both dogs with me on this occasion although, in hindsight, I haven't got a clue why I thought that Joey would possibly be up for the rigours of the Mere in the rain.

I think it was probably something to do with the fact that Sue was pregnant and she needed time without dogs all around the place so, in a moment of madness, I relented and took them both.

From the moment I arrived I had known it was a bad idea, it had been raining non-stop all night and the bushes were almost flat across the paths and bulging with their collected payload of water.

By the time we had reached the waters edge most of the kit, and both of the hounds, were sodden. Joey had tried to leg it back to the car at least twice and the more I shouted at him the more nervous and jittery he became.

Sam just looked up at me through dripping fur and had a look that pleaded for the fire in the pub, but it was only eight in the morning so that wasn't really an option, yet!

I opted for the 'Turds' point', at the narrow end of the lake, as there was a nice wind blowing up that way and Steve had bagged a lovely twenty six pound common from a little swim on the far bank, the previous week, at the time this was only the third fish to come out all year.

It never stopped raining the whole time I was there and, at one stage, it rained so hard that I thought it would flatten the brolly down on top of us. Sheets of water were being hurled along the lake and I had to cling on to the front of the umbrella to keep it down, while water coursed down my sleeves into my armpits.

By the next morning I was still fishless and still wet, the wind had abated and was definitely on the turn but it was still drizzling with rain.

The two dogs had been wringing wet for a straight twenty four hours and both of them were plastered in mud and twigs and looked thoroughly miserable.

I even considered going home, but I knew that Sue wanted a bit of 'time out' and, given the fractious nature of her expectant condition, I thought another night under a leaky brolly in monsoon conditions with two stinking hounds seemed like the softer option, so I moved to the other end of the lake where the new wind had just started to blow.

Getting set up was horrible, everything was wringing wet including all my clothes, my feet had been sloshing around in my inadequate boots ever since I'd arrived the previous morning and I dreaded to think what they must have looked like, let alone smelt like.

The bed and bedding was wet and the two dog beds that I'd stuffed in a bin liner had been the driest survivors right up until the second that the two dogs actually laid on them, and then they were as wet as everything else.

Just as I was beginning to question my sanity, a big old carp pushed itself up and out of the choppy water in the middle of the lake, straight in front of my swim.

This was all the encouragement I needed to stay, although I'm sure I heard Sam groan as she saw it jump.

Over the next few hours I saw three more fish in the same general area and I really wanted to stay on for the night, but I felt so sorry for the two dogs that I eventually decided to call it a day.

I stayed as long as I could but the bloodshot and pleading collie eyes had worn me down, I knew that as soon as darkness fell poor old Sam would be seriously cold and Joey, although younger, certainly wasn't ready for this sort of punishment.

Terry had turned up that afternoon and he'd moved into the small corner swim opposite me. Further up from the canopy tree, it was nestled in the extreme corner where the wind was blowing.

I knew that he'd not seen the fish as I could see his brolly facing the lake to keep the weather out so, on my way home, I rang him on his mobile and told him what I'd seen.

Due to work commitments I knew I couldn't get back to the lake for eight days and it was going to be like torture for me. The fish had been lethargic and unwilling to feed for so long now that it seemed unfair that I'd be absent just when they were starting to liven up.

There had been about four or five fish caught in all since we all started on the lake but it looked, now, as if the best time was upon us. The weather was on the turn and the fish I'd just seen in the middle looked well up for a feed up, it would be the longest eight days of my life.

While I was at work I kept stopping, closing my eyes, and replaying the sight of those big old warriors leaping out in the middle of the lake.

I knew that 'The Beach', where I had last been, or my favourite swim, The Canopy, were the two swims to be in as the fish had moved into the deeper water that lay between the two.

I phoned Terry every day, whilst I struggled to keep the enthusiasm up for slapping Artex over people's ceilings, it really was a messy horrible job but it paid the bills. Terry had moved into 'The Beach', which was not surprising really, given the situation, and it was at times like this that I wished I could fish whenever I wanted, as well; I knew I was missing out by not being there at that time.

One of my phone calls to Terry was met with the news I'd been dreading, there had been another one out and, not surprisingly, it had also picked up a boilie.

Dan had caught a double figure common from the canopy tree and, although it wasn't the biggest fish in the world, it was yet another one I hadn't caught, and yet another one that hinted that we may have been foolish to overlook the single pop-up approach.

I decided, there and then, that my next session would include some hand rolled, bright yellow, pineapple boilies; I just knew it was going to kick off soon and I wanted to be part of it.

Three days to go until I could fish and I was starting to dread phoning up for a report in case I'd missed the boat.

Once again there had been fish caught, this time it had been Al who had had action with two runs, both on pop-ups.

The first fish had come adrift but the second one marked a turning point that really rammed the message home; it was the first mirror to be caught on bait, a cracking looking mid twenty with huge scales across his flanks.

The next day there was more news, Al had bagged another one, this time a common of twenty nine pounds and Terry had relented as well, finally cracking under the strain he'd put boilies on the end and captured the twisted mouth common that morning.

I was pulling my hair out by this stage, as I knew the canopy tree swim was free and the fish were obviously all up at that end of the lake and properly feeding for the first time that year. I swung every trick I could that afternoon and managed to free up the next morning for a session, it was only a day early but I couldn't handle anymore, I was going mad stuck at home.

The next morning couldn't come quickly enough and I practically ran down to the lake, dragging my gear behind me, desperate for the swim to still be free as it was the only other spot at that end of the lake and I knew every inch of it.

As I reached the first corner of the lake I bumped straight into Terry who had just caught another carp, another mirror, and I didn't even have to ask what he'd caught it on.

It turned out to be the same fish that Phil had caught years before but it was a little lighter in weight at twenty eight pounds, but none the less impressive for it. I took the photos for him as quickly as possible, but all I really wanted to do was get set up and fishing.

With the camera work done, and a celebratory cuppa down my neck, I was off like a jackrabbit to the canopy tree on the far side of the lake. I'd seen fish rolling and bubbling in the middle while we drank our brew and one had sheeted up not more than thirty or forty yards from my prospective swim.

Obviously, all three rods were rigged up with the new yellow pop-ups but the big problem with the canopy tree was actually casting them out.

Due to the branches of the tree itself, it was practically impossible to get a back swing and I had to stand right at the top of the mound, behind a bush, and cast blind over the branches.

While the lead was in flight I had to whip the rod over the bush and slide down the slope into the margins, appearing from under the canopy just in time to see where I'd landed.

The first chuck was spot on and I guessed that it must be very close to the nearest bubbler. The second cast went a bit further and, although it was only a third of the way across, I saw Terry look up so I waved across with an upturned palm to ask if it was a problem, but he stuck his thumb up so I left it be, the last thing I wanted to do was start thrashing the water to a foam while they were feeding.

The third rod I swung around into the left hand margin, to a spot where I knew that a small gravel hump rose off the bottom.

The next couple of hours were electric; I'd fretted and sweated for a whole week just to be sat there at that exact moment, baits in position and the Mere carp feeding at last.

Although two mirrors had been caught already there were still three more out there somewhere, including the ultimate prize, the Black Mirror himself.

I could hardly sit still and every time the lines twitched or even moved in the breeze my heart skipped a beat. At least twice I caught sight of a chunk of carp flesh as a vortex broke on the surface over my baits, and I couldn't believe that I hadn't had a take.

After two or three hours the wind suddenly swung totally in the other direction, coming now from the South and increasing in strength rapidly, changing the game plan entirely.

I was now faced with a real dilemma, as all activity had stopped in the swim, and I was certain the fish would move on such a fresh new wind.

I decided that it was too good a chance to miss, and the Bulrush swim was the perfect spot to intercept them as the fish would have to pass straight through it.

I couldn't believe I hadn't had any action in the previous few hours and I didn't want to miss out on this unprecedented feeding spell so, after sliding down into the margins, I grabbed the rods and wound in.

I couldn't believe my eyes as I swung the rigs in to hand under the tree, the first rod I'd cast had managed to tangle around the lead, probably due to the awkward angle of the cast over the tree. The second one was even worse; it had sat out there in the perfect spot for three hours with no bloody bait on the end!

What sort of a chance had I thrown away by not tying on the pop-up tightly enough? I was more than a little bit pissed off, in fact I was fuming, a whole week of pacing up and down scheming and plotting the downfall of a Mere monster and I'd cocked it up with a simple slip knot.

Oh well, there was always another chance in the bulrushes so I shouldered the load and beat my way around there.

Before I'd even had a chance to cast out, however, I heard the shrill tone of a Stevie Neville alarm as it sung out its battle cry and I looked up the lake to where Terry was standing with rod bent into another of the Mere's secrets.

I was gutted really, not only had I ruined my chances originally but now it seemed I'd moved off the fish, which had obviously not responded to the new wind half as quickly as I had.

Round at the Beach, a few minutes later, it was obvious that Terry was attached to one of the better fish as it ran him ragged, plunging through the thick weed beds to the left of the swim. There was nothing for it in the end but to break out the boat and try and land him that way.

By hanging over the front of the boat I could tear away the weed that clung to the line as Terry took up the slack and, eventually, he was back in direct contact with a very powerful fish. It started spinning the little boat around and around as he slowly gave ground and came nearer the surface.

With just half a glance at the twisting bulk beneath the boat I could see which fish it was and I knew it was all over, the Black Mirror was just about to be beaten.

It was a nerve-wracking moment as I stretched out with the net, although not as scary as it must have been for Terry, but all went smoothly and we were soon rowing the magnificent beast back to shore.

What a moment that was, to finally see the object of all our desires in the flesh, laying there in full majesty on the mat before us, it was truly immense, a colossal carp and I swore to myself that one day it would eventually be mine.

Suddenly I had a thought and, looking inside the great fish's mouth, I saw another hook-mark. On the opposite side to Terry's there was a small dark hole where a hook had been, not fresh, but not old enough to fade completely. Had this been the fish I'd lost a few short weeks earlier? I didn't want it to be, that's for sure, although we knew everything that had been hooked and lost.

Al's fish two days earlier was the only other contender but this mark was not that fresh and instantly I wished I hadn't looked, I tried to put it out of my mind but it just wouldn't go away.

For now, though, the glory was Terry's and he'd put in a lot of time, blood, sweat and tears to get there and fair play to him for pulling it off, the Mere needed a certain sort of determination for sure.

The Black Mirror weighed in at forty-eight pounds and ten ounces although the actual weight really was immaterial, it was an awesome moment and a vision that would haunt me for years to come.

We all gathered with cameras and did the best job that we knew how before the moment was gone and the old warrior returned to the depths, but for how long?

The only thing that marred that wonderful occasion for me came a few years later when I read Terry's account of the capture and, only then, did I find out that he had actually seen my bait come off the rig as it hit the water.

Apparently, he had indeed thought that I'd cast too close when I'd waved across to check but, on seeing my bait come adrift, he stuck up his thumb, thinking it would be better to let me fish on knowing that I wasn't in with a hope in hell of getting a bite anyway.

When I think back to how anxious I had been all week to get down to the lake and the massive level of confidence I'd had whilst sitting behind those rods, watching the lines twitch as feeding fish brushed into them, it winds me up even now, many years later.

Up until then we had shared all our accumulated knowledge in the hope of unlocking the secrets of the Mere, but as soon as there was a real chance of that happening it appeared that a different set of rules had come into play. It was a turn of events that I mentally noted down and filed away for future reference under the heading of 'The yellow pop-up incident'. Years later, it would turn out to be a lesson well learned!

The Black Mirror, as it happened, only managed to last a further two weeks before his next slip up and I've often found this with big fish, before and since. It is not uncommon at all for a fish to go for months or even years without capture and then, in a short space of time, come out twice in quick succession.

Whether it's down to a break in the natural food chain, or whether the first capture throws it out of balance for a while, I don't know but it's a phenomena that I've seen over and over again.

This time it was Steve who had his just rewards when he cast at a jumping fish on the snaggy point and had an almost instant result. I just wish I could have been there to see it as Steve has become a close friend over the years and I'd have loved to share his moment of glory. We'd put in a lot of effort over the lake that year and, in fact, we continued to do so right up until the end of the autumn.

After the second capture of the Black Mirror there was only really the two of us that persevered on there for the rest of the season, and persevere we did. I fished practically every nook and cranny at some stage, although I did spend a lot of time up in the canopy, convinced that they would return for another big feed up later in the year.

One morning I arrived at dawn and headed straight for the canopy swim to put in a bit of bait and get everything ready for a day's walking and looking, but I couldn't believe what I found when I got there. Some half-wit had carved a massive path straight through the brambles and into the back of the swim. Whereas before it was totally hidden and accessible only by wading, now it was open for all to see. I knew that this was the work of the anti-angling fiend and probably the pink loo roll merchant at that, why else would somebody open up a swim for all to see?

The hypocrisy of the act belied belief, if this person wanted us gone because he was claiming we upset the natural environment of the Mere from a nature lovers point of view, then what effect did he think that hacking the place to the ground would have?

As a result of this vandalism I had to move my swim to the other side of the tree and, rather than do any more damage, I simply put up a camouflage brolly in a little clearing within a massive stinging nettle bed. This gave me somewhere to sleep and to stay out of sight during the day.

This little clearing on the other side of the tree, amongst the nettles, was nearer to the actual water line which allowed me to get closer to the lake and actually see out across the deep bay to my right, and generally spend more time watching the water without being on show myself.

Sleeping in the middle of a bed of four-foot high stinging nettles does have its disadvantages, though, and most of them crawl, hop, or fly and the one thing they all had in common was a liking for my blood!

I used to wake up most mornings doing a fair impression of the elephant man with huge lumps all over my face. There was one particular day, I recall, when I was woken by the early rays of a hot summer sun beating down on the top of the camouflage umbrella; the air within the

nettle bed was already unbearably hot and humid. I swung my feet out of the bag and sat on the edge of the bed trying to get my brain into gear.

I could feel an annoying tickle in my left nostril as if an old bogey was hanging there but, when I picked it off, I found a large rolled up spider instead. He had obviously crawled up inside my nose during the night and, in my sleep, I'd probably rubbed my nose frantically and killed him in the process. Sometimes its best not to know what comes calling when you're fast asleep and I ended up sleeping with my head buried in the pillowcase for weeks afterwards.

I was seeing the fish on a regular basis throughout the entire summer, either cruising in the sun or leaping at first light, and I was amazed that I couldn't get a pick up from any of them. It was as if they had lowered their defences just the once and instantly shut up shop again. Steve was also struggling for another bite despite being on them as well.

During the early part of autumn, as the weed began to die off, the fishing became almost impossible. Bearing in mind that most of the lake is around fifteen feet deep and the weed reaches from top to bottom, that makes for a hell of a lot of floating weed once it looses its grip on the lake bed. Some nights I would just be settling in to bed, having rowed out and baited all three rods, when the wind would pick up and bring a football pitch sized weed bed down the lake and wipe out all three rods at once.

This floating weed would be carried on the prevailing winds down to the narrow and most northerly end of the lake, where it would form an impenetrable raft, up to two feet thick in places!

This provided the perfect haven for the carp who would just lay underneath the solid green canopy for days or even weeks, picking off the snails and mussels that were packed tight into the fronds.

I used to watch them pushing their heads up through the weed and laying a cheek on the surface of the weed to push it down and flood the immediate area with water. As the water rushed onto the weed and swirled across its surface, it would wash all the crustaceans and creepy crawlies straight into the carp's mouth. There was absolutely no need for the fish to leave the sanctuary of the raft as it had its own little eco-system that could support and protect the carp right up until the weed started to sink as the temperature dropped later in the year.

It was at the back of this raft that I got my first proper look at the mythical 'Big Common'.

Every lake has one, or to be more precise, every lake has the rumour of one and usually the bigger and more inaccessible the lake then the bigger the myth will be, but here, in the flesh, behind the weed raft, I actually saw him with my own eyes.

There used to be a little pathway that resembled a rabbit hole, right at the end of the lake, and you literally had to lower yourself into a small hole in the ground to get into an old stream bed, beneath the bushes, that acted as the path to the lake. At the end of the path was a tree that leant out precariously over the margins and the weed raft. You could lie along the trunk and hang a few feet above the surface with the carp milling around right below your face.

It was a very exciting place to go and look, although actually fishing there would have been a nightmare as the weed was so thick and the swim was practically non-existent.

I had been watching a couple of thirty-pound fish appearing and then disappearing through the little viewing windows in the canopy of weed. Some of these holes were only inches across while others gave me a clear look at ninety percent of each individual carp as it moved through.

Sometimes one would appear inside the weed line, directly below me, and so close that I could have literally reached down and poked it with my finger. At times like that is was impossible even to breath for fear of spooking them, but the bole of the tree used to keep me well hidden and only the hammering of my heart threatened to give me away.

I was laying there, struggling to make sense of two new commons that had appeared a few feet away, below two ten inch windows.

There was an awful lot of head in one hole, flat and shovel like on the top with a big dark eye just visible as he scanned the underside of the weed. A massive pectoral fin waved around in the other hole off to his right but I could only make out part of that carps flank and the curve of its belly, such was the restrictions on my view through the holes.

Three feet further back I could see the top of a very thick tail lobe 'tenting' the weed as it lazily rose and fell in the warm water. I couldn't see the head of the other fish at all and it was only when the closest one turned to find a more comfortable position that I realised, with total amazement, that all the various bits and pieces belonged to the same bloody fish.

It cruised below me and I gasped as I saw the whole thing pass through the biggest viewing hole, not all at once of course, but in slow motion from head to tail as it glided along, just a few feet away. It was, without a shadow of doubt, the biggest common I have ever set eyes upon before or since, and it took my breath away.

I can still shut my eyes now and see that shovel like head in perfect detail as it settled in its new location right below the tree that I was struggling not to fall out of in amazement.

I watched him for ages and then, coming to my senses, I slipped silently from the tree and crept off in search of strong tackle and some worms.

The tackle was easily come by but the worms I had to dig from the dry ground with a pointed stick and my bare hands. My fingers were so sore by the time that I'd found two pathetic little summer worms that I could hardly even tie the hook on.

It took an eternity to get back into position silently enough so as not to scare the fish, crawling on your hands and knees through brambles is not much fun I can tell you.

The worms seemed determined to escape from the depths of my pocket at any costs and every cracked twig sounded like a gunshot.

Eventually I was back, laying face first on the tree, rod in hand with worms squirming on the hook, still tying to escape, and by some small miracle the big shovel headed common was still there in his hole.

I had only the hook for weight but there was no need to cast, the great fish was closer even than the tip of the rod as it stuck out from the side of the tree. Ever so gently I lowered the bait down on to the weed at the edge of the hole, before slowly twitching it free, allowing the two wrigglers to slowly sink the few remaining inches, where they actually landed on the side of his head. I could see them crawling across his skin, almost weightless in the water they wriggled along his face until, freefalling, they tumbled off into the clear water and sank straight through his line of vision.

This had to be it, the net was ready, I was willing to dive straight in and plunge the rod beneath the weed to land him, so surely this would be the moment. As the worms swung on the short line across the hole, brushing along the weed fronds as they sank, the big common, in one fluid motion, looked at them and blinked!

That was it, the sum total of his reaction to the best ever piece of stalking I'd performed was a simple flick of the eye and a total distain for my hard dug offering, mind you it had been worth it just to watch him for a while.

In hindsight, especially looking at the severity of the weed, I would have been better off fetching the camera instead of a rod but natural hunting instinct had taken over and I just couldn't resist.

He disappeared after a while but I saw him again a few times that year, occasionally he was with the big mirror and together they definitely ruled the roost.

Despite fishing as hard as my time (and pregnant wife) would allow, I never managed to get a single bite of any sort all year, apart from mosquito bites of course and I was absolutely covered in those.

With a couple of exceptions, there had been a ten-day period that produced ninety percent of the bites and, after that the lake hadn't produced a single fish. In fact, Steves capture of the Black Mirror turned out to be the last run of the year, it was apparent that the Mere wouldn't give up its treasures without a fight!

# Chapter 3

# A New Arrival

" *M* y year on the Mere was always going to come to an end around November time as Sue wasn't getting any less pregnant and, as comfortable as a womb undoubtedly is, the new addition to the Lane family wasn't going to stay in there forever".

As it happened I pulled off in October, just as the foliage started to drop, and I decided to spend the last few sessions before the birth having a social with the lads.

After a full out assault on the Mere I was more than ready for a break and I intended to just kick back and enjoy my fishing as often as I could manage to get away, which I suspected wouldn't be all that often!

For some reason the winter venue had already been decided as Manor Lake in Oxfordshire, on the Linear complex.

We often seem to end up spending our winters over in Oxfordshire and, when we choose a Linear fisheries water we are always made more than welcome by head bailiff, Roy Parsons, and his team of strange, but friendly, assistants.

Unfortunately for me, the lads had picked the only one water on the complex that didn't really do anything for me, either aesthetically or, as it turned out, realistically either. I blanked the entire winter, as did Keith.

Everybody else seemed to do all right and it wasn't as if we weren't pulling all the necessary strokes, we just couldn't make the indicators move whatever we tried.

Chilly was catching them on a regular basis and he really seemed to have the measure of the place, he was rolling his own hook baits around cork balls with great attention to detail, unfortunately for him he wasn't paying such great attention to them while they were left to dry out on the bank!

Every time Chilly caught another fish, either Keith or I would cast a freshly stolen hook bait right in the middle of his carefully baited swim but, even with this level of blatant stroke pulling, we just couldn't even steal a bite!

Even Reg, with his limited time spent on the bank, managed to grab a bit of the action and bag one, and not just any old one either, he somehow managed to land the lakes biggest resident; Cut Tail at a little over forty two pounds!

It was a fun time, though, despite the total lack of carp, and I suppose that the real reason I was there at all was just to chill out a bit and prepare for the sleepless nights, endless nappies and countless bottles of milk that would soon totally take over the family home.

Regular sessions of 'duelling woks' between Keith (who was going through a strange multi-coloured stage at the time) and myself, turned out a succession of culinary delights which, of course, would have been far too dry without copious amounts of beer and wine to wash them down with, so the social scene, at least, went entirely as planned.

One thing that didn't get on with the Oxford scene, however, was my battered old van; I think the journey was far too much for it to bear and one morning I awoke to find it dead in the gutter, devoid of all life and frozen stiff in a perfect automotive approximation of rigamortis!

Luckily, though, Reg had recently been trying to convince me to buy their old works Escort van, as they had upgraded, and apparently the old one was fit only for scrap or someone like me!

I didn't want to miss out on any fishing time because of the lack of wheels so I quickly hatched a plan.

Keith could bring up my bed chair, sleeping stuff and non fishing items on the next Friday evening and I'd take all the essentials by train in the morning, simple!

For some strange reason I'd convinced myself that the journey wouldn't be too bad, especially as I 'only' had the rods, rucksack, and bait bucket with me! How could that little lot cause a problem commuting through London in the rush hour, eh?

*A very happy Reg*

The first section of the journey from Three Bridges to Kings Cross did indeed go quite well, although I did spend the entire time in the guards van sitting on my rucksack, so I suppose there wasn't an awful lot that could go wrong.

Kings Cross itself though was a bloody nightmare! If you have ever travelled through London in the rush hour, or indeed at any time, then you will have some idea of the mayhem that ensues.

Picture the early morning tide of commuters as a colony of very busy penguins, all shuffling around in there own preoccupied way, all looking exactly the same and heading in one very specific direction.

If you then imagine one very bedraggled Emu type thing fighting his way against the tide in a vain attempt to find help, then that, in a nutshell, was me.

I fought for a while against the surge of pinstripe, hoping to catch a glimpse of the departure board but it was not to be, every time I turned my head around to look it was like a scene from Laurel and Hardy, with the big plank of wood as my rod bag bowling over another half a dozen Penguins!

*Keith during his multi-coloured stage*

Just when I thought all hope was lost I heard someone shouting at me, I figured it must be aimed at me because, whoever it was, knew my name!

Peering through all the irate penguins I spotted fellow carp angler, Steve Newman, waving at me from next to a telephone kiosk. He was sort of resting there in an eddy created in the flow as it split around the little cluster of phones, and hardly being jostled at all; he was obviously an old hand at this commuting game.

After a few minor collisions, involving rods being thrust up snooty noses, I managed to navigate my way across tohim and he pulled me safely from the crowd.

Unbelievably, he had a copy of my first book with him and he'd been reading it on the way to and from work every day, not only could he find the single eddy in a surging tide of suited mayhem, but he could read a book at the same time, I was even more impressed now.

Steve couldn't believe that I was attempting such a feat while laden down with fishing tackle and, after a quick coffee from a dodgy looking vendor, he wished me luck and launched himself back into the throng where, apart from the red cover on the book, he blended in and disappeared from view.

The next stage of the journey was no better. I'd eventually found the right train, which was a Great Western express service to Oxford, and full of the same snooty nosed, pinstripes I'd just spent half an hour swatting like flies with the rod bag.

The carriage layout was very posh indeed, neat little tables full of laptops, full ala carte breakfast in the dining car served by proper waiters and plenty of dirty looks from the stuck up cow opposite as I unfolded my marmite sandwiches from a piece of crumpled silver foil in the lid of my rucksack.

Mind you, when I looked down at the meagre offering I had pasted together a few hours earlier, I wasn't exactly overly impressed myself, it's amazing the bizarre shapes a sandwich can get itself into when it's been sat on from Three Bridges to Victoria!

In retrospect I should have guessed it was first class really, but the thought never occurred to me. The ticket inspector seemed to be able to tell the difference, though, and I spent the rest of the journey standing up in the corridor next to the toilet!

Eventually my ordeal was over and I met up with Reg at the station and threw my rods and rucksack into the back of Reg's motor and we set off to see my new mode of transport, I just hoped it was better than the last!

Buying a used company van off anyone is risky enough but off a mate like Reg, well, desperate times call for desperate measures, and it did have a full tank of diesel, which was something none of my motors ever usually had.

I ignored all the falling off bits and the feeble attempt to rub the sign writing off the panels, after all, there were fish to be caught.

Having had a string of dodgy vans for most of my life this one fitted like a glove, really, and by the time we reached Manor I'd managed to stick folded up bits of paper and a discarded lolly stick into the worst of the many 'rattly bits'. It would do for a while; at least until the diesel tank was empty!

That session was as uneventful on the Lane/Jenkins fish front as all of the others had been, although, we did get a visit from Phil Thomson which was a nice surprise.

Phil is one of the most eccentric carp anglers I know, not that he ever does anything outrageous, it's just his whole manner that has to be seen to be believed.

He's laid back to the extreme and his tackle is straight out of the nineteen seventies, even in the middle of winter and with hard frost on the ground he fished under a 50" brolly in an old Argos sleeping bag and paraded around all weekend in a pair of carpet slippers!

In fact the only item of gear he brought that wasn't massively out of date was a couple of crates of beer, which of course we just had to help him consume.

I can't remember if anybody caught anything other than pneumonia that session, probably not, but it was great to catch up with Phil and relive old Wraysbury lake memories once more.

As it turned out, the new van only had to make a couple of trips to and from Crawley as, on the 16th of November 1997, the long awaited event finally happened and we made our way into the maternity unit at Crawley hospital.

Sue had already bribed the nurses, by cooking them a great big bread pudding, so we were ushered straight into the one private 'birthing suite' that the unit had to offer.

I soon had the sound system working and, as Sue relaxed in the bath, Pink Floyd drifted in a comfortably numb fashion around the room, mind you so did I but that was more to do with the discovery of the 'Gas and Air' bottles!

We even had to ask the nurse for a top up half way through the afternoon. By later that evening I had witnessed that most humbling of sights, the birth of another human being, and, even more amazing it was a small part of me as well.

There is nothing quite like the feeling when the nurse hands over a little bundle and says "congratulations, you have a son", mind you he did stink something rotten!

Conor David Lane wasn't specifically timed to arrive in November but from a carp angler's point of view it did happen to be an ideal time as I had the whole winter ahead to make gurgling sounds and bounce him up and down on my knee.

By the time that Conor was six months old, and a routine had been established in his young little life, spring was beginning to be sprung outside in the big wide world.

Trees and plants were in bloom, the whole natural world was stirring from its winter stupor and the urges of a carp angler were once more on the rise.

Although fishing at the Mere is a total no-go area during the close season, I knew that a few anglers were already fishing there and I couldn't possibly see how I could just sit on my hands and wait until June.

Making a decision to be extra vigilant and camouflage absolutely everything, including my rods, I decided to risk it anyway and, before long, I was back at the place I had grown to know so well.

That first walk back through the nettles and brambles brought back a thousand memories and it was as if I had not been away at all.

I took a leisurely stroll around, loosing only a couple of layers of skin as it was still early and the undergrowth had not started in full earnest yet.

Sure enough, there were indeed anglers already there, three or four I think and, if I recall correctly, a couple of early fish had even been caught, although not any of the bigger ones.

As it turned out, the decision to risk all and start early was not one of my better ones and a few short sessions later I ended up paying the price for my impatience.

I had been sitting on the grass in the Beach swim at the Southern-most end of the lake, spending a lovely morning watching out over the lake and amusing Fat Sam by flicking single chum mixers into the long grass for her to snuffle out again.

The lake looked wonderful in its spring colours and I was convinced that a great big carp would slide out of the slightly rippled surface at any moment.

The beach swim is the first one that you come to as you walk onto the Mere, and this also meant that I was the first person the NRA bailiffs had stumbled upon as they turned up to investigate a complaint that there were anglers fishing.

Now, as it worked out, I wasn't actually caught fishing, I was just in possession of some fishing tackle!

The bizarre thing was that it wasn't even my tackle I was caught with; I was just keeping an eye on it for someone else who had popped up the café.

I didn't bother pointing this out for three reasons, firstly there was no point in dropping anyone else in it, secondly, I mistakenly thought that there couldn't possibly be a law against taking some fishing gear out for a walk, as long as you didn't use it, and finally, I was actually fishing-it was just that my rods were so well hidden they couldn't find them!

Apparently I was wrong on the second count, though, and 'intent to fish' is actually an offence of sorts.

A few weeks later I received a charge sheet from the court, which at first I contested as it was ridiculous to think I could be fined for intent to fish.

Eventually it transpired that a hidden witness was willing to go to court and speak out against me and, when I read on the sheet that his profession was a school teacher it all became clear, it was the Wraysbury dog walker after all, just as we had suspected.

So, rather than drag the proceedings out any further I pleaded guilty by letter and received a fine of three hundred and twenty pounds, which I could ill afford, considering we'd just got another mouth to feed.

I opted to pay by instalments and learn from my mistakes.

From that day on I have never even set foot on the Mere during the spring season, just to be on the safe side and, as it happened, it really sort of put me off of the place for the rest of that year.

Somehow it had spoilt the ambience of the place as, although we knew we shouldn't really be there, we hadn't ever had any real grief as such, and we had respected everything about the Mere, treating it as if it was our own.

Getting a slapped wrist by someone who had hardly ever trodden the banks, and knew none of the secrets of the lake, left a bitter taste in my mouth, so I decided that I needed a new venue for a while, and I knew just the place.

# Chapter 4

# Conningbrook

"*With* all *the grief at the Mere hanging over my head like a storm cloud, not to mention my despondency at the prospect of living like a tramp under a bush for*

*another season, I made an executive decision to bugger off down to Kent for a while and fish for a new fifty pounder on the scene known as 'Two Tone".*

Chilly was already down at Conningbrook, trying to outwit that big old mirror, and Terry had managed to catch it in quite short order the previous year after leaving the Mere, so I decided to trade the jungle for the wide open spaces and hightail it down the M20.

My old mucker 'Jenkins' had also purchased a ticket and we were reliably informed that, for once, the locals were a friendly enough bunch and the social scene was a paramount part of Kent style angling, it all sounded too good to be true.

I was really quite looking forward to fishing a lake where I could just set up a low chair next to the waters edge, crack open a cold beer and watch the sun set without fear of some uniformed little Hitler jumping out from the bushes and arresting me! The only down side was that I wasn't allowed to bring 'Fat Sam' with me as there was a no dog rule on the water, although I was certainly going to try and sneak her in at a later date.

I think the Mere had taken it out of her a bit, after all she was no spring chicken now, and in fact she'd been twelve for at least three years by then so she was probably due a little rest anyway!

My first trip down to the lake was a bit of an eye opener really. I hadn't even seen the place before, despite forking out £200 for a ticket, I'd just seen a picture of the fish and thought, sod it, that'll do for me.

As I turned up for that first session I didn't really know quite what to expect, I always paint a picture in my minds eye of a lake and it always ends up looking completely different when I actually get there.

The one thing that I never do in advance is to conjure up the smell of a new lake in my minds nose. Had I attempted that bizarre feat, then I'm sure I couldn't have been more wrong if I tried.

Nothing, before or since, could have prepared me for the full on nasal assault that hit me as I stepped from the van on that first morning.

If you can imagine, (although, god knows how!) an overpowering smell of Bachelors oxtail soup battling bravely against an onslaught of liquorish essence as it bellows across the fields in an unstoppable charge from the nearby factories.

Just when you think that you can balance these opposing forces of sensory overload in your minds nose, add an equally pungent aroma of Channel No5 and turn the 'volume' of the whole experience up from merely unbearable, to mind bendingly nauseous, and then you are nearly there with me as I stepped from the van.

It was only by a tremendous feat of will power that my insides stayed just that, inside!

I made my way around to Chilly's oval brolly, that I could see nestling in a tiny copse of stickly little trees on the far bank, holding my breath all the way.

The lake looked pretty barren after the Mere but then I suppose most places would, at least there were no bloody brambles to be seen anywhere!

That part of Kent is not exactly famed for its flora and fauna, in fact most anything that ever manages to grow above six feet from the ground gets flattened as soon as the wind changes direction.

The whole area is ravaged by various winds from the two coastlines that sit just a few miles away in either and the third side of the landscape is dominated by a large range of hills, emblazoned with a massive chalk carving of a crown, and these only serve to fire the wind back around at you again from a different angle.

It is not uncommon for storms to hang around all day, swirling around the surrounding terrain before attacking from any direction they choose.

The main botanical survivor of this unforgiving environment is Sedge grass, a tough and coarse tufted grass that surrounds the lake and, apart from this, only a few thin copses of young and wiry trees broke up the scenery.

"What the hell is that smell?" was my opening gambit as I walked into Chill's swim. "It's always like that mate, you soon get used to it" he replied, reaching for the kettle out of instinct as I pulled up a bucket to sit on.

If you ever happen to be driving up the M20 to Dover, just open the window at junction 10 and, if the wind happens to be in the North or east, you'll know exactly what I speak of, it's the most bizarre smell imaginable.

After a cuppa and a chat I decided to set up camp just along the bank from Chill, he was fishing in a plot called the 'Ghostly trees' and I plumped for the 'Lawn' next door.

After spending so long on the Mere, where there wasn't even room to swing an ant, let alone a cat, the first thing I did was run up and down the lawn waving twelve feet of carbon about like a loony, I just had to get it out of my system really.

Chilly is quite used to bearing witness to these varying forms of madness, of course, having fished with both Myself, Keith, and Reg for some years, but I think the angler on the other bank was getting a bit worried as I pirouetted up and down the lawn, swishing to and fro with merry abandon, and hollering at the top of my voice.

Over the next few weeks I gathered up as much information about Conningbrook as my poor little brain could carry, trying to make sense of it all as I went along.

Everyone was of the same opinion; that the fish ate precious little in the way of bait, due to the massive amounts of natural food in the lake.

There were next to no other fish present to share this veritable banquet with, so availability of grub had never been a real issue for them.

There were only about twenty carp in the lake and it was rich, deep, clear and occasionally very weedy, in fact, if you added about forty tons of brambles and stinging nettles along with fifty million mosquitoes to the equation, I was back at the bloody Mere!

Most anglers tended to think that single hook-baits or particles were the best approach and I was soon to agree, it really was very similar to the Mere in that respect. Unfortunately, tigers were banned, which of course only made them more appealing really!

It's always awkward fishing in these situations due to the nomadic nature that fish adopt when they are faced with a surfeit of food, they tend to drift from area to area browsing over the various beds of nourishment, a mussel here, a snail there, and a boilie along the way, that sort of 'take it or leave it' mentality.

As I have already mentioned, there were none of the usual 'nuisance' fish present so you could be forgiven for thinking that any pick up would be from a carp, it was just as well I was forewarned by Chilly that this wasn't necessarily the case or I would have thought I'd lost a fish on my very first visit!

I'd been nicely snoozing in the evening, without a single mosquito to hassle me, when suddenly one of my rods had ripped into life.

Jumping up with my head full of visions of fifty pound of carp on the other end I struck into a brief resistance and then nothing but a damaged hooklink!

A few of the other lads had apparently received blistering takes and dropped fish in the weed, quite often the hook-link had broken. Chilly knew the reason, however, having landed an incredible nine pike in his first few sessions!

All of these were taken on static bottom baits and all were hooked fair and squarely inside the mouth. I'd never come across this before in all my years of angling, sure I'd had the odd pike pick up a bait but I'd never heard of them actually feeding on anglers baits as a proper dietary supplement before, or indeed since!

After a few weeks of fishing two nights at a time for no result, apart from pike, I turned up on a Wednesday morning for another session and knew straight away that I could be in with a chance.

There were fish showing all over the lake which, all though not unusual for Conningbrook, was a good sign when coupled with the fact that there had already been three or four carp caught that week, and that certainly was unusual!

The main area of activity seemed to be in and around the 'Stadium bay', although in reality it is actually little more than a deviation in the contours of the bank.

The depth change is the most significant feature and it constitutes the only real area that could be classed as shallows, at least by contrast to the rest of the lake it can. Most of Conningbrook is around 14ft in depth so the bay, with an average depth of 9ft, passes off as the shallows of the lake.

There are various humps and small areas that equal this depth dotted around the lake, but the bay is the largest entire area of raised bottom.

As a consequence of the reduced depth, the ever-present weed really manages to get a hold over the whole region and finding anywhere to actually present a bait can be a nightmare.

On this particular occasion I turned up at the lake just as Paul Forward and his brother were finishing off an exceptionally successful session for Conningbrook.

*Looking across to 'Stadium Bay'*

Pauls brother, Nick, was down for a purely social session as, living way up there in Nottingham, he doesn't get to see his brother all that often.

For a lake that so rarely gives up it's gems it had been very kind indeed to Nick who had managed to bag two fish, both commons, one of thirty six pounds and the other around seventeen pounds. Even more incredibly, Paul had also bagged one of around twenty one pounds, so three fish between them in a couple of days angling meant that there was only one place I wanted to be fishing that session. I camped up on the grass next to them for the day and thereby staked my claim for later on in the afternoon, when they were ready to leave.

Paul, being the affable chap that he is, showed me the exact area that had been producing, which was well handy really as the weed was horrendous and it would have been only too easy to spook off the fish by thrashing around, like J.R. Hartley, in search of a clear spot.

*Paul's brother Nick bagged a 36lb common*

I usually feel very awkward sitting around waiting for somebody to vacate a swim, as it's hard not to seem as if you are pressuring them to leave as soon as possible but, on this occasion, it was a lovely day spent in good company and I was in no real hurry to get sorted out, especially as the predicted bite time wasn't until the early hours of the morning.

I had a last little stroll around the lake while the lads started to slowly pack up, but I saw no signs anywhere else, so I stuck to my original plan and moved in after Mr. F.

The bay is situated right next to a huge floodlit running track and stadium so the evenings are spent bathing in the sodium glow of massive floodlight stacks that sit only a few yards behind the swim, which is quite a surreal experience really.

The good thing is that you can see even the slightest movement on the surface among the weed and there seemed to be plenty to see that night, surely my first Conningbrook encounter was only a few hours away!

Eventually the lights were extinguished for the night and sleep became a possibility, so I drifted off to sleep to dream of big fat mirror carp running the one hundred metres around Crystal Palace running track!

By the time that dawn broke over the Kent hills I was on my third cuppa and, with the coming of light, I saw my first fish of the morning pop its head out in the swim, as if to see who was fishing for them today.

I raised my cup to him and bade him a good morning as he slipped back beneath the glass like surface, leaving a slowly spreading ripple in his wake.

He had rolled almost bang in line with the tree I was using as a back marker for my middle rod, but he seemed to be about ten yards closer in.

Over the next two hours I saw a fair few more carp show, and it was obvious that there were two separate areas that they were favoring.

One was right on the range that I was fishing, but, also, one particular common kept topping over a much closer mark.

The area I had my baits in was right on the back of the weed and the closer marks looked to be very weedy indeed, there would be no chance of plumbing for a spot as 'bite time' was upon me but I could sense an opportunity slipping by with every further roll of the fish.

To re-cast at fish like these can sometimes be the kiss of death, and 'Brownie' the bailiff, who was sat there helping me dispose of my tea rations as we watched the early morning display, regularly reinforced this point.

The more I fretted about re-casting one rod, the more that Brownie kept 'tutting' and shaking his head like a disgruntled school master.

I wasn't so sure about the sensibilities of a re-chuck myself but, as soon as he returned to his swim and I was left with only my own mind to make up, I wound one rod in and plonked it straight on the close mark.

It was just as well that I did as, within half an hour, it had rattled off and my first Conningbrook carp was hooked.

Now, as I'm sure you can appreciate, when you hook a fish in a place like Conningbrook, a place that holds a fish as big as Two-Tone, it's always going to be a very hairy experience.

Even if you know that it's probably the common you've been watching jump for two hours, there is always the chance that it may just be the big fella instead!

As a result I played the fish very gingerly but, even so, I could soon see the culprit twisting and turning around in the clear margins.

He was, indeed, the jumping common but a very welcome one all the same; the first fish from any water always seems to be the hardest one to catch.

Once the first ones caught, however, its capture seems to break down a psychological barrier and you realise, once again, that they are only carp and, just like all the others, they are all catchable in the end.

That first fish weighed twenty seven pounds and was apparently the smallest of three fish that had made there way to the 'brook' via a smaller lake at the top end, and, since their introduction, they had piled on the pounds.

The common I had caught had showed the least impressive growth rate but the other two, who were affectionately known as the 'friendly mirror' and the 'friendly common', had gone from twenty nine to thirty six pounds in under two years and, only a few years later, they were both well in excess of forty pounds!

This just helps to show what a massively rich water the 'brook' is and how much an abundance of natural food and good water quality, coupled with low stocking levels, can affect the health and growth of a carp.

If I had any illusions of having unlocked the secrets of the lake with that first capture then I was soon brought back to reality as I struggled like hell to get a second bite over the following weeks.

Despite fishing as well as I knew how, and using all the experience I had gained on the Mere regarding naturally feeding fish, I found it a real job to get bites on Conningbrook that year.

Obviously, it wasn't ever supposed to be an easy venue, but I was always putting myself in what I considered the very best swim to get a pick up at the time.

The fish would often show like crazy and, at times, you could have been forgiven for thinking that there were 120 carp present rather than just twenty fish (one per acre).

Watching the fish in the edge and discovering the level of natural caution that they displayed, however, would show exactly why the lake was so tricky.

I tried on many occasions to stalk the fish but never actually managed to get one of them to fall for a rig while I was actually 'hands on' stalking for them, although I did trip one up on a little trap set in the edge.

I remember one particular occasion; in fact I don't think that I will ever forget it!

I was quietly working my way through the small copse of trees on the east bank, just to the right of 'Ghosties', when I saw what I had been looking for. There in the margins, just behind a small clump of reeds, was the top tail lobe of a fish, small vortexes giving its presence away as the fish balanced on its nose and inspected the marginal slope.

I dropped to my hands and knees and, painfully slowly, crept closer for a better look. Through the surface film I could clearly see two mid twenty pound commons and they were both feeding happily on a small sandy patch, underneath some trailing branches.

I quietly picked my way out of the trees and returned a few minutes later with a rod and a handful of corn.

Spending ages crawling back into position, and being careful not to snap a twig or appear against the skyline, I moved from one skinny tree to another as slowly as I could, paranoid about spooking them off.

The two fish were still in the same position, so I had to wait for what seemed an eternity until they left on a small circuit of an adjacent reed bed then, as soon as they were out of sight, I lowered my hook bait and about six loose grains around the spot.

I laid the rig right at the edge so the line wouldn't be visible and made sure everything was slack and out of sight.

I laid the rod on the floor amongst the long grass and kept the tip well back from the waters edge and then took up position behind a small sapling that overlooked the spot.

After a few minutes the fish returned, only this time they had brought a third and slightly larger common with them. Whether that third fish had spotted me peering out from behind the tree, or he just sensed the danger, I don't know but what happened next was a real 'eye opener'.

The original two fish glided straight back to the spot that they had been so happily feeding on and, unperturbed by the addition of the corn, the first fish tilted straight up to feed.

It was one of those rare situations where you absolutely know, beyond doubt, that a take is imminent, or so I thought! Suddenly, and for no apparent reason, the new arrival shot forward and actually prodded the lead fish in the flank, gently pushing him off course.

Then, without visibly spooking, the three of them quickly left the area and did not return.

In fact, the few spare grains of corn stayed on that spot for weeks until it eventually turned mouldy and, as far as I could make out, they never fed there again!

With fish that look out for each other in this highly educated manner it was no surprise that bites were few and far between on the 'Brook'.

The social scene at Conningbrook, at that time, was excellent and some good friends were made in that first year.

Everybody was instantly friendly towards us and we really did have some great fun, waiting for the fish to play ball.

Among the many anglers on there that year, Paul Forward, Lee Jackson, Ian Brown, Texas Tom and many others made sure that boredom was never a serious option.

This was just as well, really, as there were often long periods of inactivity on the actual angling front and, due to the lack of weed in the main body of water that year, and the carps nonchalance towards bait, there was precious little that an angler could do to improve his chances of a pick up, it was really just a waiting game.

We had barbeques aplenty and massive social gatherings throughout the summer months with more than the odd cold lager to ease the passage of time.

The lake itself is very open around its banks and the main feature is the plethora of marsh grass and sedges that extend around most of its banks.

This leaves quite large, open grassy areas surrounding most sections, which is obviously ideal for socialising whilst being able to see most of the lake at any one time.

The only downside of the marsh grass and sedges are the thousands of 'marsh frogs' that reside within them, these little buggers can sing for England and the racket they make has to be heard to be believed!

I remember one particular evening, fishing up in the reeds swim in the NE corner of the lake, I had spent the afternoon sussing out the best spots to present my baits in the margins; carp had been very evident up and down the marginal shelf all day.

Due to the heavy silk weed that clung to the slope, I had elected to wait until the fish drifted off and then wade out the baits, dropping them by hand onto any small clear spots and, this way, ensuring perfect presentation for when they returned again later.

At least this had been the plan but, once I had stripped down to my pants and actually waded out, I found that the weed was worse than anticipated and there were no clearings at all. Trying to be as quiet as possible, I scraped the weed clear of the bottom with my toes and kept going until I felt the crunch of gravel below.

Obviously, this stirred up so much crap from the bottom that the water around me was a thick black cloud and I couldn't see a thing on the bottom.

I thought the best way to ensure I hit the spot with the bait was to stand on the clearing and lower the lead down until it was on my foot, I could then tip the rig onto the exposed gravel and even push the lead into the bottom with my toes, keeping it all neat and tidy.

A handful of bait sprinkled all around my legs completed the trap and the whole process was repeated three times, once for each rod.

It all took a lot longer than anticipated but I was happy that, should the fish ever return, I was angling as well as could ever be expected.

Just next-door in, 'mouldy corner', Keith, Paul Forward, his wife and their new child, along with and a few others had set up a barbeque so, with my sounder box in hand, I wandered around there for a bite to eat.

Halfway through my first burger I noticed that my legs were starting to feel a bit warm and itchy but I didn't really pay it much attention to start with, however, within an hour, I knew that something was definitely wrong, my legs were on fire and a faint rash had started to appear right up to the line where my pants started.

Having a young son of my own at home, and being familiar with all the associated 'nappy' stuff that goes with them, I knew that Paul's wife would have just the thing and I was soon relieving her of half a pot of 'Sudafed', a nappy rash cream that cures all manner of skin complaints. I trotted off behind a bush and smeared it all over my legs, thighs and everywhere else that hadn't been protected inside my pants!

Unfortunately for me, though, it had never been designed to combat whatever had attacked me and by the time it got dark, and everybody had made their way home or back to their swims, I felt like I was on fire!

My legs had started to swell up and great big bites or hives had appeared all over them, it was far more painful than the normal sea of mosquito bites that usually covered me throughout the summer months and I didn't sleep for a single minute all night.

Every time I got into the bag my legs would warm up and itch like mad so I had to jump out and stand in the wind, in just my pants, until they had cooled off.

Once they calmed down I would get back into bed and the whole process would start again!

By the time morning rolled around I was in a right old state, I was packed up and ready to leave but I could hardly even walk by now. If my leg so much as touched together it was agony and the itching was absolutely unbearable, I felt as if I wanted to chop my legs off to make it stop.

Somehow I managed to push the barrow around to the van, walking like John Wayne after an unfortunate accident involving too many plates of beans!

I managed to load up all my gear but the bites had gone into overdrive now, what with the heat of the day and the exertion of the walk around the lake, I was in pieces.

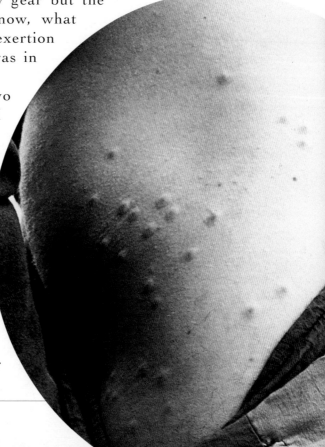

I must have had about two hundred bites on each leg and I was in agony. Showing Paul my dilemma and asking advice only resulted in fits of laughter and the camera coming out to record the event for prosperity, the resulting photo still makes me sweat even now, years later.

No more than a mile from the lake is a hospital and we decided that the best course of action would be an anti-histamine injection, either that or amputation!

As is always the way in hospitals, I arrived to find a waiting room full of sick and injured hopefuls, although I was the only one dancing around like Michael Flatly on hot coals!

Why is it that every schoolboy in a fifty-mile radius decides to get his head wedged in a saucepan on the one occasion, every ten years that I need a doctor?

A helpful neon sign on the wall informed me that I had no chance whatsoever of being seen for at least an hour, and even then the chances were slim, so I hopped, skipped, and pirouetted my way back to the van, almost chewing my fingers off in an attempt not to scratch.

The next stop was the local Tesco's, where I was praying that they sold some sort of magical potion that could render the senses in my legs totally numb and give me enough relief to make it back home to an ice cold bath, where I intended to stay for at least a week.

Hopping about in the medicine aisle, and with my skin glowing like a beacon, I ignored the incredulous looks of the passing mum's with their trollies full of wailing kids, and finally located what I was after.

There, nestling on the bottom shelf between zit lotion and that aptly named hemorrhoid ointment, 'anus-ole', was a great big tub of anti-histamine cooling cream, heaven in a jar!

I stuffed a crumpled up fiver in the hand of the cashier and ran back out to the van, not even waiting for my change, Desperation was taking a hold now and I felt like screaming.

Squeezing in between my van and the black BMW parked along side, I scanned over the rooftops for signs of life and, satisfied that the coast was clear, I quickly pulled down my shorts and started smearing great big handfuls of cream all over my bum and the tops of my legs.

The relief was instant and immense, I was practically groaning with the sudden respite that that the cream had brought, if nothing else it was cold and that alone was a godsend.

It was only when I dipped back down to retrieve my shorts, and cream up the lower half of my legs, that I realised I wasn't alone.

In the front seat of the BMW, with his horror struck face only inches away from my now liberally coated and very naked nether regions, sat an incredibly scared looking, slack jawed, business man with a lap full of paper work.

A phone that probably held a bemused, and now, ignored client on the other end, hung limply from his wrist and, had I smiled and said hello at that point, he looked as if he would have shot straight through the sunroof and run away screaming across the car park.

I did the only decent thing I could think of and pretended he didn't exist, calmly got in the van and drove away.

As soon as I was out of the car park, I pulled up and emptied the rest of the cream all over me, saving the last little bit for any of the more persistent bites on the way home.

All the way down the motorway I chanted the words "ice cold bath" in my brain to keep me going and, once inside the house, I was sat in the tub within seconds as the level of ice cold water rose around me, cutting off the agony as it did so.

The following morning, and looking like a prune from all the hours spent submerged in cold water, I trundled off down to the doctor who was amazed at the state of me and reckoned he'd never seen so many bites at once. He also informed me that I was allergic to the venom in the stings and that was why I had such an adverse reaction.

Even with a course of tablets it still took weeks for the hives to disappear; now I know why there is a 'no wading' rule at Conningbrook!

My second capture for the year was at the beginning of June and came in the form of a cracking looking mirror of twenty seven pounds, a real old character known as Scaly and one of only three original mirrors in the lake.

Never a big lover of commons, I was over the moon to catch one of the 'brooks' rare mirrors, a single buoyant bait cast to a rolling fish did the trick once again and it really did seem near on impossible to get these fish to feed on any real quantity of bait.

A few anglers were persevering with the baiting method but they were singularly unsuccessful and I didn't see a fish caught on more than one handful of offerings at any one time.

I took this second carp on a warm and wet evening from the lawn outside 'Joe's house', which is situated on the west bank of the lake.

Joe's house is an incredible property which sits just a few yards from the water, it's a large and sprawling farmhouse with its own full sized snooker room, and it really is quite a place.

Joe himself was an amazing character, a Maltese guy with a love for throwing large parties on a whim and (luckily) inviting all the anglers along as well.

Many a time we have all suddenly been rounded up like willing sheep and shepherded into Joe's for an impromptu 'jolly up'' that usually only ended when the last man fell!

A little light hearted entertainment of this sort, and the company of like minded souls helps no end on these ultra-difficult waters, if you take it all too seriously it can break your spirit in no time and it is, after all's said and done, supposed to be an enjoyable hobby!

There was another resident of Joe's house who made quite an impact on the fishing scene as well; in fact he had his own section in the Mid-Kent rulebook!

All anglers must be responsible for any loose rigs or edible foodstuffs on account of 'Bruce', the thieving Conningbrook hound.

Bruce would think nothing of raiding an empty bivvy and turning out

a rucksack in search of the merest morsel of vaguely edible fare, I have even seen him grab a can of lager, lay on his back and bite through the can while trying desperately to swallow as much of the jet of beer as possible!

He really was a bloody menace, but so affable that you just had to love him, until he ran off with your sausages that is.

In a way I've got Bruce to thank for reinstating my own carp-dog, Sam, on the scene again. It seemed that because of Bruce's presence and Joe's other dog 'Bonzo' running about all the time, the no dog rule was pretty much ignored.

In fact Pauls little dog, Jim, used to be there more often than Paul as it was a regular occurrence for him to go home and forget that he'd even brought the dog in the first place!

Quite often I'd get a late night phone call checking that somebody had taken him in for the night and asking if we'd look after him till the next evening.

Fishing with Keith again made a nice change and, although our sessions didn't always coincide, we did still manage quite a few socials, most of which involved a couple of woks full of food and a few bottles of red. In fact, it didn't take long at all for our culinary skills to become widely recognised, and we were soon constructing curries and stir-fries for all and sundry.

One particular weekend we were asked by Joe to cook a massive curry feast for a party he had planned for Saturday night. Forty people in all had been invited, some anglers and some of Joe's friends.

**ATTENTION ALL ANGLERS**

ON SATURDAY 11th OF JULY THIS SWIM
WILL BE RESERVED FOR DAVID LANE
Esq, WHO WILL BE PREPARING A
SELECTION OF FINE INDIAN CUISINE
FOR THE ANGLERS PARTY IN
CONNINGBROOK BARN. HE
THEREFORE REQUIRES A SPOT GIVING
HIM EASY ACCESS TO THE KITCHEN.
FAILURE TO COMPLY WITH THIS
REQUEST WILL RESULT IN THE
WITHDRAWAL OF FOOD PRIVILEGES.

We sweated away in the voluminous kitchen all day, preparing vats of steaming Rogan Gosht and Vindaloo.

The upside of all this was an open invite to all the anglers, two reserved swims at the bottom of Joe's garden (within eye sight and sounder box range of the rods) and as much free beer as we wanted whilst we toiled! Keith and I created trays and trays of onion bajhees, and Mr. F chipped in by dressing a whole poached salmon, complete with all the trimmings.

When it was eventually time to party, we all reeled in and joined the revellers for an excellent evenings eating, drinking and playing very bad snooker in the full sized snooker room. There was a ridiculous amount of food available but somehow it all got eaten, there was an even more ridiculous amount of booze but somehow it all got drunk, but everybody had a blinding night.

The weather had been atrocious and the big winds had whipped around the farmhouse all night but what did we care; this was one bivvy that was never getting blown away! Eventually, though, all good things come to an end and, one by one, we all staggered off to bed sometime in the wee small hours.

On the lawn outside the house I had set up a big two man bivvy, expecting female company that never arrived, but that's an entirely different story!

Next to me on the lawn was Pauls Titan brolly and the other side was Keith in a JRC Bivvy with rigid poles and plenty of pegs.

I don't suppose we had been in bed more than about an hour when a massive gust of wind flattened the walls of the bivvy against me, from the outside I must have looked like I was shrink wrapped.

At the same moment I heard I pathetic and pitiful cry from Pauls battered brolly. "Laney can I come in with you" It sounded so woeful and scared that I relented and Paul came scuttling in with his bedchair and sleeping bag. No sooner had he got comfortable than there was an almighty crack and we both looked out to see the remains of his carp house, practically inside out with only the front storm rods left standing!

The roof was totally concave and by the morning the relentless rain

had transformed it into a small swimming pool that we actually had a quick wash in before Paul, struggling against the still gale force winds, dragged the remaining bits of cloth and metal that now constituted his tackle into the van and headed off for home.

By the time everyone else had departed, a few fish had started to show in my area about one hundred yards out so I decided to leave the rods out while I slowly loaded up the van at Joe's.

Over the next hour, and with lashing rain now accompanying the wind, I saw a further six fish show over my baits, and one of these was a very big fish indeed.

I'd packed up everything, including my bivvy, and was left huddling up on my unhooking mat beside the reeds desperately trying to keep some of the rain from coursing down my neck and pouring inside my Gortex jacket. By now the wind was threatening to blow even Joe's brick shed away and eventually around three o'clock I decided to call it a day.

With the rods in sleeves and the net and buzzers in hand, I'd made it halfway across the small piece of grass separating my swim from the van when I felt the overwhelming urge for one last look and, as I turned and looked, there, hanging over my spot in mid air as if in defiance of the elements, was the biggest mirror carp that I'd ever set eyes upon.

It was a sight I'll never forget; over fifty pounds of mirror carp balanced on his tail, standing bolt upright in the wind.

As he toppled and crashed back below the waves I ran back to the swim, unzipping the rod sleeve as I went, and within moments the still baited rig was winging its way out to the mark.

For two more hours I sat there, clinging on to the ground lest I should be blown away, but all to no avail so eventually, frozen, soaked to the skin, and about six hours late, I made my way home but I knew I'd been close, oh so very, very close.

Unfortunately for me, my first year at Conningbrook was brought to an untimely end in October when a little incident involving a boat, a snagged fish and a rule book ended in a misunderstanding that relieved me of my ticket until the following April!

There was a strict 'no boat' rule at the lake at the time, although I think they have a boat there now for emergencies.

Another angler had hooked a fish which, consequently, snagged him up and he'd asked permission at the gravel workings, who own the land, if he could use an inflatable boat to free it, rather than risk leaving it tethered up to an unseen snag.

The boat had been supplied by yet another angler who happened to have it in the back of his car for use on another lake and the whole thing was really nothing to do with me at all but, being a bit bored, I went around there to watch the proceedings.

The angler, whos fish it was, used to angle at Wraysbury at the same time as me, and I clearly remembered that he couldn't swim. The reason I remembered so well was that we all had permission to use boats at the time, and his was absolutely enormous, with number 17 plastered on its side, having previously resided on a boating pond in Southend!

I remembered that his reasoning behind using such a big boat was that it was less likely to sink, as he couldn't swim a stroke.

With this in mind I offered to go out in the boat, in his place, and try and hand-line the fish free while he stayed on the bank and held the rod.

By the time the boat had been pumped up and I'd paddled out to the spot, the fish was, unfortunately, long gone and really the whole incident should have ended there but fate had other ideas.

By pure coincidence I had a photographer with me from a magazine, as we had been doing some rig photos for a monthly article.

The photographer had taken some shots of the entire goings on with the boating and stuff, which was fair enough but, without thinking he had done wrong, he then published them in the next month's magazine without me knowing.

When I received the mag a few weeks later, and first turned the page, I saw them there glaring accusingly back at me and I knew I was going to be for it, and so I was.

I have to admit, now, looking back at the whole affair that it must have looked pretty bad really and no amount of groveling or apologising could dissuade Mid Kent Fisheries that I hadn't blatantly flouted the rules, so I was banned for the rest of the season.

During my time away from the water I had a chance to reflect on my results and those of others, and tried to figure out a method of attack that would up the percentages of me capturing that one big mirror.

I hadn't done too badly really, as three fish in my first year was a good result, especially as only one other angler had caught more during that time, but what I needed was a plan that could single out the big fella.

The pit had been practically devoid of weed all year, which meant that the sandy bottom shone clean in most places, apart from the carpet of micro snails that covered great sections of it.

The deep water that covered most areas fluctuated very little, with only gentle undulations in the lakebed, making it a bit of a lottery as to where to place a bait. The whole fishing situation at the Brook was a bit strange really and I can't truthfully say, with hand on heart, that I actually enjoyed very much of it.

That's not to say that I didn't enjoy being there as I had a terrific time on the social front, but the actual fishing could become a bit soulless at times.

Looking back now on the mad parties we had and the general camaraderie of the regulars it was a crazy few months.

I remember chasing Bruce halfway around the lake one day because I'd returned to my swim and found the cardboard and silver foil remains of the packet of custard tarts I'd been saving for my lunch, they were my only food for the day, and I was furious with the thieving hound.

I couldn't figure out how come Sam, my faithful carp dog and protector, had let such a violation of our food stocks take place. It was only later I found out that Paul, in a fit of hunger and pure genius, had actually eaten them himself and then ripped and torn the packaging, before scattering it around my swim in a perfect ploy to shift the blame onto Bruce!

With the fishing, there was just nothing you could really do to improve your chances, the lake was getting busier and busier so moving swims was getting harder, and the fish just jumped for no reason so location wasn't the problem, it was just like a great big wheel of fortune really.

I suppose a lot of the problem was that I had never really fished a water where I targeted one particular fish and everybody else was also waiting for that one specific bite.

Had there been more to the actual pit, like islands or bars or something, then it may have been a bit more interesting I suppose.

The only one area that did differ dramatically was the margins, as a shallow weedy shelf ran the entire circumference of the pit, the only down side was that the big mirror had only ever been caught once from the margins and was rarely, if ever, even seen to visit them.

Bait was also something that, for the first time in years, I was unsure about so I phoned Kev at Mainline and told him of my dilemmas.

I explained that I needed something that looked and smelt like a single fruity attractor bait but in reality was a high quality bait, full of proteins and Mainline magic.

"No problem son, have I ever let you down yet?" came the welcome reply so, bathing in the warm glow of his confidence, I ordered myself a freezer full to try out.

When it turned up it was exactly what I needed, bright pill box red, stinking of Fruitella flavour but based on a really good protein base mix.

By the time that April eventually rolled around again I had come up with my master plan. I was to fish two rods always at range and on single hookbaits only. I had decided, also, to stick to bottom baits due to the lack of weed.

The third rod I'd fish in the margins if I thought that there was a chance or maybe fish particles or floaters anything really to keep me sane while the other two rods sat it out for the big fella.

On leaving the lake every week I planned to liberally scatter a kilo or two of the new bait all over the place, taking care not to bunch too many together in an attempt to get the carp used to finding single baits that weren't always attached to hooks!

My first and second trips were both totally unsuccessful and the only practice that I managed with my new rods was plumbing about in the vain hope of tracking down an early season weed bed to fish next to.

I'd scattered a fair bit of the bait about before leaving, as planned, and I heard on my return that three fish had been hooked in a mad feeding spell during the week. The good thing was that they all fell for single baits fished in the very area that I had baited the heaviest, whether this was coincidence or not I wasn't sure but it was a good confidence boost to know that my baits were probably eaten as well.

In reality I should not have even been there on that occasion, any normal person would have been too busy taking their motor to the garage instead.

Over the previous few days the old van had stared to play up a bit, which is a joke really as it was bloody awful when it was running properly! I suppose at this stage it would be prudent to reiterate my stance on motor vehicles and what I actually used to class as 'playing up a bit'.

Throughout most of my adult life I seem to have been hampered by one specific, reoccurring, nightmare.

Unlike most other nightmares this particular one seems to intensify when I actually wake up and it reaches its harrowing crescendo every morning as I reach the parking space outside my house.

Since passing my driving test, nearly twenty years ago I must have owned at least thirty different vehicles and, of these, only two have ever survived to see another owner!

Every single type of automotive disaster that can possibly transpire has transpired to one or more of my motors.

Now, obviously, if a car breaks down on the way to work it is not too much of a problem, or even on the way back from fishing it can be tolerated, but it must always be able to reach the lake.

Many a car or van has been collected on the back of a wrecking truck from the banks of various carp lakes all over the country and I've lost count of the ones that collapsed in a pile of oil and steam on motorway hard shoulders.

It is, of course, never actually my fault, I'm just a bit unlucky with engines although since I discovered where the oil and water go I seem to have become a trifle less unlucky!

I must admit though, sometimes sheer determination to reach the lake can cause me to overlook the odd mechanical problem that should, in reality, be sorted out before a sixty mile 'thrash' up the motorway.

There was something wrong with the bit that makes the Diesel end up in the bit that makes the engine work and every few miles it would just conk out and cruise to a halt.

On the day that I was due to return to Conningbrook, to continue my quest, the old van really started 'playing up'. Although I had bait a plenty, some of the other field-testers who I deliver to needed bait and I also had some pellets and other bits to collect, so there was no avoiding a trip up to Mainline in Essex to stock up a bit.

The problem was that the van really didn't seem as if it had that much traveling left in it. I had already conked out about ten times that morning and found that the only remedy was to pull over and wait for a minute before restarting the engine, this seemed to fix the problem for about ten miles and then it would conk out once more.

From my house to Mainline, at that time, was an eighty mile round trip and then down to Conningbrook was another fifty miles which, if you add it together, equals a bloody lot of break downs!

As is often the way with these things, the problem didn't seem about to solve itself and the further I drove, the more frequent the conking out became until, half way to Essex and by a blend of pure chance and sheer laziness, I discovered that I could turn off the engine while still coasting along and re-start it again with full power, hurrah!

I only had to do this about twenty times each way and pretty soon I was back in Crawley with a van full of boilies and pellets.

There was of course one slight down side to my new found cure; the steering lock was proving a bit of a problem.

It was alright if you conked out on a straight bit of road, but if you had to move the wheel at all during the re-start procedure the bloody steering lock came on and twice I nearly launched myself off the road as I fumbled frantically with the keys.

I knew that in reality it was madness to set out for Kent with the van in this condition as it was bound to completely collapse soon, but the alternative involved not going fishing. Not fishing!!

I couldn't see how that could ever be a serious alternative and decided, eventually, that if I could just make it one way then I could still fish and I'd sort out getting home later.

After all, if I became stranded at the lake then so be it, I could think of worse scenarios.

The journey down the M23, M25, M26 and finally the M20 was horrendous and I conked out about every five or ten minutes, all the way there but eventually, by sheer persistence, I coasted down the track and into the car park next to Joe's house.

Its funny isn't it, but by the time I'd stepped three feet from the motor I'd forgotten all about it!

I was far more interested to see that a generator and a big old water pump had been set up on the top bank of the lake since my last visit and that the pipes led from a relatively new pit behind, straight into the small reed lined bay.

It hadn't actually been switched on as yet but it looked encouraging, as it had obviously been put there for a reason.

My experience of pumps and carp in the past led me to believe that, if my theory were correct, as soon as it was turned on it would prove to be an irresistible draw to the carp's natural curiosity.

The best place to fish the pump would be from 'The Island', although it's a bit of a stupid name really as, not only is it plainly not an island, but there are no islands on the lake at all!

Lee Jackson was in there at the time but he was due to leave the next morning, so I vowed to keep a good eye out for any activity from the workman at the gravel company and be ready to move as soon as need be.

At the crack of dawn the following morning (or somewhere thereabouts) I was rudely awakened by a JCB trundling along the track behind me. As I peered around the edge of the brolly I just caught sight of a bowser full of diesel being towed up towards the generator, I didn't need telling twice! I grabbed my kit and practically ran around to the island, just in time to see poor old Lee disappear off to work, this was more like it. The generator spluttered into life and I sat and watched as the coloured water stirred up from the margins and streaked out across the pit.

The force of the water from the pipe quickly dug a deep 'plunge pool' into the marginal shelf as it scoured the bottom, down to the rock below.

I could envisage the mud trail acting like a beacon to the fish, calling them in from all over the pit, and when it started to abate later in the day I duly stirred the bottom up with a big stick to restart the flow of chocolate colored attractor.

I positioned my baits at twenty yard intervals along the coloured strip of water with the furthest one being just into clear water, at about seventy yards range.

The day quickly passed in anticipation and, before I knew it, it was evening time and Lee was back again, after a hard days work in the shop.

He decided to set up further around the lake, in the lifebelt swim, and apart from the two of us only one other angler watched the sun set over the lake that evening.

Just before the darkness had totally enveloped the bay, I noticed that the muddy water from the pipe had started to run clear again so,

borrowing a discarded shovel, I simply filled my barrow with earth from the recent excavations on the back lake and tipped it into the flow, repeating this a few times at regular intervals right up until midnight.

During the course of the evening I had seen a number of fish showing in and around the bay but one fish in particular kept showing at long distance.

He was on the same line as the muddy trail but just beyond it, where the water cleared a little, and probably about one hundred yards out from my swim.

The fact that I could still see him at all as it grew dark, let alone at that range, suggested that it must be a very big fish indeed.

I had intended to leave all three rods in the mud trail but, eventually, I could resist it no longer so, just before bedtime, I reeled in one rod and sent a single bait out as close as I could to the spot.

It was a job to see the lead and bait land, but it looked and felt right, so I left it there for the night and retired to the brolly.

It seemed as if I had only been asleep for a few minutes when the most almighty splash tore me from the land of naked women and seventy-pound carp, and I peered tentatively out from under the sleeping bag.

The water in the margins was rocking from the re-entry of a big old carp and it looked as if my plan was coming together.

By the colour of the sky I knew that it could be no later than about five in the morning so I just lay there staring out, waiting for him to jump again, when a single beep on the long-range rod brought me fully awake.

As I struggled out of the bag I watched the rod tip pull slowly down towards the water and then, as I was halfway across the grass with the bag flapping at my heels, my alarm tore the morning in half as the baitrunner kicked in to play.

As soon as I leant into the fish I knew it was a 'goodun', the line cut higher and higher in the water until, over one hundred yards out, a big humped back broke the mirror calm surface.

What happened next will always be indelibly etched in my memory; he turned and, at full acceleration, charged back into the bay with a spume of water breaking across his shoulders.

He must have surged along like this for sixty yards or so but luckily, due to the angle, I was gaining line all the time.

The water, having settled over night, was crystal clear and as he turned back out of the bay I could see him, inches under the surface as he passed in front of me, every scale and marking was evident and, as I realised what I'd hooked, I don't mind admitting I was scared half to death by the whole affair.

Its funny how you dream of the moment for months or years but when it finally comes, it's fraught with so many possible disasters that it becomes almost too much to bear!

Somehow, though, I managed to gain control of both the fish and myself and coaxed him, painfully slowly, towards the net.

At first it looked as if it was going to go as smoothly as clockwork and I guided the big old fella right up to the net cord and halfway over it.

The feeling of dread was just being exchanged for one of pure ecstasy, the first stirrings of a victory cry were dancing around my lips when, with an almighty explosion of water, he woke up to what was happening and powered back out of danger. I was so close now that I wasn't losing this battle for anything so, unwilling to give him any line back, I marched straight into the lake with the fish raging on a short line but staying just out of reach of the flailing net.

Out across the marginal shelf we went until I was up to my chest in water and then we reached a stalemate, he was too tired to make another run and I was sinking fast in the silt and unable to get the net underneath his considerable bulk.

As if all of this was not farcical enough, once I had eventually managed to coax him over the net I couldn't get the leverage to ensnare him.

Every time I tried to lift, my feet slid further down the marginal slope until, eventually, I threw the rod down in the water beside me and, holding only the tip, unceremoniously wrestled my prize into the mesh.

The words to describe that transition of body and mind as you realise that the battle is over and you have won it, have not yet been invented so I had to rely on screaming "LIGHT MY FIRE!!" as loudly as was humanly possible across the lake, startling coots, moorhens, and Lee Jackson as I did so.

The latter appeared, at a jog, into the swim five minutes later knowing, beyond doubt, what it was in my net, especially as I was dancing around singing 'I'm Free' at the top of my voice.

Such was the release of pressure at finally catching the biggun that I felt released in some way, as if I'd just been freed early from a long sentence.

It made me realise, much later on, that I'd been fishing in a way that really didn't suit me at all.

Not for me is the camping out and waiting my turn at the one biggun in the lake, and I vowed never to get that embroiled in the 'bounty hunting' side of things again.

At the time, however, I just felt elated and we set about phoning anybody we could wake.

After much trying we managed to raise Paul Forward from the comfort of his bed, he'd heard the phone going and going and known the outcome before he'd even picked it up, it was either Lee or me and today, it was me.

Paul arrived at the lake shortly afterwards to do the photos and the

first thing we realised was that we didn't have enough film, so I left the lads in charge of the sacked fish while I nicked Pauls motor to shoot up the shops and grab a few rolls.

I was absolutely buzzing and a few minutes alone gave it all a chance to sink in, at last my quest was over and the big girl was mine!

I flicked on the radio and wound up the volume as the DJ played 'The Beautiful South' and a track called 'Perfect Ten', it's a song in praise of over sized women and it fitted perfectly, seeing as what I had waiting for me back at the lake. When the line "I like to hold something I can see" came on, I was singing away at the top of my voice and grinning like a Cheshire cat. Everything was laid out waiting for me on my return, and we weighed her in at a hefty fifty four pounds.

The photo session went like a dream and the fish suffered the oohs and aahs of the assembled crowd like a pro.

It's a great feeling when you bag the biggun that you've set your stall out to catch for so long, it's even better if you bag it early in the morning or during the night as you have a whole day of rejoicing ahead of you.

The sun was shining, the phones were going non-stop as the word spread and everything was right with the world.

Later on that day, as I was floating around the lake in a cloud of euphoria, Mrs. Joe called me over, while hanging her washing out and asked, "Who caught it then?"

"I did" I proudly replied, sticking my chest out a bit.

"Yes, I heard you," she said smiling. "It was five twenty seven precisely and I turned to Joe and said 'someone's had the biggun dear'"

A steady stream of people came over to congratulate me throughout the day, some brought champagne, some brought cold beer, and no fishing was done but, then, what was the point?

True to form, the bloody van wouldn't start again the next morning but I'd already made contingency plans for just such an eventuality and 'borrowed' Paul's AA card number.

Rather than wait at Joes house, after phoning the 'very nice man in a breakdown truck; I used my final half an hour to sit down by the lake and reflect on the previous years angling and remember the good times along the way.

It was a lovely morning and I was totally lost in my own little world, so I didn't hear the arrival of the AA, I didn't even notice the flashing yellow lights and I was only broken from my reverie by the sound of Mrs. Joe shouting "Dave" across the field at me.

It wasn't really the best way to start out my charade of being called Paul, but the 'very nice man' kindly overlooked this minor detail and, after a rather long and complicated procedure, he managed to coax the old girl into life again (the van, not Mrs. Joe) and I was back off down the motorway for the last time.

# Chapter 5

# *The Secret Garden*

"*After the buzz of Conningbrook had settled down a bit and I'd actually got a new fuel pump fitted to the old van, I started to think about where to fish next. I didn't have a clue where to go but one thing was for sure and that was that it would not be busy, would definitely not be another circuit water and I wanted a bit of mystery back in the equation*".

Size of the fish was pretty irrelevant really; I just wanted somewhere to chill out for a while and fish for the unknown rather than sit it out for one particular, known, big fish.

I did think about the Mere, but it was still the spring season and I certainly wasn't going to risk another, much larger, fine by falling into that trap again.

I was also feeling a bit jaded with the whole big carp scene really and needed somewhere to recharge my batteries before immersing myself in another big challenge.

In fact, if I put the whole thing into perspective, I suppose it was 'The Mere' that ruined me in the first place; the pure, wild, and unspoilt environment, the unknown quantity and the thrill of the chase.

Conningbrook, although a lovely fishery and one of the friendliest places I have ever angled, didn't really do it for me and I realised that I was fishing for the fish and not my own personal pleasure.

At the end of the day I fish for pleasure and, if I have to question whether the end justifies the means, then maybe I already know the answer.

Nowadays I find that the mystery factor is what really gets my pulse racing, the unknown, the thrill of a run on a water full of dreams, even if the realities turn out to be less than expected, the excitement you experienced at the time remains vivid in your memory.

I didn't have to wait long to find the perfect venue, in fact Reg had been pestering us to come and look at a certain lake for ages.

We, being Keith, Chilly, and myself had thought at first that he was just trying to lure us up to his neck of the woods to save himself a bit of petrol money but, with time on my hands, I decided to humour him and pop-up there for a little look.

As it was still the closed season in the Cotswolds all four of us had decided to meet up at the lake and hopefully we'd see a few of the fish that lived there while they were comfortably safe from anglers lines.

After pulling up in the car park, having followed Reg's terrible directions from the back of an old beer mat, I crossed the road and walked up to a large privet style hedge with a rustic country entrance, akin to the wooden doorway in that classic children's book 'The Secret Garden'.

Once across the threshold, it was like stepping back in time, a quaint wooden hut stood on my left and inside I found a slotted front that looked out in a pillbox style across the lake, a bird watchers paradise.

Every type of waterfowl and exotic bird life imaginable was depicted on the inside hut walls and, even with the restricted view of the lake beyond, I could see that it was, as Reg had described, a place of outstanding beauty.

I hurried outside and bumped straight into Chilly who was leaning against the bole of a large oak tree and smoking a fag while staring out over the pond. He was obviously as impressed at first sight as I was and together we set off for our first walk around.

Visible gravel bars, islands, reed beds and small bays made up the bulk of the lake and a large, round, deeper section had been stitched on to one end, as if by way of an afterthought.

When the four of us were all assembled we took in the full tour as Reg filled us in on the small amount of history he had been able to glean.

Although it had only been very lightly fished over the preceding few years, there was a local rumour that a thirty eight pound carp had been caught some years earlier and was now, unfortunately, in a bow fronted case adorning the walls of a nearby pub!

The lake itself was outstanding and one of those places that you just can't wait to fish every different nook and cranny of. I could just envisage my brolly set up next to the massive reed bed at the southern end or nestled under the oak tree as I fished up against the islands etc.

The far bank section was out of bounds and given over to a nature reserve, it was this that the hut looked out over so any little 'sorties' into this area would have to be kept very low key.

We soon found some fish, milling around under a tree in the Back Bay. As it was still the closed season the carp were acting very naturally and soon mopping up the baits we'd sprinkled beneath the branches that the four of us were hanging out of.

Most of the carp seemed to be around the low to mid twenty-pound bracket, mostly very scaly old mirrors, but four of them stood out from the crowd.

It transpired that Reg had seen these bigger ones before and, he later told us, two other big grey mirrors that were not present on this particular afternoon.

He had been hesitant to say on the phone how big he thought these larger ones were for fear of ridicule if he had turned out to be sadly mistaken.

I know myself how hard it can be to size fish on a lake where you know none of the stock, and have no point of reference to compare to.

Regardless of that, I was convinced that all four were upper thirties and the bigger one by some margin, and if they hadn't been caught (at least not for donkey's years) that was enough for me; where do I buy my ticket!

We nicknamed the place 'Charlie's' for some reason, and set about laying plans for the coming season.

We decided to have a sort of pre-baiting campaign throughout the rest of the closed season, just to get the fish used to finding a bit of bait. I used to drive up there early in the morning and spend the day just looking about before baiting up and then driving home, which was bloody hard work, considering the distances involved.

It was a total round trip of about 250 miles from my house so it took a bit of doing but I was sure it would be worth it in the end, also it was such a relaxing place to be that it was more of a pleasure than chore.

Keith and Chilly had other plans set out already but Reg and I were well up for it, also Graham, another friend of ours, was to start the season on there with us.

Although spending all of our spare time at Charlie's, we curiously never saw the big mirrors again at all that spring and started the season with only that one single sighting to remember them by.

From the first moment that I cast a line into that pond, on June the sixteenth, I started to learn a valuable lesson about un-pressured fish and the way they react to the interferences of the outside world.

Carp that are not used to being put under scrutiny by anglers, carp that are not accustomed to finding traps at every meal table are not, by any means, easier to catch than their more worldly wise cousins!

I think the problem lays in the fact that they treat each and every little anomaly in their normal environment as a sign of danger and as a result they spook from lines, bait, or even the sight of a person where a person usually isn't found.

We managed to trick a couple of early fish into picking up a bait, while they were still a bit unsuspecting, and by the end of the first weekend I had managed a twenty six pound, heavily plated mirror and lost one while Reg outwitted a twenty four pound linear.

From that moment on the fish just seemed to exist in a state of perpetual paranoia and, before long, they restricted their movements to the out of bounds bank and a small secluded bay that lay within it.

If ever we were lucky enough to come across them in the fishable sections they would instantly disappear as soon as we started fishing for them.

We eventually spent most of June and July just chasing them fruitlessly around the lake! It was all extremely frustrating but, at the same time, massively challenging and the more we struggled the more determined we became.

Strangely, though, although we still saw the odd fish (especially if we snuck around to the Back Bay and peered in there) we never saw the four big fish again, it was as if they had a secret passageway into another lake somewhere.

It wasn't as if it was a massive pit or anything, I suppose it totalled about 17 acres if you took all the bays into account, but it was amazing how well the fish could hide within it.

Apart from us three there was only really one other carp angler on there and we obviously got to know him really well over the course of the summer.

Kevo had been fishing the pit, on and off, for years and was our only really reliable source of information on the place.

Amazingly he said he had been re-catching a very small proportion of the fish for years and, like us, had seen much bigger fish throughout his time on there but only the occasional sightings, and usually in the closed season.

It seemed to be the general consensus of opinion, among the few locals who had fished the place in the past, that the out of bounds bank was practically a permanent residence for the better fish during the actual fishing season.

Later on in the summer, Keith came over for a couple of sessions as I think all the talk of how relaxed and beautiful it was had finally persuaded him to pay the odd visit.

Although he didn't manage a 'Charlie's' carp he enjoyed it no end and together we had a couple of incredible 'nature moments'.

The first was on the south bank, where a large reed bed grows out from the margins. We were walking a circuit, looking for signs of fish, when we both heard a small splash on the other side of the reeds. Creeping up as quietly as we possibly could we simultaneously leant out over the thick reeds, hoping to get a glimpse of a carp in the margins when suddenly, and with a blood curdling squawk, a bloody great bird flew straight out of Jurassic park and nearly clobbered us in its haste to escape.

Neither of us had ever seen anything like it before, it was at least the size of a heron but fully spotted and more than a little cross!

We had to go into the bird watching hut and look it up on the charts on the wall before we discovered it was a Bittern.

The second occurrence was during a sneaky trip around to the out of bounds, we weren't fishing or anything, just looking to see if we could find any of the missing monsters.

Keeping as quiet as possible, for more than just the carps sake, we crept through the long undergrowth on our way to the Back Bay.

With only a few yards to go we had to cross a piece of ground that was on view from the bird hut, so we were hardly even breathing in our attempts to become invisible when, as if from nowhere, a bloody great deer just flew up from under our feet, one second nothing and the next, a full sized roe deer in mid air in front of us!

He must have 'gone to ground' when he first heard us approaching, hoping we'd pass by and only bolted as we almost trod on the bloody thing.

All thoughts of keeping quiet were soon forgotten then, we almost wet ourselves in shock.

By the middle of August, and with no further fish to show for my efforts, I had had enough for a while, plus the permanent draw that the Mere held over me was starting to have a bizarre effect.

Every time I dreamt about fishing it would be at the Mere, even though I hadn't been there for ages I still couldn't get it out of my mind, I'd often wake up suddenly in the night and be totally surprised at being somewhere else.

The more I thought and dreamt about that Black Mirror, the more I knew that I couldn't possibly rest until I'd caught him.

It wasn't just him either, the vision of the big common was a haunting one and, although he'd never been caught, that didn't mean that he never would.

Eventually I gave in to the temptation and returned to the jungle for a series of six or seven trips that can only be described as hell on earth.

I'd left it far too late in the year really as the weed and the brambles had grown with a triffid-like enthusiasm and strangled the whole lake.

Added to this the thick blue/green algae had really taken a hold and visibility was next to non-existent.

Straight away I knew I'd need a boat, as Terry's little one had been re-claimed from its hiding place in the bushes, and the weed would make finding clear areas almost impossible without one.

On a trip round to Keith's house one evening I stumbled across the perfect vessel, just languishing under the willow tree at the bottom of his garden. Apparently he had borrowed it from Adam Penning for a trip abroad and it was just sort of 'resting' in his garden for a while.

It was an eight foot fibreglass rowing boat with proper row-locks, seat and everything, a Rolls Royce of a boat compared to my normal efforts.

The only down side was the colour, as I didn't think bright blue and white would blend in with the verdant back drop of the Mere too well, but half an hour with a big pot of green paint soon sorted that out.

I was sure Adam wouldn't mind too much, after all he is a carp angler too and we all love green, don't we?

Getting anything on or off the Mere is a nightmare as the road that runs past the entrance is regularly travelled by spies, or at least that's how it feels when you are trying to sneak on there pretending that a rod bag or rucksack is really a walking stick or a big bag of sandwiches.

A bloody great big boat, though, is beyond the bounds of subterfuge and there is just no way can it ever be anything except a bloody great big boat!

Consequently, it was two thirty on a Monday morning when I eventually pulled up in the lay by with a badly painted green boat roped to the old van roof. I didn't have a roof rack so it was held in place using many different cords, all knotted together and wound through the open windows and around the hull.

It had been a windy old drive up the M25, with the windows half open and the van had been lurching all over the place.

Taking my van out on an open road was a scary enough prospect anyway, let alone with the added encumbrance of an upturned boat on the roof.

I'd left the dogs at home on this trip as it was going to be hard enough work as it was, turning up in the dark and rowing across the neighbouring lake to reach the Mere.

The lay-by is not actually anywhere near the lake but, instead, it lies along side the far bank of a big lagoon next to the Mere itself.

To reach the Mere by boat you have to start by dragging the boat, and all your gear, over an old iron fence and dropping it next to the ditch.

The ditch is a good six feet deep and surrounded by nettles so the only sensible way across is to clamber down into the bottom of it and pass your gear over head from one side to the other, easier said then done in the pitch dark.

As soon as I pushed the boat over the railing and let go of the back it plunged nose first into the ditch and firmly wedged itself there, it seemed to take forever to free it as I stood at the bottom of the muddy ditch in the pitch black, struggling to lift eight foot of boat back out on to the other side whilst being stung to death at every turn.

After the boat came the supplies, life jacket, oars, bait and everything else that all need chucking in or over the ditch and then dragging up the other side and off into the bushes with the boat.

Eventually, I had the boat and all the associated clobber safely out of sight and, after driving the van up the road and parking up, I set about launching it all out onto the lagoon.

Then it was a simple matter of rowing about five hundred yards to the back of the Mere before unloading all the boat, dragging it over another causeway, loading it all up again and finally drifting silently onto the magical, but somehow spookily dark waters of the Mere.

I had a rough idea of where I wanted to set up my main camp, I'd been thinking long and hard about the 'long run' and I couldn't get the image of that lost fish out of my mind.

Somehow I was sure that it almost owed me another chance so I struck out the oar and headed down the lake.

Even in the half light of pre-dawn I could make out the unmistakable shape of a small marker bobbing about in the middle of the lake, between the reeds and my intended swim on the back bank.

Somebody had obviously beaten me to it and, as I rowed onwards, I wondered who might be here already, as you could never tell until you actually bumped into them, such was the hidden nature of the swims.

As I grew nearer the tiny marker it was suddenly eclipsed as a big silhouette of a carp slid silently from the water, rocking the marker back and forth with the wash from its re-entry. Whoever was fishing there must have been pretty excited at the sight of that and I started planning and re-planning where I would fish.

As I arrived at the 'long run' I could see the rod tips just peeking out from the bushes but there was no answer to my whistle and no obvious signs of life.

There was also no boat in the little hidden parking bush either, and this was strange as the only access was by boat.

Rather than hang about, I made my way to the opposite side of the lake where the reeds bulge out from the end of the point and give plenty of cover for parking up the boat and tackle, while I looked about for signs of life.

As I arrived on the outer stems I could make out a tiny, camouflaged craft already pulled up tight into the reed bed but still no signs of life.

Pulling up beside it I tied up to an old tree stump and picked out the small path in the dark, heading upwards out of the undergrowth to higher ground.

Once I was up on the high bank I made myself comfy on the grass and watched the sun come up, this is always a special moment on the Mere as everything slowly stirs to life and the odd carp hurls itself out of the water sending huge ripples across the surface.

As soon as it was fully light I picked up my little rucksack full of water and a few bit's of food and set off walking the banks in search of carp and anglers alike.

By mid morning, and with the sun beating down from a clear blue sky, I had managed to find one but not the other as there was still no sign of the mystery angler and owner of the abandoned boat.

Further along the bank, in front of 'Turds Point', there was a large floating weedbed and there, just poking out from the edge of the canopy, was the unmistakable flat lobed tail of the big Black Mirror himself.

From my dangerous perch, at the top of a bendy little willow, I could just make out his frame as it lifted the profile of the weed when he rose and fell with the gentle ripple. He wasn't alone either, for circling the back of the weed was the equally unmistakable form of the big, shovel head common!

The two biggest carp in the lake and I'd found them within a few hours of starting back on the Mere, all thoughts of Charlie's lake disappeared in the wink of an eye, I was back at the Mere and it was as if I'd never been away!

By mid afternoon I was in full stalking mode, dangling a single large snail from a short piece of candle, directly down through the top of the weed bed.

I knew from experience that the Mere carp love picking snails and mussels from the bottom of these floating canopies, and also that they would be almost impossible to catch while they were doing so.

Whoever the absent, mystery angler was obviously knew this as well because one of the only items left in his boat was a jam jar half full of water, snails and a few zebra mussels!

I had been a bit concerned at first that maybe somebody had drowned or something terrible like that but, when I'd thought about it a bit more, I figured that it very unlikely they would have tied the boat up in the reeds first!

Eventually the mystery was solved when I bumped into Little Ritchie, sneaking about on the path and looking even more furtive than usual.

He told me of the events of the previous night and how the lake had been raided by the authorities, which I found a bit strange as the spring had long since passed and usually only the old bailiff was left in charge by now.

Ritchie, fearing capture, had been forced into a complicated getaway involving rowing across the lake and sneaking off through the bushes, abandoning all his tackle as he did so. In reality, he had probably forsaken the safest spot on the lake anyway as, in the night, without a boat, nobody was ever going to find you in the 'Long run'.

After Ritchie had departed I spent the afternoon sitting up in the spindly little tree, watching the Shovel Head common and the Black Mirror playing a game of cat and mouse with the resident Cob Swan.

The swan was determined to force his way onto the weed raft to inspect my piece of candle, to test it's edibility, but the two big fish were extremely protective of their little piece of real estate. The swan regularly harassed either one of the fish, actually surging towards them and spooking them off, but it was outclassed when the two leviathans teamed up and surged back.

At one stage the swan actually back peddled and got really flustered as the two carp kept closing in on him, forcing him away from the weed but, eventually, the fish had enough agro for the day and drifted off deeper into the little end bay and the thick weed that had settled there.

With only a swan left to fish for I wound in and set about tucking myself away for the night.

I'd found a perfect hiding place for the boat and I decided to spend a bit of time fishing in and around the bay, as the fish obviously liked it there at that time.

The weed that builds up in the area every year proves an irresistible draw to the fish and they usually end up spending weeks at a time holed up in the thick beds of floating Canadian pondweed, safe from the attentions of anglers and swans alike!

I managed a couple of sessions over the next weeks and started to see fish regularly in the area, although getting them to pick up a bait was a different matter entirely.

Unfortunately, though, I never got the chance to exploit my findings as it seemed that there were forces working very hard this year to stop any angling taking place, even during the summer months of the old 'normal' season.

At this time of year we were usually left alone to get on with it but, just a couple of weeks after the incident with Ritchie, and just before one of my planned sessions, I received a phone call from a friend informing me that my boat had been discovered and confiscated and some of the more 'hidden areas' had been exposed.

Unwilling to risk adding more debt to the family purse by appearing in court again, I opted to give it a miss for a while and return to Charlie's for one last concerted effort.

I would have gladly walked away from the Mere for good if I could have, it was so much hassle to fish on there that I regularly questioned my own sanity.

Not only was it owned by people who really didn't want us there anyway, but the whole logistical nightmare of moving your kit about through the hideous brambles and nettles, the hiding away and jumping at your own shadow, not to mention the unbearable humidity of the swims, made it sheer madness to even consider calling it enjoyable.

The problem, of course, was the Black Mirror himself; there was, and still is, no other carp like him. It was an impossible situation, really, as I knew that there was just no way that I could possibly walk away, he haunted my every dream, and I just had to catch him no matter how long it took.

It was with mixed emotions that I returned to Charlie's again after my short break at the Mere. I was glad to be fishing back in the company of

Reg again, glad to be allowed to sit out in the open next to the rods and sip a cold beer as the sun went down, but my thoughts were still at the Mere, watching the Black Mirror glide in and out of the weed beds.

In general, all our efforts on Charlie's since the first week of the season had drawn a big fat blank and, as far as I was concerned, there was really only one plan left to try.

We had tried chasing them around the lake, tried stalking them, and even tried poaching them from the out of bounds areas, so the time had come to seriously bait up.

Not a few kilos here and there or a bucket full once a week, but to absolutely fill it in every other day for weeks!

With Reg only living a few miles from the lake and me being able to get hold of the 'good gear' from Mainline at the right price the plan was simple, I'd supply a mountain of Assassinate boilies and pellets and Reg would spod it all out there, in the evenings after work.

We picked two adjacent swims at the deeper end of the pit and set about bringing the fish into them on our terms!

The bottom, at this end, was a lot different to the rest of the lake, apart from being deeper it was also a lot siltier and at first we struggled for bites, even though there were obviously tench and bream, along with the odd carp visiting the area on a regular basis.

After two weeks of solid baiting we could see the carp rolling over and head and shouldering every evening as darkness fell.

They were bang on top of the baits but only the odd single bleep would register on the alarms. Both our fish earlier in the year had fallen to pop-up presentations and, what with the extra silt, I still thought that this would be the way forward but, as it turned out, I was so very wrong.

One evening, after watching a dozen tench and two fair sized carp roll over the spot, I could take no more and wound in one rod, sitting there staring accusingly at the terminal tackle hoping for inspiration.

After a while I pulled out a pair of scissors and cut straight through the mainline, letting the whole lot fall in a tangled mess in the bottom of the rucksack, time for a change!

I tied up a straight forward bottom bait rig but with an extra long mono hook link, probably at least fourteen inches, and a standard long hair with an eighteen mm bottom bait, straight out of the bag.

Taking aim at the latest set of ripples emanating from the spot, I cast the rig out into the zone.

It's amazing just how much difference a rig can actually make isn't it?

I mean, you read all the time about how a change in presentation can make all the difference, but not to the extent of blanking for weeks and

then five runs in a night to one rod, but that's exactly what happened.

By the time that morning rolled around, I had netted two carp and three tench and the next week's session couldn't come around quickly enough.

The swim itself had become a mud bath over the previous few weeks, what with all the spodding sessions and bivvying up two nights a week, and I couldn't face the thought of setting up in a swamp so I went for a walk to try and find some leaves or something to lie in the puddles.

At the back of the car park I found the perfect thing, they had just cut the long grass in the nearby field and piled up a huge mound of fresh cuttings there.

I was soon back at the lake with a wheelbarrow loaded up with nice dry grass and my swim was soon covered with a thick wall to wall carpet of the stuff.

Apart from the onslaught that evening from all the various bugs that I'd brought with me in the grass, the session was another success on the new rigs.

This time I caught another two carp, including a cracking common of twenty eight pounds, which was the biggest one so far.

Reg soon changed rigs as well and he also bagged a mid twenty mirror before the fish decided enough was enough and retreated, once more, to the sanctuary of the far bank.

I know that fish of this size might seem like small fry when compared to the Black Mirror or Two Tone, but I still take everything on it's own merits and those Charlie's carp had earned a lot of respect as far as I was concerned.

The fish I'd had were all commons, a couple of doubles, a low twenty and a lovely twenty-eight pounder.

Reg's fish was the same one that I'd caught at twenty-six pounds at the start of the season.

In fact when we compared photos with Kevo it turned out that all the fish we'd caught were the same ones he'd been catching for years and the great, un-caught leviathans that we'd seen in the closed season were determined to stay just that, un-caught!

The winter came and went, taking us off with it, off to search for easier ponds for the coldest months and then back again for the last two weeks.

Incredibly, both Reg and I managed to fool one more carp each, both mid twenties and mine, amazingly, the same bloody fish I'd started with, and the one Reg had caught off the baited area!

My capture had come as a result of Kevo's amazing fish finding skills and had, realistically, been handed to me on a plate.

I'd been struggling away at the deep end and Kev, just down for a social, came running back from a stroll around to say he'd found a few fish on the shallows.

Not having any tackle with him it fell to me to do the actual angling (somehow I forgot to tell Reg!) so I was around there like a shot.

From up a small tree, overlooking the spot, I could clearly see about five fish, all feeding on an area no bigger than a tea tray, they were actually stacked on top of each other waiting for a turn at whatever it was that held their interest so badly.

Why it should still be that the same, individual fish took the hook bait I don't know; whether he was more stupid, or the others were more intelligent, or whether it was only him that had a preference for an alternative food supply remains to be seen but the result was the same, an

old friend on the mat and all the others melting off into the distance once again!

As things turned out, that was to be my only season on the pit, the next year the place was rammed out with a new influx of anglers and the rumours were that I had caught herds of carp up to upper thirties and Keith had popped down and had a low forty mirror.

Even Chilly, who had barely trodden the banks, had apparently had a few, not to mention the monsters that got away!

It's a shame, really, as it was such a tranquil place and, although I never mentioned it in print and never publicised my meagre results, I still feel partly responsible for filling it full of anglers and bivvies.

Without doubt there were a few better fish in there but nothing like the rumours relayed after we left, it seems that people find it incomprehensible that anglers like Keith or I would even think about fishing a lake that isn't stuffed with unknown forty and fifty pounder's.

Unknown fifty pound carp are pretty thin on the ground at the best of times but, when one does come along, then it's obviously going to cause massive ripples in the carp fishing community and attract a lot of attention.

Unbeknown to me, as I drove away from Charlie's at the end of that season, there was exactly that waiting on the horizon and a fish was soon to surface that would change my entire fishing plans for the following couple of years.

But, what of Charlie's and the new influx of big fish hunters?

Later the next summer, when I was firmly installed in my new quest, I heard from Kevo that between all of the various groups of new anglers they managed a handful of small fish, with the best two being a nice twenty-eight pound common and a certain heavily plated twenty-six pound mirror, by August there wasn't an angler left on the place!

# Chapter 6

# Sonning, the great unknown

"*It was early May, in the year of the millennium, and I sat at the dining room table sorting the bills from the pile of post when the phone started ringing. I*  put down the letter I'd been reading and picked up the receiver and, by doing so, set the wheels in motion for one of my most enjoyable and exciting campaigns since the early days, when Phil and I had set off together to tackle the great Wraysbury lakes*".*

Keith was on the other end of the line; all fired up and excited having just got off the phone with somebody at the Carp Talk offices.

Apparently, the next week's paper would have details of a new and previously unpublished fish in excess of fifty pounds that had been caught from Sonning Eye pit in Berkshire.

The angler was a guy named Andy Dodd, a bailiff for Reading Angling and, apparently, he had also caught a forty-pound mirror a few days previously.

In very short order we had arranged for a fax of the picture to be sent over and we started ringing around, trying to get tickets before the mad rush started.

The ironic and slightly annoying thing was that Keith and I had so nearly joined the lake about four years earlier after a rumour of a big common had come to our ears.

Something or someone had put us off at the time, dispelling it all as mere conjecture, oh how we wished now that we'd followed it up more closely when it first came to light.

As soon as the paper hit the shops, the grapevine was buzzing with the news but, fortunately, the fact that the pit covered an area of more than 350 acres put a lot of people off the idea from the start.

There would still be a fair few anglers who were either hard core or just plain crazy enough to try their hand though, regardless of the size of the place, and I was definitely going to be one of them!

There seemed to be nobody on the normal grapevine who knew anything at all about the pit, other than the original rumors Keith and I had heard a few years previously.

The only other information I could find out was that there were a couple of lads, known locally as 'The Hippies', already fishing the lake and they had a reputation of being extremely 'unfriendly' towards other anglers who wanted to fish there. Well, if this was true then they were certainly going to be busy with the amount of anglers now wanting a ticket!

The very next week I set off on Monday morning, armed with a map and the cut out picture of Andy and his new fifty pounder, to see what it was all about.

Eventually, after a few wrong turns and dead ends, I came to the entrance marked 'Sonning Eye Sailing Club'.

I was getting more and more excited as I bumped down the lane, knowing that at any moment I would get my first glimpse of what might just turn out to be the answer to all my dreams.

It could also turn out to be a complete 'hell hole' of course.

As the trees thinned and gave way to the glorious sight of water, I parked the motor up against a small fence, filled my pockets with bait, and hopped over the rickety wooden posts.

I followed an old footpath around a tiny 'lagoon' of less than an acre and pushed my way through the trees on the far side, emerging onto a small and secluded swim that looked out over a large bay of about 25 acres in size.

The near side of the bay was made up of jungle and tall reed beds while the far side had a gravel workings half obscured by the trees. A large gravel dredger and two barges were moored on the far bank but appeared tiny to look at, which gave me some idea of the sheer scale of the place, after all, this was only a tiny section of the entire pit.

I climbed a small and decidedly dead looking tree on the water line and gazed down through the clear water, spotting gravel humps and small bars dotted about at various distances.

Right below my feet was a polished section of gravel about six feet square in two or three feet of water. It looked so inviting that I sprinkled a handful of boilies onto it before setting off to find the rest of the lake.

I did not have to look far and it soon became apparent that this first corner was only a small piece of a much larger bay. The whole area was old and well established with large climbing trees and dense undergrowth all around-it looked bloody wonderful!

Back in the motor I continued down the bumpy path until it, and the lake, turned sharply left and the main body of water stretched out in front of me. I parked up once more and stood in the first available swim, it was a bit like standing on Brighton beach and trying to focus on the horizon, and I'd thought that Wraysbury was big!

Three hundred and fifty acres is certainly one hell of a pond and I just hoped that there was a decent head of fish in there or location was going to be an absolute nightmare.

Vast islands dotted the scene before me and, through the gaps between them, even more water was visible, in fact it was not easy to ascertain where the far bank actually was!

Rather than be put off by the size, though, I could only feel excitement at the amount of different places I could try and the vast level of input that would be coming my way, as I'd already decided that this was, most definitely, the place for me.

After driving around to the official car park, next to the sailing club, I set about walking the bank beyond. I knew that most of the lake was out of bounds to Reading angling club but figured that there would be some sort of a sign that dictated the boundaries. I must have walked for about half an hour, looking in every little nook and cranny before finally reaching the top end and the boundary marker.

From this top end the lake looked even bigger and I called up Keith on the mobile and tried, in vain, to put it all into words, all I could do was keep repeating "it's bloody massive mate, absolutely bloody massive".

Beyond the top bank, and the limit of the Reading angling section, laid a large gravel workings and the road that serviced this workings bore away in a different direction from the far bank of the lake. There seemed to be no access to the far side without strolling right through the workings and picking your way through an area of fresh gravel extraction at the back of the lake.

Realising that I could go no further, I made my way slowly back to the sailing club, although I dearly wanted to go over to the far bank and explore over there as well.

I would need a local ordinance survey map to figure out exactly how to get there though, as both ends of the lake were dead ends and the roads seemed to lead you away from the area. I suppose that is some sort of an indication of the size of the place, if you need a map to find the far bank then how the hell are you supposed to find the fish!

As it happened I was just about to find that out and, as I stepped back into the small bay swim at the beginning of the lake, there were about four carp all milling about near the gravel patch I'd baited.

As I watched, one of the bigger ones, a mirror of about twenty-five pounds, came straight in and tilted up over the spot, hoovering up a handful of bait as he did so.

That was good enough for me and I was off at a trot, back to the motor, where I just happened to have all my fishing gear stashed away under a ground sheet in the back.

I was in a bit of a quandary now as, if I was caught fishing without a ticket then I might risk losing the chance to fish here at all, so I decided to drive over to Reading Angling Center and get a permit before I started.

The ticket was just a local club card and there was no problem in getting one, but it turned out that the night fishing was run on a syndicate basis and required a bit more work to obtain.

There was a separate form that needed signing and then sending off in advance so I grabbed the club ticket, stuck the night form in the glove box, and drove back to the bay as fast as I possibly could.

It goes without saying that the fish had moved out of reach by the time that I returned, although I did find another different group a bit later in the day, about half a mile away!

I spent an enjoyable afternoon stalking for them in a reed lined bay just past the sailing club and, although I didn't manage to hook any of them, I couldn't wait to sort out the night ticket and start to fish it properly.

By the late afternoon I started to realise that I hadn't seen another soul all day, where were all the other anglers, after all, everybody who could read knew all about the fifty by now, but I was the only person fishing on the entire 350 acre pit!

I decided to chance my arm and phone up the guy who ran the night syndicate to see if I could drive over to his house and join there and then, that way I'd be able to stay for a couple of days and really start to get to grips with the place.

I found his number in the club book and rung him from my mobile while I sat on the grass watching a couple of small commons cruising around the bay.

He seemed a bit confused as to why I was in such a hurry to join, (I didn't want to say that I was already fishing there, just in case I sounded a bit too keen) he explained that it would make no difference anyway as the new permits didn't start until the 16th of June and, as it was only the second week of May, there was still plenty of time to post off the form.

Suddenly the penny dropped and, after thanking him and turning off the phone, I checked the front of the permit and there it was in black and white, this permit runs from June the 16th 2000!

No wonder the lake had been so quiet; I'd been happily poaching in the close season all afternoon.

I was a bit put out that the guy in the angling centre hadn't told me when I bought the permit, in fact he'd even sold me a pair of waders as I'd explained I'd left mine at home and would need some to wade around the reeds in the bay, so he must have realised I was intending to fish straight away!

Apparently, though, there were only a handful of members from the previous season who'd bothered to apply for a spring ticket and everybody else had to wait until the start of the new season in June.

I quickly packed all my stuff away, suddenly paranoid about getting caught with such a pathetic excuse, even if it was true.

Luckily I made it back to the car unchallenged and I drove back out the gate and headed for home, laughing all the way!

The first day of the season couldn't come around quickly enough, a new season on a new and unknown pit, and I was so excited that I thought I was going to burst into flames on the drive down there.

As is always the way when I'm buzzing about a new lake, I hadn't been able to sleep at all and, consequently, it was still only four o'clock in the morning when I rolled through the gate and pulled up next to the point swim in the bay.

There wasn't another angler in sight, which was what I'd been praying for all the way down the motorway, so I quickly bagged the little swim on the point for the coming few days. I had been so determined to get that spot, especially since I'd seen those fish so close in, earlier in the spring, and again on almost every occasion that I'd visited since, there had been some sort of activity in the bay.

It was blatantly a lot shallower than most of the other areas and there was evidence of an old gravel washing plant in the top corner (just out of bounds) and these areas on big pits often provide the spawning areas.

I set up my umbrella and dumped a few items of less expensive tackle under it to mark the swim as taken, and then set off for a day of walking and looking.

Further along the track, in the main section of the lake, I came across a guy who was set up and fishing up against the long island near the sailing club. I assumed he was an existing member as the new season didn't actually start until midnight but, after a quick chat, it transpired that he'd fallen into the same trap that I had a few weeks earlier and he also thought he could start as soon as he bought his ticket.

It was none of my concern and I told him that it didn't worry me either way; I already had my swim sorted so I was well happy. In the end, though, he decided that instead of risking being banned before he'd even started, he'd pack away the rods and wait until midnight as well.

We sat and chatted for a while about the possibilities the lake held but, when I told him where I was fishing, he said that he'd been informed the previous day that it was an out of bounds area.

Now, I could see from the swim and the worn ground that it must get fished, in fact there were even some old used teabags in the bushes next to where I'd put my brolly, but this guy was adamant that a bailiff had actually stood with him, in that very swim the afternoon before, and declared it out of bounds for Reading anglers.

I was now in a right old quandary, I was in the top swim on the lake but now I didn't even know if I was allowed to fish there or not.

The little map in the back of the handbook was next to useless as far as the boundaries were concerned, the entire 350 acres had been condensed into a two-inch map and you couldn't make out a thing. I didn't want all the next best swims taken throughout the day only, for me to be ousted by a bailiff at the last minute and left to fit in wherever I could.

Over the next hour, three more anglers turned up and two of these set up in swims further down the same bay that I was in, which put even more pressure on me to make a decision.

I could see fish cruising about in the point swim and I just knew I was going to catch something if I stayed there but, eventually, after much consultation with the others and the rule book, I decided to move while I had the chance.

Within an hour of me moving out, there was somebody firmly ensconced in exactly the spot I'd just taken my brolly up from and, when I tried telling him that the area was off limits, he said that was rubbish and it was one of the best swims on the lake.

He went on to say that it was also the area that Andy Dodd had caught the forty pound mirror from in the spring and there was no way he was moving out as that was the swim he'd been after in the first place.

No amount of discussion was going to move him now, and the fact that I'd been wrongly turfed out on the say so of a bailiff that didn't even know the bloody rules didn't seem to make any difference to the bloke's resolve.

I was absolutely fuming, I'd been there since four o'clock in the morning to secure that swim and now somebody else was going to fish it.

Eventually, after a hopeless conversation with a bailiff, Andy Dodd himself turned up to try and make sense of it all. He was actually one of the bailiffs as well so I was half hoping that everything might end up all right after all.

It turned out that the original bailiff had actually thought the swim was off limits and everyone was very sorry but then, unbelievably, they decided that the best way to sort it out was to toss a coin, which, inevitably, I lost!

This really put a downer on the whole start to the season, as the fish were blatantly obvious all over the swim, in fact one crashed out a few yards in front of us while we were trying to sort it all out.

There was some measure of justice in the end, though, as the guy who fished there somehow managed to stay for eleven nights on the trot and not catch a single thing, although quite how he managed this feat I'll never know as there were herds of fish in front of him the whole time!

I set up a bit further along the bank in a small overgrown swim, but a small island to my right meant that the fish were inaccessible really.

Later that day, Keith turned up as well and he set up further down to my left so at least I'd have a sympathetic ear to moan into.

Paul Forward and Nick Helleur were also about, and they chose swims even further along the track to Keith's left, making them close enough to share a drink or two with in the evening, so at least the social scene would be good.

We had a string of visitors that day and the phones never stopped ringing, everybody wanting to know about the new pit on the block.

It seemed that just about everybody had bought a ticket for the place, as the buzz of a new fifty pounder had whipped the big carp fraternity into a frenzy.

I don't think that Reading Angling really knew what had hit them; they had advertised the big fish in a bid to raise ticket revenue so as to be able to continue paying the lease but, in reality they had thrown a snowball and started an avalanche!

As is often the way with these large pits, talk is cheap and resolve is easily broken.

By the end of the first two weeks there had been no fish caught and ninety percent of the keenies had gone forever, but from Reading Anglings

point of view at least the lease was paid for another year, and we had a nice quiet pit to fish.

At the start most of the fish had stayed in the big bay, drifting in and out of the area in front of the point, although they did appear to be mainly the small ones.

The rest of the shallow end of the lake was fished at a big disadvantage from the 'in bounds' section as the bar systems, that the fish could blatantly be seen using, were at extreme range. This meant that the level of accuracy needed to place a bait on top of a bar at well over one hundred yards could not be attained from the bank, and boats were not allowed.

The first big winds of the season came at the end of the second week and howled across a hundred acres of open water, sending massive white-capped waves crashing spectacularly into the sailing/ski club bank.

This was more like it and surely location was just a matter of finding the frothiest bit of water.

By standing on the ski club jetty, as it pitched and tossed in the waves, I managed to glimpse a couple of shapes moving deep down below the swell, the jetty bank was out of bounds to angling but I could fish the adjacent bank that also faced into the teeth of the gale.

The swim I chose was in an area that was, technically, off limits to the ticket holders as it was leased by the skiers but a quick chat with the guy who ran the ski club left me in no doubt that nobody particularly cared what I did as long as I kept my head down, which was fine by me.

It was not so much a swim as a hole in the bushes and it absolutely screamed CARP!

There was thick froth blowing up the bank where the waves had whipped the surface up and the water rocked with the effects of the big South Westerly wind, pounding into this small corner of an inland sea!

A small culvert to my left let excess river water into the lake and the opposing forces of water rocked and peaked the surface. I simply flicked two baits out in front of me, both bottom baits and 20mm in size, one on the shelf and one at the bottom, where it seemed to drop off into ten feet or so of water. It was hard to ascertain anything in the conditions, so I threw a handful of bait around each one and hid myself by laying face down on the floor next to the rods with a camo jacket pulled up over my head.

As with a lot of the off limits areas at Sonning, it was only really the bailiffs that seemed to care about what was in and what was out, the ski club and sailors seemed amiable enough and there was no real reason at all why some of the spots were deemed out of bounds at all.

Speaking to the local lads it seemed that, in the past, the anglers had been left totally to their own devices but, now that there were a lot more new faces around, the old rule book had been taken off the shelf and dusted down again.

I was sure that it wouldn't last long, though, and already there were far less interested bailiffs and far fewer people to check up on.

I decided to play the game anyway, and keep low and hidden in my new found hideaway, while the spray cascaded over my head as I watched the rod tips bouncing in the wind.

The thrill of that first run on a new water is indescribable, especially when you have no idea what may be on the end, it was totally imminent that it was going to happen, given the conditions, and the fact that I could see the odd one cruise past in the turbulent margins. Never the less I still nearly suffered a coronary when it did eventually rip off.

I was still lying on my belly, with my head peering over the edge of the bank, straining for another glimpse of a fish in the coloured water, with the rod tips right next to my head when one of them whipped around and line flew from the spool. The wind was so strong that it was all I could do to stand up against it, let alone play a very angry carp.

The fish raged for a good ten minutes before I managed to net him, fighting as if he had never felt a hook before and his very life depended on it (which, in reality, might well have been the case!).

He really did put up an extraordinarily hard scrap and my knuckles were physically bleeding across my left hand, from the spinning reel handle as I tried to drag him into the margins for netting.

The actual netting was the worse part of the lot; physically pushing the net under the waves was a nightmare as the wind kept throwing it back up in the air and into the branches above me. The gusts were so strong that clouds of spray were being thrown up from the margins and soaking me in the process.

What a feeling, though, as my first Sonning carp finally hit the mesh, my first fish from a new water and it was an immaculate, and new personal best, common of thirty-three and a half pounds!

I was stuck with a dilemma now, I had a stunning carp secured in a

sack behind an overhanging tree to keep him from the worse of the weather and I was all alone in this tiny secluded section of the lake.

Luckily I knew a man who could help, and a quick phone call to CP had him bundling Storm the carp dog into his little red van and driving the few miles from his house to do the honours with the camera.

I have always had a 'slow starting' problem on lakes and it usually takes me months to start catching the better fish, sometimes I can spend a whole season in the metaphorical kitchen before being allowed into the actual party but, here I was with my biggest ever common carp as my first capture; I was dancing on the ceiling straight from the off!

Even more so, a few hours later when I took another common of twenty five pounds from the same spot, and I even managed to follow this up with a scraper twenty the next morning as well!

It was a massive feeling of relief to know that I had a rig and a bait that would, and could, do the business, all that remained to do was find a few more spots that might produce, after all I could hardly rely on a gale force South Westerly every week of the season could I?

Regarding the actual captures, I made a decision there and then, to tell nobody about my results (apart from Keith, and CP who took the photos), this was not done maliciously but I saw no reason to encourage the competition. Even though only two or three weeks of the season had elapsed, I had seen plenty of anglers give up already so I thought I'd let 'natural selection' run it's course before advertising my results, especially as mine were the only three fish landed so far!

# Chapter 7

# *Close Encounters*

"*In the past I have been very mobile in my approach to big pits, always putting myself where I thought the fish were at any given time, and at first, bolstered by my recent results with the commons, I thought this would also be the method on Sonning. As it turned out, though, this was definitely not the case, and before long it became obvious that I would need to adopt a very different outlook altogether*".

Although I think that my own personal strength as an angler lies in my mobility and willingness to constantly move around, it soon became apparent on Sonning that the best way to trap these fish would be to establish a feeding area of my own.

There is so much water that is either 'out of bounds' or merely 'out of range' that mobility would only work when the fish were actually accessible. Vast areas were untouchable and location alone would not be enough to secure any sort of regular results.

Only one or two wind directions would bring the fish within range of the 'in-bounds bank' and most of the visible bars and features were at too great a range.

Finding out the exact layout of the pit and it's inherent bar system can provide a valuable short cut to potential feeding areas.

It can't, unfortunately, tell you where the bigger fish are definitely going to feed but it can show you where they might, albeit with a bit of persuasion and a lot of bait.

This was to be the plan on Sonning, although the area that we put it into operation originally came about as much by luck as the result of any strategic planning and plumbing.

By now there was only really Jenks and myself, Fat Sam the carp dog and a handful of stragglers left doing any real time.

In fact poor old Sam was only doing the odd session nowadays as age had finally taken its toll on the poor old girl, she'd been 12 years old for at least five years that I could think of, she had trouble walking and was as blind as a bat!

Most weeks she'd happily stay at home in the comfort of her bed but occasionally she'd still jump up and wag her tail as I loaded the motor so, on these occasions, I'd bring her along but we had to make sure she didn't keep walking straight into the lake!

The week following my capture of the three commons, a fortuitous move onto a new and enthusiastic wind saw Keith bank his first Sonning fish.

The main section of water, where the sailing boats raced, was the largest section of 'in bounds' water but it didn't look as if it had been fished much in the past. There were a few old grown over swims but mostly it was a long straight bank with wild grass and nettles running amok all over it.

There were no real divides or trees to split it up and it must have looked a bit daunting, really, I suppose. At the start of this section was a corner bay and the wind was piling into it with merry abandon.

I'd set up in the last small copse of trees before the open bank, just on the mouth of the bay and facing straight into the wind.

Keith had made his own swim by battering down the long wild grass about thirty yards further along to my left and, also, discovered a small feature rising off the bottom, in an otherwise massive and open expanse of water.

My swim looked absolutely perfect, particularly with the new and roaring North Westerly wind tearing into it and, to be totally honest, I wouldn't have swapped swims with anybody, not for all the tea in China, and I love tea! Throughout the day I had various visitors and I could tell that every single one of them wanted to be sat exactly where I was at that moment, watching the waves lapping up around my front bank sticks.

Visitors were quite common in the early days, as it took no effort to just come and look, I think a lot of people were just waiting in the wings for something special to happen, which was another reason for keeping quiet about any results we might have.

Some of the visitors though were just plain strange, and had probably been waiting patiently for someone to punish for years. One of the strangest was a bloke who turned up in my swim that afternoon in a pure white safari suit and hat, he could have walked straight out of the 1940's Burmese jungle, and I was quite surprised he didn't have a regimental stick under his arm.

He marched straight up to me, stopping only a foot away from my face, and proceeded to tell me the entire history of Sonning and the surrounding area, including the five fifty pounders he and his friend had caught and, of course, the monster that had got way by wrapping itself around a passing gravel barge!

The thing was, all I could think about was the one massive hair that grew out from his left nostril, and curled halfway up his face, I kid you not; it was practically working its way back into his eye socket!

How he could have missed that in the mirror while adjusting his Pith Helmet I will never know, but I was fascinated by it and I couldn't stop staring. Eventually he ran out of stories, bid me farewell and strode off towards Keith. I just shook my head in amazement, checked my nose for stray hairs and hid under my brolly for a while, imagining poor old Keith trying not to stare at the protruding follicle.

The swim just looked better and better as the afternoon turned into evening and the wind strengthened ever more, eventually lifting the front of the brolly and bending the trees to my right.

It just goes to show that there is always more under the surface than meets the eye because I blanked in the perfect swim, while, just a short distance away Keith opened his account in memorable style.

Like mine, his first fish was also something very special. I don't think I will ever forget the sight of either Keith, fit to burst, or that wonderful 33lb linear on the mat at his feet as I ran into his swim at midnight.

The noise of Keith trying to remain calm and secretive had woken me from 100 yards away!

The poor bloke had been going through a massive 'lean spell' for ages and the total release of all that frustration and anticipation had manifested itself in a cry that would have woken the dead! As I appeared in the swim he grabbed hold of me by the shoulders and bounced me around the place like a lunatic, a fantastic moment and one that still makes my giggle even now, every time I think back.

Obviously we thought that we had stumbled across a lake full of thirty pounders but how could we have possibly known at the time, or ever imagined, that our first two fish were possibly two of the six biggest fish in the entire 360 acre lake!

The feature that Keith had caught from appeared, at first, to stretch along the bank at a range of about thirty yards. I could pick it up from my swim about sixty yards further down the bank, but it did not appear to be a continuous 'bar'.

The surrounding area was very thick Canadian pondweed and this made it hard to decipher exactly what it was that we'd found.

The area was subsequently plumbed to death over the next few weeks and we discovered, eventually, a system of five bars that, after weaving their way from miles out in the lake, all ended up a mere thirty yards from our two new swims.

We'd cut a second swim so that we could fish a rod on each bar between us and cover all possibilities.

The various humps and bumps at their ends were heavily weeded all around but perfectly fishable on the tops. At first they had appeared as one bar running across in front of us but careful plumbing had provided us with the knowledge that would lead us to a string of captures and the perfect area for our campaign.

The bars actually ran away from us, off into the middle of the lake, like huge road ways, and hopefully they would be full of traffic once we started our baiting in earnest.

Although we both love 'a bit of bait' I don't think we had ever baited like that before, or since. We realised very quickly that the only way to make a real difference was going to be using 'lots' of bait.

Massive bream were also present in numbers and no amount of bait appeared to deter them, vast quantities of 20mm Mainline boilies were deposited onto the bars and subsequently eaten, by something or another, every night.

I was turning up with a wheelbarrow full of loose boilies and six catapults hanging from the handles every night that I fished.

I would just stand there and fire out bait as fast as I could, each time a catapult broke I would drop it on the deck, grab the next one and carry on, stopping only when all six were broken or the barrow was empty! The fish were obviously using the bars as roads and making their way down the lake under the cover of darkness.

The strange thing was that they would only use one or two of the roads per night, and never come at all in the daytime.

I picked off the odd one in the morning to start with but, pretty soon, the bite time shrank to a period between eleven pm and about three in the morning. It was as if the fish were happy enough to stay at massive range beyond the weed during the day, or even lurk in one of the huge bays in the out of bounds areas on the far bank, and every night they would pick a road or two and make their way along for a feed up.

It got so predictable in the end that I changed my entire sessions to coincide with the feeding spells.

I usually fished a Thursday morning through until Saturday lunchtime, as my time was limited to two nights per week. Due to the nocturnal habits of the carp, however, I started turning up very late on a Wednesday evening or, even in the middle of the night, to grab the chance of another bite. My wife used to go out on a Wednesday evening and I was at home looking after the kids but I started packing up all the gear in the van ready, leaving the house when she returned about 11pm.

This way I could arrive at midnight and be in with a chance straight away. I'd sussed out that the gate in the car park that prevented you driving around the lake was only really there for show. Although it was firmly chained and bolted on one side, the actual hinges had no pins in them so you could easily open and close it from the other side.

I'd first seen the guys from the electricity board using this tactic, to service one of the pylons further along the river bank, and it was knowledge that came in handy on many an occasion.

If there was nobody about it was so easy to pop the gate and drive all the way down to the back of the swim, saving a walk of at least fifteen minutes with all the gear, and a minor hernia every time.

There was a big mound of earth about twenty feet high to hide the car behind and, as long as it was back in the car park by morning, then no one was any the wiser for it.

I was always a bit paranoid about the headlights, though, as you would be able to see them from all over the lake, so I used to turn them off and stick my head out of the window to see where I was going.

It was a bit hairy, driving through waist high wild grasses in the pitch black while standing up with most of my upper body outside the car!

A hay fever sufferer would have been reduced to tears, as the cloud of pollen coming up over the bonnet had to be seen to be believed.

I remember one particular night when I turned up about 12.30pm and, after bouncing along the track to the swim wearing sunglasses to keep the seeds out of my eyes, I pulled up behind the mound and walked the short distance to the swim in the dark. The rods were all clipped up ready at the right distances and I put them straight out on the spots. After firing a few baits around each one I set about putting up my house but, before I even got it out from the holdall, I had a take and landed a 31lb common!

I was sitting there on the damp grass with a big fat carp in the net, all alone on a 360-acre pit and I'd only been there half an hour. It is moments like this that I go fishing for, and I sat there and laughed out loud like a madman!

A succession of twenty pounder's fell to my rods over the next ten weeks, in fact I notched up an incredible nineteen carp from Sonning that first year. Some nights I would have six bream on the trot and then a carp about midnight, bait up again in the dark, and then suffer another couple of bream before bagging another carp in the early hours.

Not all of my fish were from that one swim, as I found it really hard to be pinned down, even though the method was obviously working, but the majority came from there and they seemed well up for the 'big bait' method.

Most of the carp were incredible looking beasts, long and lean mirrors and commons that appeared to be of a strain more suited to the adjacent river Thames than to the pit itself. I am sure that a lot of the fish in Sonning originated in the river and were either introduced by flooding or by slightly less natural methods, via a match anglers keep net.

Keith's area, although only yards away, produced less fish in total but was still far and away the second most productive spot on the lake that year. As a result of our successes we were having a bit of a problem ensuring our swims stayed 'our swims' and a couple of times I missed out and had to sit by while another angler reaped the rewards of my baiting up.

Poor old Keith had it even harder, as he could not get down to the lake before about 5pm on a Friday and, although I tried all the usual strokes, I couldn't always keep his spot free for him. One such weekend, at the beginning of September, our old mate Steve Allcott had arranged to come over for a social session on the Friday night and the plan was to all fish in a row along the area we had been baiting. Steve arrived long before Keith and I met him in the car park. Already, two anglers had asked me if anyone was fishing 'Keith's swim' and the second of these was all loaded up and ready to trot around there, so I quickly blurted out that Steve had

already dropped some gear in there. Steve didn't know what I was talking about, but realised there was something going on, so just played along. The swim was too far away for matey to see the truth and Steve and I carried his gear around there a bit sharpish. As a result of this, Steve actually ended up in the swim for his one night visit and Keith set up next door, intending to move back in when Steve left in the morning.

It's funny how fickle the hand of fate can be sometimes isn't it?

That night I had two fish, both mid twenties, Keith had nothing, while Steve had his first and only bite from Sonning and landed his first and only Sonning carp, all 52lb of it!

I felt sorry for the both of them really, poor old Jenks didn't know what to say (for once) and Steve seemed more than a little embarrassed about the whole affair as well but he was still understandably over the moon as he had just caught a mahoosive mirror carp.

Unfortunately, it was as if that capture had closed the door on Keith's swim and it practically stopped producing after that, the fish were definitely showing a preference for one particular 'road' that sat bang in the middle of my swim. Because of this, we decided to concentrate mainly on the three bars in front of this swim, fishing it almost on a rota in the end.

I would turn up in the night on a Wednesday and leave either Friday, when Keith arrived, or first thing Saturday morning. Then Keith would cover the whole area when I left, through till Sunday afternoon. He kept the bait going in over his marks as well, just in case the fish spooked off of the main bar, or just picked a different route for a change. Between us we were putting out an incredible amount of bait now, and supplementing it with pellets as well. In fact, there were only two days of the week when no bait at all was being introduced and we just knew that the 'Big Fella' would turn up again eventually. We were just hoping that it wasn't one of the fish we had already lost, as the odd one would come adrift occasionally.

Due to the heavy weed we had dropped a few, not many, but one of these I felt convinced was a very big fish.

Those few weeks spent on the sun-baked top bank at Sonning were wonderful, painful at times due to the unrelenting attentions of mosquitos and horse flies, but so memorable never the less.

On the Fridays that I stayed I'd socialize with Jenks, usually involving curry and wine, and in the week I'd often be joined by my old

mate CP who had bought himself a ticket the very next week after photographing that first common for me on the sailing club lawn.

In fact, CP had kicked off in fine style, although a little cheekily really. He had turned up for one of his first sessions and set up in the bay near the two buoy and, during the night, had heard quite a few fish crashing over my spots.

For once, neither Keith nor I were on the lake so he'd snuck in and bagged a forty pound mirror before I turned up.

This was a much bigger fish than the ones we'd been getting amongst and on further inspection of the photo's, it turned out to be the same fish that Andy Dodd had caught just prior to the fifty.

The only low point of that whole summer was the very sad, but, I suppose inevitable, demise of my greatest ever friend.

Sam the Carp Dog, who had happily affected so many peoples lives during her seventeen years on the bank, and who had been a constant companion to me for so much of my life, finally passed away.

We had secretly been waiting, and I suppose if I'm honest, hoping, that she would move on quietly in her sleep, thereby releasing her from the pain and suffering that her old age was starting to bring. However, like the stubborn old cow she had always been, she steadfastly refused to let go, so I had to commit the ultimate betrayal.

One morning I had a phone call from home, explaining that all was not well, and poor old Sam could hardly even stand up, so I immediately packed up my stuff and drove home with a heavy heart, knowing the task that lay ahead. After all those years of loyalty it broke my heart to have to drive her to the vets, pretending to her all was well when I knew, beyond a shadow of doubt, that it was to be her last ever outing.

For years afterwards I still felt guilty, although I knew in reality there had been no other humane option.

Months later, during a winter's session on Pingewood, I stood there, in the pitch black, looking out over the lake when I became aware of a shape next to me. I knew it was just a grassy mound but, with half a bottle of red wine inside me and a vivid imagination, it seemed like she was once again by my side. Not wanting to turn and look, thereby shattering the illusion, I ran through a whole host of memories of how she'd robbed and pillaged everyone's food stocks, sneakily drank their tea while they looked the other way and beaten off all other canine competition to be the Queen of every lake she'd ever fished. I don't suppose there is an angler who ever met her who doesn't still have a story to tell and, ultimately, it was this knowledge that helped me come to terms with her passing.

I took her ashes and mixed them in the potted soil of a beautiful red maple tree, that I still refuse to actually plant in the ground, just in case I move house again, as she will obviously be coming along wherever I go.

Even now, years later, I still miss her, and seldom bump into old friends who don't start one story or another with 'do you remember the time Fat Sam did this or that'.

I think you only ever have one chance at a friendship like that, and she had been mine.

When I finally managed to pluck up the enthusiasm to fish again I returned to my quest in the 2 buoy, and Keith and I drank many a toast to Fat Sam as the sun set over the distant trees.

The day times at Sonning were singularly fruitless, as far as the fishing was concerned, so it was a regular occurrence to wind in about 11am and drive up to the 'Square Deal' café on the Bath road for a big fry up, or just spend a few hours strolling around with a rod, hoping for a rare stalking opportunity somewhere.

Stalked fish were hard to come by that first year and I was convinced that they spent most of their days over on the far bank, the forbidden lands as it were.

I'd never fished a lake before where I hadn't even walked all the way around and the frustration was starting to have an effect.

I was sure I could make more things happen if I only had total access to all of the lake, and the stories of how well protected the far side of the lake were had started to wear a bit thin, it could only be a matter of time before curiosity got the better of me.

We did have some stalking opportunities on our side of the pond though, and one particularly hot afternoon in mid summer, Keith and I had an experience to remember on the extreme shallows beyond Punisher's Point, as the little point at the entrance to the lake had now become called.

On this occasion Keith had elected to set up in the point as there were a few fish about and, during a visit in the day, I'd spotted a bit of movement on the shallows so we'd decided to investigate.

Down to Keith's right at the bottom of the bay, and firmly in the out of bounds section, the floating weed had gathered up in a big raft against the reeds. We knew the fish got down there, as we could often see them from the top of the tree, and I had snuck down there once or twice before

for a closer look, seeing the odd one cruising about on the shallow margins.

Right at the bottom of the bank we were standing on was a small bay, that deepened off a bit before swinging around into the shallows, and the old gravel washing area of shallow sand. It was actually at the bottom of somebody's garden, which obviously made it a bit tricky to stalk, but the big old trees and the distance from the house to the bank helped a bit.

It was in this bay, full of weed that we came across the fish all pugged up under the weed and looking very approachable.

We had been wading through the out of bounds reed beds, generally just doing what we shouldn't and looking for a quick chance of a bite, when we emerged into the tiny bay.

It was a fair old wade through the swampy reed beds to get there and we were up to our waists in water by the time we reached the weed. There in front of us, lying in a small hole in the weed, was a carp and, as we focussed more closely, another one behind it and another and another!

Everywhere we looked there were sections of fish flesh showing through the holes in the big raft of weed and we were understandably excited about the whole affair.

Hidden from the house and the bank, we were comparatively safe within the reeds and the floater rods were soon being rigged up for what would obviously be lambs to the slaughter!

Creeping back to the weed, we flicked the floating boilies into our respective holes and stood, side-by-side, swatting mosquitos from our sweaty little faces while we stared intently at the baits and carp, willing them to make closer contact.

Mine went first; a mouth appeared from nowhere, a small swirl, anticipation, a strike, and a rig hanging pathetically in a tree behind my head!

How the bloody hell had I missed that?

Keith was next, and his attempt met with the same pathetic result as mine and then it was as if a switch had been thrown, the fish were still there but now they knew that we were as well.

Try as we might we couldn't get them interested in anything and then, from the weed to my left, we saw the beast!

Compared to the others in the weed bed he was massive, it was a job to tell how big any of them were, really, as the weed was so thick we could only see sections of each fish at any one time but, however big they were, this one was much bigger.

Struck by one of my usual fits of genius, I suddenly came up with answer to the bait problem; worms, that's what I needed, worms!

As quietly as I could, I crept back into the reeds, trying not to push too much of a vortex as I waded through chest high water and weed, slowly making my way to the marshy shallows at the far edge of the swamp. After finding an old plastic pot that had been washed up there many years before, I set about digging for worms. Of course, I didn't have a shovel, and all the bits of branches and wood that lay around were rotten as a pear and useless for digging with.

There was nothing for it but to kneel down in the shallow water in my waders and tear at the stinking black ooze of the bank with my bare hands.

Punishers point

Ten minutes later and I was back at the waters edge, totally covered in flies this time as the black sludge had splashed up all over my face as I'd torn through roots and reeds in my search for worms.

My fingernails were jet black and I stank to high heaven but, hanging proudly from the hook, were two straggly little worms, and a small red pop-up to keep them afloat.

A sorrier looking pair of invertebrates it would be hard to imagine, and the worms didn't look too healthy either!

The biggun was still there, his head filling one of the holes and he was looking in the other direction which, hopefully, would make matters easier.

I flicked the 'worm surprise' just beyond him onto the weed and, praying it didn't snag up, I inched it back into the hole.

I don't think the carp was overly impressed by the sudden invasion of two drowning wrigglers and a bright red pop-up, as he instantly sank from view, but I had half expected that really and, sighing in a 'resigned to blanking' sort of way, I lay the rod on a clump of reeds and we resorted to watching the fish sunbathing.

I could tell by the look on Keith's face that something was happening over my shoulder and, before he found the right words, I turned to see the most enormous pair of lips trying to engulf the worms, pop-up, weed bed and all!

The bait had drifted to the edge of the hole and the slight breeze had lifted it up onto the raft, the big lips wanted it but the weed was matted across its face and it was preventing the rig from going in. With trembling hands I picked up the rod and waited as the little red boilie was being juggled through the weed, ever so slowly it sank further through the weave like an aquatic game of 'Jack Straws' and then it happened. Suddenly, the red boilie disappeared from view as the lips shut, I instinctively whipped the rod up in the air but, mid strike, there was a flash of red as he opened his mouth to get a better grip and the bait came hurtling out of the weed, flew over our heads and landed ten yards behind us in the swamp; bugger!

We couldn't believe it as it had been so close, that big old carp had really wanted those worms and I'd cocked it up.

In retrospect, I think we'd have had a right old game landing it anyway as the weed was so thick, and the bottom dropped away quite quickly beneath it.

As it happened, we didn't have too much time to muse over what might or might not have been as, just then, I saw a person step into Keith's swim and look down towards the reeds where we were now standing, blatantly on view.

Instinctively, I sank down onto my knees in the water with the level just lapping at the top of the chest waders, but had I been seen?

Keith was a bit slower off the mark and got captured 'bang to rights' by the, now, very obvious bailiff type person who was looking less than pleased about the whole affair.

As Keith made his way out of the reeds to meet his captor he signalled with his hand for me to stay low, somehow I'd not been spotted.

I stayed in there for about fifteen minutes and then slowly crept out (still on my knees) until I reached the gardens, before sneaking across the lawn, over the fence back onto the lagoon before finally strolling nonchalantly into Keith's swim from the in bounds side.

As it turned out, I had just missed the departing bailiff anyway but Keith suffered the indignity of having to take a telling off like a naughty school boy, I even think he got some sort of official 'yellow card' or something equally ridiculous.

Full grown men, creeping around in the bushes and getting slapped wrists when we're caught, you've got to laugh really!

I'd had a few trips down to the Punishers Point myself over the previous weeks and, although I was keeping the two buoy baited and still catching from there, I'd started making a plan B, just in case the attentions of other anglers became too much at the far end of the lake.

The point was very weedy and the bars were incredibly hard to find from the bank, but plan B didn't exactly rely on staying on the bank!

For the mean time, though, I was happy to keep plugging away with plan A as all that bait would surely have to pay off and eventually it did.

It was the week of the petrol crisis and mob hysteria had well and truly taken a hold, food shortages had been threatened and people were fighting in the aisles over a carton of semi-skimmed!

I was lucky enough to have filled my tank with unleaded on day one and, obviously, I'd saved enough for at least a one way journey to the lake. I phoned Chrissie on the Wednesday and was very dismayed to hear that somebody was already ensconced in the two buoy and he was showing all the signs of staying for a few days at least.

It looked as if I would have to put plan B in to action a lot sooner than I had anticipated.

I hated it when somebody else was in my carefully nurtured swim, as I was always fretful that they may end up with the result that I had been working so diligently towards.

I'd taken a dozen fish out of the swim so far and probably used in excess of one hundred kilos of boilies in an attempt to keep them visiting the marks. I knew that, eventually, the biggun would come back as a fish

like that just can't resist a nice big pile of bait; I just hoped it would not be this weekend.

The afternoon and evening were spent preparing the boat and markers for the coming expedition.

With my previous experience in boating on Wraysbury and the Mere I knew that I could pull off the whole operation in double quick time, even under the cover of darkness. Normally I wouldn't go to such lengths to pull a stroke, (honestly) but I had to set up another area soon as the popularity of my first one was gaining in momentum every week.

I could teach the millennium trust a thing or two about pulling in the crowds!

The other thing that made it even more frustrating was that the 'Hippies' could be seen every weekend on the other bank, blatantly boating around and doing exactly what they liked while we were restricted to staying within a set of rules.

In previous years I think the whole lake had been fished in this way and it really was the only way to get to grips with a lot of the areas.

As well as the Hippies there was also another guy who seemed to fish wherever and however he liked, and we'd managed to get to know him quite well over the previous months.

One of the first times we'd run in to him we were sitting in the two buoy, just after dark, sharing a glass of two or red wine when we heard the unmistakable sound of paddling.

Out of the gloom a little boat appeared, loaded up with various buckets and markers, he just moored up next door and popped in for a chat as if it was the most normal thing in the world which, of course, it was for someone who had fished there before the re-emergence of the rule book.

We'd nicknamed him The Steeplejack, and during many chats he'd told us a lot about the lake and its history.

It appeared there was actually no permission for the far bank at all, but people had always fished it anyway and, as long as you kept your head down, then it was quite an easy thing to get away with.

Boats had also been used quite extensively over the years and it had only ever been the sailing club that objected, so as long as they'd made sure there were no sails on the water beforehand, there had never been a problem.

It appeared we were now fishing the lake at a massive disadvantage and he, for one, was amazed we were all so well behaved!

The area in front of the Punishers Point was absolutely choked with weed, so to start a second baiting campaign I needed to find at least a small area that I knew was reasonably clear to begin with.

The Steeplejacks chats had left me realising just how inefficiently we were fishing, compared with the methods used in the past, and I knew that I could learn more in an hour afloat than I had all season from the bank.

Luckily, just before my departure, Kev phoned from Mainline to tell me that some new hemp pellets had finally arrived.

Apparently Kev had found somewhere that could manufacture pure crushed hemp into a pellet form; this was hemp of a high food grade and totally different to any other product around at the time.

He convinced me on the phone that I just had to have it so, dropping everything, I used even more precious fuel and shot over to Essex on the double to grab fifty kilos of pellet and another forty kilos of boilies, Christ I was getting through some bait!

I left the bait in the motor and loaded all but the rods on top of it, a nice home cooked meal and off to bed, ready for an early departure in the morning. I was halfway through a strange dream where longboats filled with lanterns discovered hidden cities below bizarre green seas, that were, of course, alive with huge carp.

Just as the largest of these denizens of the deep cruised up towards me I was suddenly awoken by a two year old foot stuffing itself in my ear.

Shaking the last confused images from my brain and the foot from my ear, I dressed in a lovely little camo number and set off for the lake.

The motor was fully laden with tackle, boat, and a mountain of bait, which only helped to further drain my dwindling fuel supply.

I had one stop to make on the way, at a small dive shop in Slough, to buy an underwater halogen lamp; maybe the lanterns in my dream were an omen!

The plan was to first prod around with a stick to locate the bars and then give them a quick flash with the torch to make sure that they were clean. With this done I could push a long stick into the soft silt at the back of the bar and trim it down, just above the water line, forming a permanent marker to bait around. My first job on arrival, though, was to discover the identity of the 'two buoy poacher', that way I'd know if I'd been gazumped on purpose or purely by a cruel twist of fate involving a newcomer.

As I pulled into the car park, I clocked the new and shiny red BMW and realised that it was the former of the two options.

Mark, one of the 'Wolverhampton wanderers', had got down a day early to beat me to it, what was worse was that he had already bagged one from my newest, and heavily baited, spot.

The fish was a fully scaled mirror of twenty three pounds, typical of the size of fish in this area and a fair sign that all of Keith's and my bait had been polished off in the week.

Mark informed me of the wonderful new area that he had 'found', completely stripped of weed and only thirty yards out! I tried to make him feel guilty by telling him the reason why, but obviously it fell on deaf ears as I'm sure he already knew exactly what had been going on.

I considered moving into Keith's swim next door, but I knew, in reality, I was settling for second best so, torturing myself no longer, I set off for the point swim at the other end.

The day was poor, overcast and drizzly and I spent most of it preparing for the night to come. Buckets were filled with bait, prodders and marker sticks were cut and sharpened, and large temporary markers were made out of plastic drink bottles, attached via a length of cord to crisp packets full of stones. These could be jettisoned as soon as a likely spot was found, to add a point of reference to work to. It can be an impossible task, especially at night and in the wind, to identify one particular patch of the surface once you have passed over it. A spot can be found and then lost again in the blink of an eye if it is not marked up quickly.

Somehow, I managed to wait until ten o'clock at night before making the final drive up the lane for a last 'car check' before dragging the boat out.

All was quiet, or at least it was until I started pumping it up!

It's only when you are trying to operate in total subterfuge that you realise how noisy a foot pump can be, do you slowly and quietly pump it, creating less noise but also a lot less air, or thrash away at it, noisily, getting the job done as quickly as possible?

I settled for the 'thrashing' option and within five minutes I was loading her up in the margins. I must admit I was very excited at the prospect of being afloat once more, and so giggling like a school boy, I pushed off and paddled against the strengthening South Westerly wind. Using the prodder, it didn't take long to find the bars running in parallel lines below the weed and by following them along I soon located the unmistakable scrunching feeling of clean gravel. The whole operation ran like clockwork, even the torch managed to stay taped to the stick as I held it under the water, illuminating the yellow glow of the sand and gravel.

Within an hour and a half I was sitting back on the bed chair drinking tea, and feeling a lot more confident than before, I couldn't wait for day break to see where the markers were in relation to the swim.

The wind piled in all night and I slept in fits and starts until just before dawn when I bagged a couple of bream which had me up and ready to cast on my new 'hot spot'.

I waited, drinking tea, while daylight weakly filtered through the heavy cloud-filled sky until, there in the gloom, I saw the markers.

The areas I'd chosen were, unfortunately, all situated on the same bar about sixty yards out, as one glance at the markers showed, but still a massive advantage and the only marks that I knew of over about twenty yards out.

I cast around them, marking the line at the best spots before retiring to the café for a much needed breakfast. By lunchtime I'd walked around and chatted to the two other anglers present and had a text conversation with Steve, who was due down about one o'clock.

Nothing further had been caught, but the two buoy still looked good and I hung around only temporarily before making my way back to cast out. I was up to my waist in the pond, just sorting out the last rod, when Steve arrived and everything stopped for tea.

The wind was still pushing in nicely, but Steve assured me that it was due to swing to a Northerly soon. This, of course, was the worst news possible as the two buoy would be an absolute dead cert in a new wind, an occupied dead cert!

No sooner had he finished casting doubts in my mind than he was proved right, as if working from a script the wind changed and lifted the front of my brolly, briefly, before filling it full of driving rain! Cheers Steve! Steve set off in pursuit of a swim and no sooner had he left than the Steeplejack appeared at the door. I could tell from his face that something was amiss and it soon transpired that this was, indeed, the case.

Trying to hit the shallows
from Punishers point

The old in bounds/out of bounds scenario with the point had, once again, raised it's ugly head only this time it was, apparently, in conclusion and the swim was no longer on the Reading ticket!

The swim that I had just gone to all those lengths to learn and prepare was off the map before it was even on it!

True to his word, a Redlands bailiff duly arrived and informed me (in the nicest possible way) that due to complaints from the nearby houses of 'torches on their windows at night and people in their gardens after dark' the swim had been deemed out of bounds.

I tried to explain that burglars were a more likely explanation than anglers, as you could not even see the houses from the lake, but all to no avail, I was allowed to finish my session and that was that.

I think I can figure out what had really happened, it was that bloody dog!

The nearest house had a yappy little mutt that used to stand behind the fence at the bottom of the garden and bark for no reason whatsoever at anybody or anything in the point swim.

All that barking had driven the house owners crazy, as well as the anglers, and some old 'cock and bull' story of midnight raiders would alleviate the problem in one very foul swoop.

Really, I should have upped and moved there and then, but it was pissing down and I was more than happy with my marks, especially when, during a lull in the rain, I spotted a fish not far from my right hand marker!

Steve set his house up further along the road bank and then produced a bottle of champagne to toast his capture of 'The Eye', unfortunately for my head he also pulled two bottles of red wine out of the hat to follow.

That's how we spent the last night of the 'point', like Custers last stand. Steve, the newly arrived Des and I, sitting there drinking and chatting the evening away (well actually, Des chatted and we occasionally burst in with the odd snippet of conversation when we got a chance!).

At some time in the wee small hours a bream decided to hang itself on one rod and I very begrudgingly climbed out of bed and into a cold and clammy set of chest waders.

Standing out there in the lake in the pitch black, with a splitting headache whilst playing a bream was bad enough, but in a near gale force wind it was a bloody nightmare.

Half an hour later I had to repeat the whole procedure again for another of our snotty backed friends, the North wind was severe now and I really wished that I was sat in the two buoy, holding on to the bivvy for dear life, knowing something was bound to happen.

Just then, out of the bushes behind me appeared Mark. I looked at the clock; it was half past four in the morning and blowing a wild hooligan of a wind. Had my prayers been answered?

Had his bivvy been wrecked and he was off home?

Unfortunately not, the words he spoke were like hammer blows and after the first few I just wanted him to stop, I knew what was coming and dreaded every syllable.

"Have you got any big scales I can borrow? I've just had a lump from the 'two buoy' I think it's The Eye".

I tried to blurt out some form of congratulations but the words stuck to my mouth like dried up Madeira cake, all I could manage was "Whhgggmmmmb,b,b, eh?"

I stared at a slug on the floor while he recounted the tale, my mind numb, unable to believe that I felt so robbed.

I'd never felt like this before when a fish that I wanted had been caught by another angler, or when a swim that I had been fishing had produced to different rods.

I suppose the difference was that never before in my entire angling 'career' had I fished and baited one swim with such a level of tenacity and sheer 'bloody mindedness', determined that the biggun would, eventually, come calling.

Unfortunately, when he had come calling, I hadn't even been home to open the door, oh well, shit happens.

I told Mark I'd be up in the morning to do the photos for him and I crawled, dejectedly, back into my damp bed.

I was up at first light and gagging for a cup of tea. The previous night's celebrations with Steve had left a less than desirable taste in my mouth and probably stained my teeth purple as well.

I pumped the Colman's up while wondering if the early morning visit from Mark may have been some sort of alcohol fuelled delirium, hoping beyond hope I suppose.

I reached for the milk, which had tumbled on it's side but, being in a bottle, had not lost all of it's contents, in fact as I picked it up I realised that it had, actually, gained some extra contents of it's own. A great big black slug was happily drowning in what was left of my liquid lifesaver.

Grannies in Tesco's would have fought to the death over those few fluid ounces of cow juice but I was having none of it now!

I was thoroughly pissed off and all I had to look forward to was a long wet walk up to my normal swim to photograph the biggest fish in the lake for somebody else!

I packed up all my kit, while braced against the strong North wind, I half remembered an old saying about an ill wind that blows no good, if that old saying held any truth then this wind had been ill'er than a dead cat!

I ponced tea from Steve and then made my way up to the two buoy to do the photos.

Mark was over the moon, as you would expect but, although I tried hard, I couldn't lift my own spirits very high. I think it was a case of the teeth smiling but not the eyes!

Usually I laugh at people who think they own a swim and have this belief that the lake, in some way, 'owes' them something, but I am nothing if not honest and I'm not afraid to own up to my feelings whether I actually agree with them or not.

I felt absolutely 'Robbed' and totally 'Gutted', I couldn't wait for it all to be over so that I could go to the pub and get completely smashed!

It was all so wrong, the bivvy was set up on the flat piece of grass that my bivvy had created, the unhooking mat was laid out on the little clearing I had battered down with a bank stick weeks before, even the purple loosestrife that I had transplanted into the bushes behind to cheer up many a photo was still there, if a little brown around the edges now.

It was like watching a remake of a film with different actors and I really had to grit my teeth to get through it, I wasn't happy!

With the deed done there was nothing left but the drive home which, for once, went without mishap and I was soon boring Sooz with my tale of woe.

I think that she was almost as gutted as me, being, of course, under the illusion that catching a fifty pounder would have signaled a let up in my relentless pursuit for a while, poor deluded girl!

The very next week saw me back in the two buoy again, to hell with stable doors and bolting horses, I would carry on regardless.

I had a master plan up my sleeve which involved creating a new area at range that could be fished from the next swim along as well, this way I could increase my options from the two buoy and also give myself a back up should it be taken. I knew that nobody else would even consider plumbing for a spot out there in the thick weed, but I had a boat!

In fact I had two boats, the big grey Narwhale that I had used the previous week and my little inflatable beach dingy that had been languishing in the bushes all season.

The following week I was back again, all alone in the two buoy and trying to kid myself that there would be another chance but, deep in my heart I think I knew it was all over.

I still tried hard though, employing the boat and nearly killing myself in the process!

I had stashed an old inflatable 'Mere' special in the bushes months before, badly painted with camo paint and rolled up in an old canvass sack, before being buried behind a pile of stinging nettles, and now was the perfect opportunity for a maiden voyage.

Reckoning that the EYE would not be silly enough to return to the big clear area again, I was determined to find a spot further out, intercepting the fish as they moved along the bars.

I waited until well after dark before dragging out the sack, which in hindsight was my first mistake.

Everything seemed fine in the gloom as I pumped away and the dark shape on the grass slowly grew and grew to resemble a boat.

Even in the margins it still resembled a boat and it was only about thirty yards out into the pitch dark lake that it started to bear more resemblance to a tea strainer!

The ominous hissing of air that had started so gently suddenly intensified and the sides started to feel decidedly spongier as I rowed forwards. I searched with my hand for the root of the noise, unwilling to put on the head torch for fear of drawing attention to myself.

As my finger came in contact with the split in the seam it only made it worse and all thoughts of mapping out the swim were abandoned in favour of a hasty return to dry land.

The hissing grew louder and the front and back of the boat started to lift as the pressure dropped in the centre and then, just when I thought nothing could get worse I felt a sharp pain in my leg, as if a needle had been jabbed in my thigh.

Before I had a chance to wonder what it was, another one scored a hit on my side and then three more on my back, whatever it was it bloody well hurt and suddenly there were loads of them. Not giving a monkeys about secrecy any longer I flicked the switch on the headtorch and the beam revealed a colony of ants, great big red ones crawling all over me and, because of the temperature, I was only dressed in a pair of shorts!

Now I was in trouble, I was still twenty yards from shore and the boat was nearly flat, the front and back were almost vertical, sandwiching me between them.

I had one finger jammed in the hole trying to save the last of the air and any attempts at rowing with the other hand were pretty futile, really, as what was left of the boat was only going one way, and that was down.

The ants must have been living in the canvas bag, staying hidden until the water started flooding in and now they were furious and somehow they blamed me for everything.

I was audibly yelping in pain by the time I got close enough to shore

to abandon 'pancake' and roll into the cooling waters of the margins, dragging the ant infested Frisbee that used to be my boat up the bank behind me.

Sitting there in the pitch dark on the grass, rubbing doc leaves on all the lumps and bumps that covered my body, I convinced myself that the close in marks didn't look so bad after all and just maybe the biggun would come back for another go!

My pain induced enthusiasm only lasted as long as the bumps took to subside, though, and I soon came to the conclusion that, in reality, it would be another year before there was any chance of seeing that big old mirror carp again.

# Chapter 8

# The Forbidden Lands

"**D**uring the winter of 2000, England was awash, monsoon conditions had swept the country and flooding was widespread, every day the news opening to footage of somebody paddling a canoe up the high street or building an ark out of match sticks!".

From a fishing point of view it was a disaster and over at Sonning you could hardly even get in the gates, let alone fish. I remember wading along the main car track and the water coming up to my waist!

Down at the two buoy end, the Thames had breached its banks and the flood water was hitting the reeds with such force that a permanent cascade of water jetted a clear eight feet in the air, before crashing into the margins of the swim.

The flow was so strong that, as I waded across the river where my bivvy usually stood, my legs were almost swept out from underneath me.

We were just hoping that the 'Big Fella' had not decided to up sticks and move on to a new home in the Thames, although he would have had to learn to swim like a salmon if he was going to leave the Lake at the top end, against the flow.

Stories are always rife, after floods, of fish seen swimming over the pathways and bow waving across fields. Personally I've never seen it myself although I remember Pit Four in the Colne Valley losing about a third of it's stock one year into the river.

We briefly considered the possibility that the Eye may have made a break for it by crossing the road into the trout lake next door and then out the other end into the weir pool, but then we decided that he was probably too damn fat to make it under the fence.

After the flood water subsided we started again in earnest, walking the pit and looking for early sightings of carp. This year, however, we were a bit dubious about baiting the same old areas again, as they were now well known and would be under constant pressure.

First of all, though, we had the spring season to contend with and we wouldn't start baiting just yet as we had no idea where the fish would choose to spend the next few months.

Spring is my favorite time on the big gravel pits, and as we had no experience of spring on Sonning at all it was, once again, all very fresh and exciting.

The mobile approach seemed to be the best option to start with, as fish in big pits tend to move around a lot at this time of year, especially before the spawning urges set in.

Different areas come in to play and a new wind can literally move fish for miles!

In the first few weeks of spring, as the temperatures started to rise, I managed about three or four small fish by fishing on the new winds but I was up against some serious opposition this year as Chilly had decided to put in a concerted effort on the lake starting this April.

Chilly, being the sort of angler he is, and having a fair amount of time at his disposal, was getting in the right areas and making good use of his time.

The fish were obviously building in numbers at the shallow end of the lake and, unfortunately, only the Punishers Point really gave you a chance at reaching them.

The swim had undergone yet another bizarre twist of rules since the previous year and this time it made even less sense than ever.

The swim had been reopened to Reading anglers, but they had chopped a load of trees down from the woods behind and blocked off the front of the swim so that you could only cast into the small channel to the left of the swim.

Quite how this would stop the dog barking or prevent the mystery torches in the neighbour's garden I never figured out; maybe they were averse to the sound of leads hitting the water!

The out of bounds bank on the far side was by far the better looking

*Chilly showing me how it's done*

area during these early weeks, as the natural route down to the shallows lay on that side of the lake, and the frustration at being confined to the Reading Angling bank really started to kick in.

I made one tentative excursion to the far side during April but came up against a rather hostile reaction from one of the 'Hippies', who we now knew had no more right to be there than I did.

The fish continued to stack up on the shallows and then, over a four-day period in late April, they fed in earnest.

Unfortunately for me, I was relegated to being Chilly's photographer (I know how poor old Keith had felt the previous year, now).

Big pits really can be this 'swimmy' at this time of year and, try as I might, I just couldn't get anywhere near them.

He was fishing from the Punishers point and casting out to the old areas in front, by putting the rods in front of the new 'barrier' of chopped trees and casting sideways into the open, shallow area, exactly as everyone else had done and would continue to do until the barrier mysteriously disappeared one night and the swim was returned to normal.

Unfortunately for Chilly his time was cut short when his wife Lynn who has been suffering in silence for years with a serious illness had to return to hospital and he, obviously, put his fishing on hold to be with her as much as possible.

I think he only managed to fish a total of about ten nights on Sonning but he put them to very good effect, catching five fish in quick succession, the biggest being a common of thirty two pounds (the same spawn bound fish I had caught on the previous summer) although one or two of the mid twenty mirrors were absolutely stunning examples of big pit carp!

By the end of that month (ten months into my campaign) the fish had started to appear regularly in other areas, dotted around the pit, and warming their bodies in the strengthening sunlight.

What usually happens in big pits throughout May is that the fish start to split noticeably into two or three 'size' groups for spawning. Although the actual ritual is still someway off, the fish start to congregate with others of their own stamp to feed, laze, and generally prepare for the glorious, once a year, orgy that inevitably follows.

This is obviously the time when you can see exactly what it is that you are angling for, if there are any unknown whackers in the pit then now is the time that you will see them.

As I've said, size grouping is a major factor of their behavior at this time of year and it is commonplace for the various groups to be very far apart and, as it turned out, when I did find them on Sonning, you could practically measure it in miles!

The fish on here had been merrily doing there own thing for years, with only a handful of anglers in the past to disturb them, so I was gambling that they were well set in their ways. Unfortunately I knew almost nothing about what 'their ways' were and finding the bigger fish took a lot of time and leg work. It was obvious that only the small ones were left out in front of the point where Chilly had his hit so it was time to go exploring, looking for that inevitable 'safe area' where the biggest and strongest would be preparing themselves for a big feed up and then wild sex! I walked my little legs down to stumps over the next two weeks, looking in all the likely spots that I could gain access to.

It was about this time that the unwritten 'access laws' took a strange and unexpected turn and this eventually led to a far better scenario for the coming seasons angling.

Sometime in the early spring, apparently, a pair of anglers had decided to set up a hidden camp on one of the larger islands in the middle of the lake. Miles from anywhere and totally secluded, they had carved an encampment and set up a bivvy and base camp.

This made no odds either way to me, Keith or any of the other poor buggers stranded on the boring old in-bounds bank as the island was so far away we could barely see it in any detail, let alone cast near it.

For some reason, though, it did seem to matter to certain individuals on the other side of the lake and the bivvy ended up getting burnt down, or at least this was the story we heard on the grapevine from the in-bounds bank!

The atmosphere was more than a little tense after this strange and incredibly outrageous reaction to what was, in all reality, just a bit of fishing.

For a couple of weeks we watched from afar the comings and goings on the far bank and wondered what, if anything would happen next.

Eventually, the inevitable did happen and the saga continued in earnest.

It was a Friday evening, about an hour after dark, when we all heard an incredible commotion from the far bank swims.

A sudden burst of shouting and swearing was quickly replaced by a ferocious sounding dog, barking and snarling, a few more shouted snippets about 'teaching someone not to burn my bloody bivvy down' drifted across the water and then, all was deathly quiet.

In the morning it was as if nothing had happened, the only visible difference on the horizon was the lack of hippies!

The next week was the same, and so was the next, so I thought it was about time to take another little trip around to the far side of the pond and see if I could find any evidence of life, or indeed death!

Since the 'Friday Night Massacre' there had been no sign of any more hostilities; in fact there had been no sign of anybody at all!

Talk had started to circulate about the fact that there may be an opening for a bit of surreptitious angling and, if the 'Hippies' had really gone, then maybe a few of the members could sneak around there and fish from the greener grass that it obviously held.

The fact that nobody had ever even seen any of the lake beyond the gravel works didn't seem to come into it and, to be truthful, most people didn't have a clue how to even get around there. It was all just talk, as it often is, but I was seriously interested in at least having a little look.

It wasn't as if you could just follow the bank around, though, as in a normal lake, as the workings at each end formed a natural barrier.

Now, I knew that the hippies had been known about by the angling club, and indeed the gravel company for a long while, but had been 'tolerated' for whatever reason.

In fact, somebody that seemed to know had once told me that it was their unsavoury character and total refusal to budge that created a situation whereby it was easier to just ignore them.

This 'head in the sand' attitude, however, would not be extended to a whole bunch of 'new' anglers traipsing around all over the place, so I hatched a little plan.

As plans go it was quite a cunning plot, also a little selfish I suppose, but what the hell. I needed somewhere that I could do my thing without the constant worry that somebody else was going to jump in and reap the benefits again.

As well as this, I was also of the opinion that the grass really was that much more verdant and lush on the other side of the pond!

The plan involved an old bivvy that I had in the cupboard at home, an old bivvy that looked exactly like the Hippies bivvy that had been set up permanently for the whole year, especially when viewed from five hundred yards away!

Strategically placed on the precise location of the old one, and with the odd candle left burning on a Friday night, it would soon lead everybody to believe that it was business as usual back at the 'encampment' and, obviously, all plans for visiting would be instantly shelved.

I suppose, in reality, I was doing the angling club a favour by keeping all their members firmly back where they belonged, and also the Gravel Company would not have to deal with a load of lost and camouflage clad anglers wandering around on their land looking for Nirvana!

I, on the other hand, could quietly come and go as I pleased and keep a good eye on the area to see if the fish found it 'greener' as well.

With this new and cunning plan in mind I set off for another reconnaissance mission.

This time I made it unchallenged and I was soon making my way through the thick woods into territory that I had previously only seen through high-powered binoculars.

That whole side of the lake was so much more interesting than the section that Reading Angling had permission for; there were woods and fields, points, bays and a whole cluster of islands and gravel bars.

Making my way through the thickest woods I eventually emerged in the old 'Hippy camp'.

It was like coming across a cowboy camp after the Indians had chased them off up the canyon, all that was missing was a scalp on a spear and a hat with an arrow in it, (although there was a toilet roll on a branch)!

Old discarded bottles of 'fire water', or at least 'Brown ale', were scattered around in the bushes and a couple of tins of soup were still stashed in the fork of a tree. There was even the remains of a small camp fire, although it lacked the characteristic glowing embers that let John Wayne guess how long ago the massacre took place!

There was a short ladder in the steep margins at the lakes edge that allowed access to the boat that had been used, and the patch of ground that lay at the entrance to where the bivvy would have stood was worn to leather. The swim itself looked wonderful and I sat there trying to imagine what it must have been like to fish Sonning from such a different perspective. I also felt like a bit of a thief in the night and couldn't help but think that I was trespassing, not on gravel company property, but on the 'Hippies' territory which, in one way I suppose I was.

It was a shame that everything had turned out in this way, really, as we were all only after catching a few fish, at the end of the day. It would have been so much easier to all get along, but I could still understand the resentment to share their hard found prize.

After all, I wasn't exactly planning to shout about anything that I might come across and, in previous years on the Mere, I had fallen under the spell of 'false ownership' myself!

Further along the bank was a carbon copy of the first swim, although set more into a corner, but it was still a cracking looking area. Sticks were protruding above the water level, marking the ends of the bars as they cut through the bay in a typical fashion.

After having a good look around I set off to look for areas where I may be able to do a bit of fishing in the future. I didn't intend on fishing the 'Hippy' swims, I just wanted to make it look as if they still were, I was on the look out for something new, something tucked away and exciting where the fish could actually be seen for a change.

Back along the bank, off towards the shallows, I found a small swim that looked as if it had been cut out in years gone by, but not fished for a fair while since as there was quite long grass on the ground and undisturbed bank side reeds and grasses.

It was shielded from the field behind by a thick 'hedgerow' of bramble and saplings, all intertwined with nettles and bindweed. The field was wild and unkempt and stretched across a three hundred yard area, towards the back entrance to the workings and a new and exposed gravel pit that had recently been dug there.

The swim itself was well hidden, and I stood there looking out from it for quite a while, imaging the rods sitting in front of me and the peace and tranquillity I could have if I were tucked nicely away in there for a few days. After about half an hour I decided to continue my tour so I walked through the small gap in the hedge, emerging back onto the field behind.

As I did so, I spotted a pair of bright orange 'Building site jackets' near to a water pump at the side of the new pit and, unfortunately, right next to the exit through the far bushes, my only route back to the car.

I quickly ducked down behind a log pile of cleared trees that had been bulldozed up in a big heap and watched from the safety of my 'hide'.

I could see the workers easily in their day-glow tops but, from this distance, there was no way on earth they would pick out my camouflage attire, particularly as I was hidden behind a ten foot high mountain of tangled branches. Unfortunately I had not come away prepared for a long day out and I'd run out of drink ages beforehand. I was absolutely gasping for some water, the sun was beating down, and the 'jackets' didn't seem to be in any particular hurry to do anything at all!

They had a land rover with them and they seemed content to just lean on the bonnet chatting and smoking- lazy buggers, why couldn't they go off and do some work!

It was at least another hour before they decided that somebody, somewhere, would be missing them and they clambered back in the land rover and trundled off in a cloud of dust.

I could see already that this side of the pond, although rosy, held its fair share of thorns and it would be very possible to become stranded in paradise for long periods.

I spent the whole of the next week at home, and work, thinking about the new areas and the possibilities they held, planning and plotting my attack. All I had to do now was find the fish and I was pretty sure it would be somewhere on the far side.

The margins in the main bay over there had looked extremely deep and snaggy and not the sort of place that you would imagine to be overly warm, at least not in comparison to the sheltered shallower areas that the smaller fish were currently using.

The one big advantage was the fact that they faced the sun and, as such, would be the first areas to warm up every morning.

So, the next week, I loaded the van with the normal gear but added a false bivvy and a rucksack full of camouflage before setting off on the familiar drive up the motorway.

I parked the car well out of view down a little cul-de-sac on a nearby estate and walked up the road to the back entrance.

I was still a bit nervous about crossing the open area to reach the woods, as I didn't really know who or what to look out for, but I made it across without being spotted and I was soon picking my way through nettles and brambles along the new and unfamiliar margins, peering in under every bush and tree hoping to catch a glimpse of the infamous 'Sonning Eye'.

I battled my way through one patch of stinging nettles and came out directly behind a large section of snags, the sun was shining straight into the branches and the heat of the rays had made the air sticky and alive with insects.

The surface of the water was calm and dark with the reflected depths below and, as I poked my head through the first gap in the bushes, I saw him.

He was just laying there, five feet below me, just under the surface in crystal clear water. I had never, ever, seen anything so impressive in my life!

I sort of just crumpled up into a ball and tried to become invisible by hugging my knees and making myself as small as possible, all the while biting my thumbs so as not to scream out the words that kept repeating themselves on a loop through my head.

"Bloody Hell, Bloody Hell, Bloody Hell"!

I'd never seen a carp so wide in my life before, probably for the pure reason that there wasn't another carp that wide in the entire country, it was immense, monstrous, almost ridiculous and, for some reason very scary!

Further along in the snags I could see other good fish as well, and after a quick and very shaky reconnaissance crawl, I knew I'd found the area where they would sun themselves and warm up prior to spawning in a few weeks time.

There was no way on earth that they were ever going to actually feed in the snags and, even if they did, landing them would be a nightmare.

A network of bars made their way into this snaggy area and it was obviously here, along these transit routes, that I'd pick the fish off as they came in and left every morning and evening, at least that was the plan!

It was lucky that I had thought to bring the camo netting as I was so close to the fish that I would need to hide from them as well as everybody else!

I ran most of the way back to the van, suddenly nothing else mattered, all I could see was that one enormous carp laying there, suspended in the gin clear water as if he were flying.

Getting everything across the open ground and into the woods was the most nerve racking experience imaginable, not that I cared about the consequences of being caught but, what if I got thrown off before I had a chance to fish for the beast?

I managed to get enough gear back into the woods behind the snags and crept forward into the clearing from where I would fish, taking my time and picking out spots on the bars to position the baits.

By late afternoon I was all settled in, hiding behind a large tree trunk just in the cover of the woods, but with a good view of most of the bay through the fork of the tree.

That first night spent in the woods was a bit strange and slightly unnerving; I didn't know whether I was doing the right thing by hiding in the woods, so as not to be on view from the lake, or whether it would be better to hide from anyone approaching through the woods by sitting out next to the lake?

Every minute I expected some crazed hippy to come charging around the corner, looking for revenge, and there I'd be like a sitting duck.

The island off to my left didn't exactly help matters either, every time I got settled down there would be a blood curdling scream from the little copse of trees in the middle. Some of the noises I recognised as Herons, which really do make the most horrendous noises when spooked, but what was spooking them?

As for the other things going on out there, well, all I knew was it certainly wasn't a Heron and, whatever it was, it was torturing a very scared squealing thing that was soon to become it's evening meal.

Eventually I retracted my head into my shoulders like a tortoise, pulled everything I had over the top of me and fell into a strange, dream filled sleep.

It was a good job that I did sleep so fitfully as I awoke easily to the sound of the clutch on one of my reels kicking into life, I don't know why the alarm didn't sound but I didn't wait to find out.

Struggling from under the various suits of armour, I staggered out into the open and bent into the fish. As I took in my surroundings I could see

that it had probably been light for no more than half an hour and the sun was far from up, which would make it about half past four in the morning.

The lake was flat calm, as it often is at that time of day, and I could clearly make out the bamboo canes marking the tops of the first three bars.

Heading up the lake to my right between the second and third stick was a large bow wave and my line was cutting through the water after it, giving off an audible hiss as it did so. It was imperative to keep the line high as I didn't know how sharp the closest bars were and the last thing I wanted was to be cut off.

Winding like a maniac I kept the line high and tight and managed to get the fish over one bar with no dramas.

The next bar proved a little trickier but, eventually, I bullied him over it and into the close gully where, in theory, things should have started to get a bit easier. The reality of the situation was totally different though and a sudden jerk through the rod, and a coil of line flying through the rings, had me looking at the reel for the first time in the fight and what I saw was not good.

Somehow the spool, which should have been smoothly rising and falling during the retrieve, thereby aiding the perfect line lay, had jammed solid in the extended position and eighty yards of line was piled on top of itself in a big line mountain at the back of the spool.

As I watched in horror another big coil slipped off the reel and rattled up the rod, it would only take one coil to jam in an eye, and the fish to bolt and then it would all be over.

In a sudden fit of genius I decided to whack the spool as hard as I could to try to get it back down again, which in all fairness was the immediate result, it was just a matter of quite how far back down it went that presented a problem!

With the spool now jammed tight against the reel body, and the entire mechanism seized up I was starting to doubt the wisdom of my actions.

The fish had obligingly stopped trying to escape and was probably wondering what the hell I was up to, as I pulled and pushed bits of metal in all directions in an attempt to gain a bit of line. Suddenly, the spool clicked forward a bit and I was back in business, so I just cranked as much line onto the mashed up spool as possible and dragged the fish straight into the net before the next disaster struck.

In the net I could see the most wonderful looking carp I'd caught for almost a year, the exact amount of time since the last time I'd caught it, as it was my first recapture from Sonning, but it was also one of the most classic looking carp imaginable.

He was up a bit in weight since the last time we met, pulling the scales

*A classic Sonning mirror*

around to twenty-seven pounds, and it was a very encouraging start to a new campaign in a new area.

Throughout the morning I began to realise the appeal of fishing over on this side of the lake and, to some extent, the Hippies reluctance to let anybody else even look at it. More and more fish made their way across the bars and into the snags along to my right, and I saw more carp in the first two hours than I had seen the entire previous season on the Reading bank.

I only had the one night to fish that week but I stashed all the gear in the woods, erected the decoy bivvy in the main swim, and made everything ready before I left so it would all be easier on my return, which wouldn't be very far away if I had anything to do with it.

As soon as I got home I took everything that I would need, bivvy, rods, buckets, bags and everything that would be on show, into my garden and painted the whole lot with camouflage paints. I also sewed another large section of army netting together to form a hide from which to fish.

My mind was racing with the possibilities for the rest of the spring and I couldn't wait to get back and have a more concerted effort.

I decided not to bait the area heavily, as the fish were already coming there, and I was assuming that they would return there every day until they spawned.

This would only take place when the water temperatures stabilised at a level that they found ideal to drop their load, probably out amongst the weed beds at the back of this large bay.

I knew that my mate CP was heavily baiting an area in the next section of lake along from here, about four hundred yards away by water and the other side of a chain of islands, so I decided to fish by another method entirely and use attractor bait pop-up's, placed on the highest points of the various bars, hoping to ambush the carp in transit.

It had worked well enough on the first attempt so there was no reason to assume that it wouldn't carry on working.

Rigs were simple helicopter set ups with extended shank hooks and bright pop-ups; I even treated the reels to a bit of a service after the previous week's disaster.

I had buckets, bags and covers all sprayed up with green, brown and black aerosols to leave the various, less expensive items, stashed in the woods. There was no way I was dragging the entire kit back and forth across no mans land every week.

In the middle of this open workings section of flattened gravel and sand was also a small lake of about six acres, and this new excavation

joined onto the big lake by a small channel, perfectly large enough to allow the fish easy passage in and out. This discovery just brought it home to me how much of a disadvantage we'd been fishing under by sticking to the one area on the far side of the lake, after all, here was a completely separate but annexed lake that we never even knew about. If the fish decided to spend a month in there we would have had no chance.

As luck would have it I returned to find the scene exactly as I had left it, I'd told no one of my capture and the fish were still there, unmolested and lazing in the sun.

That session was a disaster, I lost two fish the first morning and one on the second before landing a lovely looking mid twenty mirror, which was some compensation but not enough.

The lost fish irked me no end, in one way or another they were all lost due to the stick markers in the top of the gravel bars. I assumed these were a legacy left over from the hippies angling years but, being made of solid cane they were causing problems with kiting fish.

Because I wasn't using a boat to land the fish it was easy for them to wrap around the canes during the fight.

One consolation with the lost fish was that the big fella was still in the snags and obviously not one of the ones that I'd lost.

I spent the second day trying to tempt him into taking a worm that I'd dangled over the extreme, outside branch but, despite it actually crawling over his head at one stage, he showed no interest whatsoever. It was an incredible sight to be so close to such a colossal carp, I couldn't even guess at the weight he may have been, all I knew was that he was far bigger than anything I'd ever seen before.

What a way to spend a day, though, laying on my belly staring eyeball to swollen eyeball with a big, fifty-pound plus fish.

It was also a good opportunity to see what other beasts the lake held as well, although I was surprised to see just how few other large fish there were.

The second biggest was the known forty that Chrissie had captured, at just over 40lb, the previous year from the two buoy. Next up was another fish that didn't look far short of that mark, although she was obviously holding a fair amount of spawn; it had a distinctive large plate scale near the vent that I knew I'd recognise on the bank.

From these fish down it was really only a couple of mid thirty mirrors and two or three good commons, two of which I had already had at thirty-three and thirty one pounds.

It seemed that the big one was a breed on its own and was obviously a completely different strain to any of the other fish there; he was also in a

*Me, storm dog and CP waiting for the inevitable*

completely different size bracket and really did 'dwarf' everything else he swam past.

That evening, the fish made their way out of the bay along their normal routes, the biggun was the last to leave as usual and was really getting obscenely large now, surely it couldn't be long before they started to spawn; the weather was very settled and constantly warm and sunny.

That night I went and spent some time in CP's swim, I hadn't even told him about all the action I'd received that session, I was a bit pissed off about losing so many fish and I wanted a chance at the biggun before shouting too loud about the takes I was receiving.

I suppose it was a case of once bitten twice shy after the previous year's fiasco!

CP was getting a bit apprehensive about his swim, as he had put a hell of a lot of effort and bait into it for next to no result; in fact he had only had one small common in the last few weeks!

He was talking about moving around into my bay with me and I couldn't really blame him, I know that I would have done it long before as there was a perfectly good swim fifty yards along from mine that wasn't being fished at all.

Keith had also started fishing the bay, doing a bit in my swim when I wasn't there but had yet to catch.

As it transpired, CP 'not moving' into my bay that night, but deciding to give it one more shot, would prove to be the best move that he 'never' made.

The next morning I was sitting up and waiting, at first light, for the fish to appear as usual but they never showed, and by eight o'clock I knew something was wrong.

Just as I was beginning to fear the worst and that the spawning had started, CP ran into the swim all excited saying he'd just had a thirty seven pounder and lost a big common at the net! I told him I'd be around in an hour when I was sure that my daily chance of a take was definitely not coming.

After half an hour and with no sightings I gave up early, I knew it had all changed and they just weren't coming back. I made my way around to his swim, passing him in the fields on the way, he was over the other side of the long grasses, running around yelling and punching the air and I knew!

*CP with a spawn laden 37*

*The second biggest Carp in England!!*

What I couldn't have known was the weight, the fish that I had had in my swim like a pet dog for two weeks turned out to be the second largest carp in the land and weighed in at a colossal 57lb! What a morning for CP, all that hard work had paid off in the end and I had learnt a valuable lesson, unfortunately it was one that I already knew but had ignored.

The big fish always come to the big, pre-baited areas, time and time again it happens and CP had certainly put some bait in his swim over the last few weeks and that had obviously been where they went every night. It had just been this final morning before spawning that they threw caution to the wind and ate everything in sight.

A fifty seven pound mirror, a thirty seven pound mirror and a big common lost at the net, Bloody Hell!

Once again I had been so close, only this time I had no thought of having been 'robbed'. CP had played it right, done the hard work and had his just rewards.

As predicted, the spawning took place a couple of days later and it was once again a new ball game.

I consoled myself with the knowledge that my turn would surely come, eventually, wouldn't it?

Leaving the large bivvy in the Hippy bay I gave up on the snags area, knowing that they would not be back now and started searching for a new area to fish.

I briefly returned to Punishers point, and indeed the two buoy area, but it all seemed so dull after the wonders of the snags bay, there must have been somewhere that the fish hid out?

On a chance meeting one day with the Steeplejack, I picked up a few pointers that sounded very interesting and tied in with the sighting of fish that CP had witnessed, leading up to his captures.

Apparently, out in the middle of the lake, there was a large plateau area that the Steeplejack had fished years before by boating out from the nearest swim. Nowadays, with the new regime, this wasn't possible but a small and close-in island looked out to the same area and, from there, it would only be an easy cast to reach the plateau, which was marked with an old scaffold tube sticking out from it.

The near side of the island was very close to CP's swim and quite well hidden, the other side looked out at the area I needed to reach but, unfortunately, it was right on show from the distant Ski and Sailing club. In fact the Ski Club used it as a roundabout, so I would have to stay totally hidden during daylight hours.

The other, slightly off-putting aspect of fishing this particular island was that it was home to the green eyed monster!

The Green eyed monster, or so we had convinced ourselves, was the instigator of all the hideous torturing and slaughter that took place every night amongst the screeching Herons on the island.

We had heard the noises for weeks and never quite been able to work out what was creating them.

One night, CP had been sitting on his low chair drinking tea and staring out at the Island, when a pair of green eyes started staring back at him.

At first, I thought he'd just been smoking the wrong fags or something, but he kept on seeing them on a regular basis and then, one fateful night, so did I.

We had been standing at the front of his swim, looking at the screeching island as it grew darker and the first sounds of battle emerged when, as plain as the nose on my face, I saw a pair of slanted green eyes appear in the bushes, a few feet off ground level, staring straight at me. I looked quickly at CP who just nodded and said "Green eyed monsters about"

It didn't end there either as, about an hour into darkness as we still stood there chatting, a strange light beam reflected in the water in front of us and then shot along the bank, passing straight between our two sets of feet before disappearing behind us!

CP turned and looked at me wide eyed in shock and, quick as a flash said,

"Oh shit, Green eyed Monsters got a head torch"

At which we both burst into fits of laughter, so much so that I could hardly breath and tears rolled down my face, although it all didn't seem quite as funny that fateful afternoon, a few weeks later, as I stood there loading up the boat for my first actual trip out there to meet him!

Packing myself an overnight kit, and a big sheet of camouflage netting, I arranged with CP that he'd drop me off there by boat that evening, and I'd phone him for a lift back the next day, before the ski boats started up. This way I would have no boat on show and I could tuck myself neatly away in the bushes, out of sight from anyone, whether they were on land or water.

By tea-time, and with no sign of the ski club showing up on the far bank, I decided that I may as well go out there early so, CP, his dog Storm dog and myself, were soon floating across the little gap, keeping the island between ourselves and the far bank so as not to be spotted.

I don't know what we expected to find on the island but, as we pulled

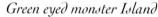

*Green eyed monster Island*

up under the overhanging trees and looked into the clearing for the first time, we nearly died of heart failure as there in the middle of the island, sitting on an old plastic chair, was a bloke in an old cap, donkey jacket and track suit trousers!

I nearly fell out of the bloody boat in shock, especially as he looked as dead as a dodo.

It was only when I realised that his training shoes weren't actually attached to his feet that I sussed it, it was a dummy that had been placed there as a bizarre deterrent to somebody or another, and it held all the hallmarks of the Steeplejacks strange sense of humour.

Once again, fear turned to laughter and we rocked about for a bit before off loading me, and my kit, under the trees.

I will say one thing though, CP never actually got out of the boat and he set off for shore a damn sight quicker than he had rowed out there!

I spent the evening creating a hide that involved butting my brolly opening directly up against a row of trees and then camo netting over the lot, it was a bit treacherous and, if I did get a run in the night, there was a good chance I'd wake up a lot uglier than when I went to bed.

As it turned out, though, sleep was not a realistic option and I spent the strangest night you could imagine.

The whole island stank of acrid piss and the trees were stained with an oily sheen on the bottom foot, all around the margins, as something had marked it's territory good and proper.

I guessed the Green eyed Monster must have been some sort of big Mink or Otter, or even a Fox or Black Panther, but whatever he was he'd been busy as there were no shortage of bones and skulls laying about all over the place.

I didn't really relish the thought of finding out, face to face, exactly what sort of monster he really was, and I kept a watchful eye on old Dummy as well, just in case!

The island was more like a big hill and I was camped at the bottom where the ground was fairly bare, except for the trees. The middle of the island rose up and was totally covered in bigger trees, brambles and mixed undergrowth of every conceivable variety.

It was in this thicket that the Herons and Geese roosted and, after darkness fell, they started their intolerable racket as they argued and screamed at each other over who was sleeping where, it seemed that none of them wanted to be on the outside for some reason!

By about one in the morning, long after CP had stopped answering his phone, I decided that, as I was still alive I must be safe, so I grew a bit bolder and decided to investigate the racket a bit closer. Most of the screeching had died down by then, but there were still plenty of other noises going on.

I crept, on hands and knees, up the steep slope behind me, headed into pitch darkness at the top of the hill in the middle.

I reached the summit and stood up, taking a tentative step into the thicket, straining my eyes for a glimpse of whatever lay within, when suddenly, the ground erupted in front of me and something far bigger than a Heron charged off into the darkness, cracking it's leg on a branch as it went and scaring the shit out of me, twenty Herons, thirty Canadian geese, and even old Dummy as it went.

I could hear CP laughing as I slid back down the slope to the comparative safety of the bivvy, convincing myself it was only a stray deer or something, but I stayed in the sleeping bag the rest of the night just in case I was wrong.

By mid morning I had decided that the plateau was a rubbish place to fish anyway but, unfortunately, just as I was thinking of abandoning the island for good the skiers set out and I had to stay stashed away with Dummy while they whizzed past only a few yards in front of me.

At one stage, one fell off right next to me and was hollering at the top of his voice to his mate on the boat.

He was so close that, if I'd have even whispered Boo to him, I reckon he would have shot out of the water like an exocet!

Eventually, they went back in for lunch and CP snuck around the back of the island, in the little boat to rescue me. By god we had a giggle over dinner that night as I recounted the tales of my one and only night on the Green Eyed Monsters Island.

The next day I set off to search for a decent land based spot to continue my campaign and put my new theory of lots and lots of bait into full effect.

After much deliberation, and planning the routes I'd seen the fish use up until now I picked a quiet spot, where I was positive I could make something happen.

It was far enough away from the bay area and near to a small gap where the fish had to pass through, to get from one side of the lake to the other. After plumbing around for a while I found the perfect feature in the form of a double hump at about sixty yards range. It was in the middle of the 'route', and the fish could hardly fail to notice it as they moved up and down the pit.

The swim itself was little more than a gap in the trees with a flooded margin that left a small hump of land, just big enough to house the rods.

I didn't fancy wading to and fro across the flood so I talked Chrissie

*My swim, 'The Hump'*

into helping me cart an old railway sleeper from a nearby wood pile into the swim.

It took a bit of carrying across the bumpy overgrown terrain, it took even more effort to chuck it into place and I ended up soaked and stinking from the flood water but, eventually, I had my bridge.

From an aerial view of the lake it looked to be the 'perfect' spot for a big ambush and I didn't muck about with the bait either.

I had used the Assassinate the previous season to great effect, but now I had a new bait, 'NRG', from Mainline to test so I started off by mixing the two and slowly weaning off one onto the other, to give myself the best of both worlds as it were.

I piled in as much as I could carry around to the swim every week and, over a four-week period, I must have put in one hundred and fifty kilos of boilie and pellet. Now, this may seem an awful lot of bait to some people, especially as I was only catching bream from the spot, but I could tell that it was being eaten. Every week the spot would have changed dramatically, and the actual silt and clay that held the stones together to form the hump was being eroded by the constant attentions of fish. What started out as a clay hump, with gravel and stones mixed in, ended up as a pile of bricks and rubble. In fact, if I had continued all summer, I think it may well have collapsed!

During my few weeks fishing that little swim that I had cut out for myself, I picked off about eight carp by fishing pop-up's at range on the bar systems.

I had located a bed of the stringy Potmogoten weed that I love so much; in fact it was only when this weed started to die off that I saw visible signs of carp at night over the hump.

There really is an irresistible 'draw' to this kind of weed at the right time of year and as soon as I found it I knew it would produce a few fish.

The swim itself was totally hidden away and could not be seen from anywhere, I was not being 'poached' again this year!

Much to the amazement of my neighbors at home, I had carefully dug up buckets and buckets of 'bindweed' out of my garden and the bushes at the end of my street, and started to train them over the camo painted bivvy that I left in the swim as a permanent fixture.

I also planted willow switches along the margins to screen my position from the other bank and concealed every sign of me being there, from every angle; my gear was still camouflaged from the old swim so it all blended in nicely.

*A Hobby hunting over Hippy Bay*

All of the fish that I had picked off from the bars at range had been small ones but I was determined that, eventually, the bait would draw the big fella in, and this time I was not going to miss out on my result.

Wherever the fish went in this section of the lake they would have to pass through this gap to change areas or to utilise the main section of water.

There were only two ways in and out and, from my observations in the early part of spring, I knew that this route was used frequently.

In fact, it was this gap that I was now sat next to that I had watched them appear through on that first morning in the snag bay when I had bagged the 24lb mirror.

Although the hump I was baiting was not part of the actual bar system or 'roadways', it lay only twenty yards short of a bar that could qualify as a virtual 'motorway' for the fish and I was confident that it would be visited, the actual bar system in this area was fast becoming choked with weed and I knew that I would start to have problems landing the fish before long, if I was fishing at range.

The false bivvy I had erected in the main swim was still doing it's job and we had next to no visitors the entire time we were there, only CP and his mate Jamie, Keith and I ever seemed to tread the banks, apart from the odd visit from the Steeplejack as he made his way off to bait up some spot or another, as he was always 'up to' something.

We now had a new car park as well, purely for the select few, and it had come about more by accident and chance than anything else. There was an old locked gate at the back of the garden centre on the main road, behind the lake, and by some fluke somebody had discovered that an old key they had actually fitted the lock perfectly. We could now pull off the road, through the gate, and park up on an old gravel track that would have once led to the workings, but was now abandoned and hidden by bushes and trees. Before this it had been either a case of leaving the van in a nearby street or actually driving head first into the brambles and then, after escaping out through the back door, covering the back of the motor in camo sheeting and old branches!

One week I arrived on a Sunday and decided to leave the van in the local pub car park, obviously it would have been rude not to have stayed for an afternoon carvery and a few pints of Guinness, so it was some few hours later when I eventually clambered over the gate at the back of the 'new' lake and made my way across the exposed gravel workings area to the woods on the far side, where my tackle was hidden.

On the way past the exposed square pit, I noticed a movement in the corner of the lake and, on closer investigation, there were three or four carp cruising along the exposed marginal shelf, only a few feet out from the bank this had to be worth a go.

I stood and watched for a bit and, as I did, there was a thump on the path behind me and I turned to see a young Canadian goose laying there, looking just as confused as I was, trying to figure where he'd come from.

Looking up, as you would do when a goose lands with a thump on the ground next to you, I saw the power cables still shaking and it was obvious what had happened.

I had half noticed a big flock of geese going overhead a few minutes earlier and this poor little fella had obviously twanged off the wires and crash landed. Feeling a bit like the good Samaritan, I carefully picked him up and put him in the lake to join his mates.

With my good deed done for the day I ran through the nettles and long grass to the back of my swim, where I had the tackle and dried bait hidden away in various bushes and trees. There was even a big round reed bed that grew on dry land where I could stash the rods without even having to break them down. The only bit of tackle that was tricky was the life jacket, every time it rained it would self inflate and what was a nicely hidden green jacket would suddenly become a bloody great bright yellow balloon!

With a couple of rods, and a mat full of bits and pieces, I went back to the new pit where the fish were still milling about in the corner, but approaching them was a nightmare. There was no cover whatsoever and the gravel underfoot was so loud it spooked them straight away, the only way was to set a trap and sit and wait for them to return.

With the baits in position I looked across to the far side of the lake and I could see the little goose, all alone and looking very lost as he paddled up and down the margin, calling for his mates. I stood up on a mound of gravel and I could instantly see the problem, I'd put him back in the wrong lake!

The other side of the gravel road to the new lake was another fresh dug pit with about a thousand geese nesting on it, or, at the moment, nine hundred and ninety nine.

I felt so guilty that I spent the next half and hour creeping up on the lost fella with a landing net before pouncing out from a pile of stones and netting him first attempt. I bet he wondered what the hell was going on, but he soon sussed it out when I slipped him into the margin of the correct lake and he caught sight of all his mates.

I suppose, what with the beer, the big dinner and the strange goose hunting affair in the afternoon sun, I must been a bit tired and dozed off for a while in the long grass.

Some amount of time later I awoke to a screaming run and jumped up all groggy, not having a clue where I was at first.

The fish had somehow managed to find the only bit of weed in a totally barren environment, but it was only short, new weed so I soon had him on the move again.

He wasn't a big fish, typical of the bulk of Sonning's stock; I suppose he was about twenty four pounds but a good way to start a session none the less.

The next day I decided to move the van onto the track as leaving it at the pub for two days was asking for trouble. I'd caught two more carp in the night from the bar way out the back of my baited swim and, once again, they were both scaley mid twenties, I was still to catch one off the main hump area, though.

By lunchtime there were no more signs of fish so I started to get a few bits together to take back to the van, unfortunately, though, there were also no signs of my van keys!

I searched and searched, all through my bags, pockets, along the path and all around the gate area but they were nowhere to be found.

Later that afternoon I bumped into Jamie and he assured me that one of the massive selection of keys he had in his van would fit mine and, knowing how unsecure old Astras can be, I tended to agree.

As it turned out, the only key that did fit was a hammer and chisel and we eventually had to remove the whole barrel, fitting a stubby screwdriver into the gaping hole as a new key.

Halfway through, the landlord of the pub came out to see what all the noise was about, and I started to explain that it was my van and we weren't stealing it but he just laughed and said, looking at the state of it, he'd assumed it had been dumped anyway, bloody cheek!

The worse thing was, two weeks later, the engine blew up anyway and the very next trip to the lake, in yet another new van, I bumped into a dog walker who produced a set of keys she'd found, from her bag, and asked if I knew anyone who'd lost them!

Towards the end of July, I had a feature to do for a magazine so I moved a couple of rods over to the Punishers Point on the Reading bank for the morning, to take a few pictures and stuff.

I saw quite a few fish over there but they were mainly small ones. Never the less, I did actually consider a move for a few days but I had arranged to meet Keith the next day over in the encampment so, after the photographer had gone, I drove back round to the garden centre and parked up near the back gate.

Keith had booked a rare day off work the following day, which was a Thursday, and we'd planned a big curry and a few beers for that night.

Although we did fish together, as it were, we seldom actually fished at the same time, Keith works five days a week and only gets weekends free and at the time I was self employed and took two days on a Sunday\Monday or a Thursday\Friday, to avoid the busier times.

This session I wanted to put out a lot of bait, and then fish over the top of it for a few days to see what was visiting the hump.

Often, I would bait heaviest when I left but, this week, I intended to really 'go for it' so I loaded up the wheelbarrow with twenty-five kilos of bait, consisting of, 10k of NRG boilies and 15k of response pellet treated with the same attractors.

I was determined to see my plan through, regardless of the fact that the hump still hadn't produced a single carp!

By the time I'd walked it all across to the swim, and then fired it out, I was knackered and soaked in sweat, which only worsened the mosquito problem.

They were a nightmare in my swim due to the amount of undergrowth and the swampy river that made up the front of the plot.

I have been plagued all my life by the little buggers and the Sonning variety was second only to Colnemere in their ferocity, and they absolutely loved the taste of my blood!

By the time Keith arrived in the evening I was wiped out already but, by about midnight, after a curry and more than the odd 'social' beer with Jenks, I was feeling very strange indeed.

Total sleep depravation and near malaria from a thousand mosquito bites was beginning to take its toll and I staggered back to my swim for some much needed kip.

As soon as I got there I realised that I had left my sounder box on Keith's bivvy roof, but I wasn't going back for it then, so I turned up the alarm heads that I usually have on low, and crawled into bed.

It was so hot that I was sleeping under a mosquito net affair that I had rigged up outside the bivvy, made mainly from sticks and a piece of old onion sacking! It felt as if I had only been asleep for a few minutes when a squawking alarm sent me hurtling into the makeshift netting and then deposited me, thrashing, onto the floor trying to free myself. Eventually I broke free, ran across the bridge and struck into my first run from the hump.

I must have actually been asleep for longer than I thought, as the total silence all around told me it was that dead time of night, around 3am, when nothing seems to dare to make a sound.

Nothing, that is, apart from a big old carp that was making a sound like a drowning pig as I attempted to drag him into the net. The fight had just been a display of kiting and plodding that, had I been more awake, would have told me it was a big fish, but it was only when I stuck my hand in the net for a 'feel' and felt a bloody great pop-eye against my palm that I realised for sure that I'd eventually got him.

A total of three hundred and fifty acres of water, twelve months of hard work and a lorry load of bait and finally I'd got him! I struggled up the bank with my hard earned prize and lay him down on the mat at the back of the swim. Although I hadn't called him, Keith arrived in the swim minutes later holding the sounder box that had sent him halfway through his bivvy roof in search of the offending rod, before he'd realised what was happening and ran down to me.

He came in the swim to find me laying across a mountain of beached whale, shouting "I've got him, I've Bloody got him!" over and over again until I was finally convinced that I wasn't hallucinating.

By the time we had sacked him safely, and then woken up everybody

who'd answer their phone, yelling at them all in turn (to varying levels of encouragement, as it was very early), it was getting light enough to do the rituals of weighing and photographing.

I couldn't even lift him off the ground I was so tired, it was only adrenalin keeping me from passing out! Keith hoisted him up on the scales and he spun the needle around to fifty five pounds, which made him a new personal best 'whale', as well as the culmination of the most intense and bizarre 'campaign' that I think I've ever undertaken.

Once again the big baited spot produced the biggun but this time it was the only fish to come from it! It made me wonder how many times he'd visited the area before, and how he had managed to 'get away with it' every time, but they were thoughts for another day. Today was a day for celebrating, although I seriously needed some sleep first before I could even think about that side of things.

After the photos had been taken, and the great beast had swam back to the sanctuary of Sonning, I wound the remaining rods in and got my head down for a few hours, although it was hard to sleep with all that adrenalin in my blood!

Throughout the day friends visited me, all wishing me the best and most of them bringing beer. By the next morning it had started to sink in that my business at Sonning had come to an end and it was time to find another pit with another, different, set of rules to play by and challenges of its own, although I knew I probably wouldn't be seeing a bigger carp than that one for a while!

# Chapter 9

# End of an Era

"*After my capture of the Eye from Sonning I had intended to move on to pastures new and, for a short while, I tried to find a suitable pit to move straight on to, unfortunately there are not that many lakes left with untapped potential and great big fat mirror carp swimming around unmolested within their depths*".

There was of course one, The Mere, but I was trying to keep away from there as I wasn't sure if I could take another round of that just yet.

Sonning was certainly going to be a hard act to follow and the thing that made it even harder was that, mentally, I wasn't even that sure that I had finished my business on there at all.

Just catching the one biggest fish in a lake has never been the driving force behind my angling, of course that is ultimately what I am aiming for but I like to feel that I have caught all that I 'need' from a lake before moving on.

I like to have caught from different areas of big pits and in different conditions, I like to feel that I have really come to terms with the place, but I don't like to catch the same fish again, so there I was, faced with a bit of a paradox and unsure what to do about it.

I think that, when you put so much time and effort into coming to terms with a water and learning its very moods, it becomes somehow entwined within your soul!

All that time spent trying to understand and even pre-empt every move made by the lake and its inhabitants forms a bond that is not easily broken.

My mind was still full of Sonning and there were fish that I still dearly wanted to catch, on the other hand I didn't want to take away Keith's chance of catching the 'Big Girl' by risking a re-capture, which would be terrible angling!

In my short time on the pit I had managed to winkle out twenty eight carp, but of these only three were over thirty pounds, also the second and third biggest fish that I knew of in the lake had both still eluded me so there was still plenty to go for.

I spent a week or two up in the Cambridgeshire area looking at a massive pit complex that I was lining up for the following spring, a real unknown entity with next to no history whatsoever.

It was in an area that gets quite heavily fished but, as is often the way, it was left alone due to its vast size and lack of previous form, which suited me just fine!

It looked to be an ideal next move but it would need a decent reconnaissance session in the springtime before I could realistically commit myself, especially considering the distances involved in traveling up there and back. So, three weeks after my capture of the Eye I found myself, once again, treading the banks of Sonning.

During the period leading up to the 'Eye' I had, fairly regularly, been seeing a few fish using one of the small bays formed by the angled banks in a corner of the pit. Each time I had looked there had been between four and seven fish patrolling the marginal shelf and generally hanging around the reed beds in the corner. I hadn't fished for them before as I could clearly see that the big girl wasn't among their number but now, of course, that was exactly the situation I was after!

Hoping that they were still using the area, I loaded up a small stalking kit and made my way around the muddy banks, the rain of the previous night had really softened up the ground and, due to the low-laying nature of this area, it had become very bog like. Maybe it was something in the drain off from the land that had attracted the fish here in the first place; who knows how their little fishy minds work, eh?

In the first spot that I checked I almost stepped right on top of one as I pushed through the reeds and came across him, right under the bank, milling about and looking very catchable indeed. As I watched I spotted others, there were a total of six fish in the group with the biggest one looking like an upper twenty pound common, at least.

It was practically a guaranteed bite situation if I played my cards right and, somehow; they had failed to notice me looming up above them so I quickly sank back into the undergrowth planning my attack.

With the fish being at such close quarters I didn't want to blunder in and spook them before I'd even had a chance of a bite so I sat back and watched them for a while before getting the rods out.

I find that this period of watching can often be the difference between success and failure. There will always be one little spot that the fish prefer, even when floater fishing there are sections of surface area that produce all the bites, on the bottom it is even more noticeable.

Unfortunately it is always so tempting to just plonk a bait down there straight away and then be forced to try and move it into a better position when it's too late and the fish are feeding confidently, this is when you are most likely to ruin the whole thing.

The best way is to try and identify that little 'hot spot' first and then sneak the hook bait in there when their backs are turned, it's just the actual waiting that can be a nightmare. Half of my mind knows that I am doing the right thing and keeps reminding me that they have been here for hours, days, even weeks but the other half is screaming at me to get a bait in the water quick, before they all bugger off and never return!

As I watched this little group it became obvious that they were unwilling to grub about on the small, yellow, exposed sand patch that was the main feature of the margins but instead they kept tilting up over a small silty patch that lay tight up against a two foot square clump of weed. There must have been some form of natural food there as the fish were almost swimming in formation circles, one behind the other, and every now and then one would drop down and suck at the silt or rub its belly on the bottom to disturb some food for the next one in line!

With the spot identified I snuck back to the tackle that I'd left in the bushes behind me and fetched a rod and a can of 'Jolly Green Giant' along with a handful of 10mm NRG baits and a tiny yellow pop-up to balance the rig. As the fish made off for another circuit I lowered the rig on the spot (it was only four feet from the bank), I sprinkled a handful of bait over it and set the alarm up with a remote sounder before sneaking back under cover.

Isn't it bizarre that it can take so long for a trap to be sprung in this situation, or is it just that it seems like an eternity while you crouch there behind the reeds waiting? You would think that the very next fish to visit the spot would just 'hang itself' but it's seldom the case and they seem to be so good at ignoring the hook bait or leaving it until it's the very last morsel of food on the spot.

The urge to go and take a look is almost unbearable but you dare not in case a broken twig or a fallen shadow spooks the fish, pacing up and down doesn't really help matters either so it's just the fingernails that have to take a hammering.

I was on about my seventh finger when, eventually, the alarm screeched and I leaped through the reeds and into action. I was praying that the big common had been the greediest and pushed ahead of the others to snaffle the bait, the initial bend in the rod, didn't indicate that this was the case.

The fish didn't seem to know what was going on and practically beached itself further along the margins and, with no particular drama, was soon in the net. It practically goes without saying that it was one of the smallest of the bunch, a little common that probably would have made about eighteen or nineteen pounds if I'd had any scales with me, it was a very dark streamlined fish, typical of the Sonning strain, and I gave him a little 'thank you' pat on the head before slipping him back. I'd forgotten how much fun stalking could be as I'd had precious little chance to do any on Sonning, what with the sheer size of the place and the strict baiting campaign I'd been involved in.

It was almost like I was now fishing another lake entirely, I was not tied to any one swim and intended to make the most of the warm weather and just drift about with a rod, net and a few bits of tackle, for a couple of sessions at least!

By night I was unsure what to do, the fish had moved out from the reeds but, being a Friday, I knew that Keith would be set up in his usual swim so I decided to pack up and spend the night with him and have a nice chilled out social before setting off stalking again in the morning. We sat out in a large open area just behind his swim and devoured a meal of chicken and chips washed down with ice cold Beck's beers that I had fetched from the local shops, and we chatted about all manner of things, but mainly about when the 'Eye" would turn in his direction and how big would it be by then!

I slept out in the field that night with no Brolly or covering, savoring the star studded summer sky above my head, which was full of thoughts of my next venture and where it may take me, at last I was beginning to think beyond Sonning and I knew that it would not be long before I could leave.

The next day, in an almost identical situation in the same swim, I managed to outwit the second one of the same group of fish, a mirror of nineteen pounds and my thirtieth Sonning carp. In all honesty I would have been content to leave it at that and try again to find another water to fish. I already felt that I was deliberately targeting the tiddlers in an effort

*Entrance to the Back Bay*

to avoid the nightmare scenario of ruining Keiths chances with a fluke repeat capture of the Eye.

If I fished blind and over any amount of bait then there was always the chance, however slim, that the wrong one would pick it up.

As I was returning the nineteen-pounder though, another mirror rolled over on the surface at the back of the spot, I didn't get a brilliant look but I could tell from the characteristic 'flat back' that it was a 'good-un', definitely over thirty pounds. The dorsal fin seemed 'stubbier' than is normal and the coloration left me in no doubt that it wasn't the 'Eye' himself so, therefore, it must have been one of my remaining target fish.

Although my session was over for the week (Saturday is the latest I ever stay) I knew that I could get back down again in about four days time and the way things had been going I felt confident that the same group of fish would still be here. I fed them the rest of the corn and about a pound of crumbled up NRG boilies before I left and covered my tracks by 'fluffing up' the reeds and grass where I had been fishing. Only Keith and one other angler, who had taken my photos for me, even knew I had been fishing at all, let alone where, and I wanted to keep it that way as well.

The weather had been perfect for stalking for weeks, hot and humid with occasional downpours to freshen the air up. Unfortunately, now, with another biggun in my sights, it decided to turn and give way to proper torrential rain. The day before my session it started to piss down with a vengeance, I couldn't really see the fish hanging around in the edge in those conditions so I made a decision to look at another couple of lakes in the area instead. I spent all morning driving around the Reading peripheries looking at perspective pits, I walked around 'The Causeway', 'Barnett's' and three or four other pits that I can't even remember the name of now, but none took my fancy. Every now and then the rain would let up and the sun would poke out through the clouds making my thoughts turn to the little reed bed in the corner of the bay back at Sonning, but no sooner had I considered it than the skies would open once more. By mid afternoon I had walked myself to a standstill and decided, on the spur of the moment, to drive over to Sonning and check out the bay, whatever the weather. It was still chucking it down as I trudged along the bank in a set of clothes that had long ago given in to the elements and clung to me like soggy rags.

Half-heartedly I peered over the reeds, just as the upper twenty common decided to leap clear of the water right under my nose! I nearly jumped out of my skin, not content with one leap he went on to do it three more times in quick succession! I couldn't believe my luck, although I could have kicked myself for not coming here first. The rod was still set up from last session and the little yellow boilie still looked ok so I crept out into the open and lowered it down from the tip onto the hot spot. I risked a little sprinkle of crumbed bait before setting well back from the water and taking shelter from the rain. I was so wet and uncomfortable by now that I had to change into my last pair of dry socks and an old, smelly but dry, t-shirt I had in the stalking bag.

As if working to a script the bite alarm burst into life just as I was struggling into the shirt, no jacket, no boots, and within seconds' no more dry clothes!

I did however have a healthy bend in the rod as a powerful carp charged out from the margins. I was obviously expecting an upper twenty-pound common to be attached to the other end so it came as right shock when a big mirror rolled over in the margins, I could see at a glance which fish it was and my heart was in my mouth.

The Linear that Keith had caught on our first season, that glorious old warrior with the big golden plates set into his flanks, was currently attached to my line and I was just praying that he stayed that way long enough for me to bundle him into the net. As it turned out luck was still firmly cheering in my corner and with a final spray of water from his tail he plunged into the folds of the net and was mine!

Ironically, the fish that had started off Keiths Sonning saga looked like being the one that would end mine! Along with 'The forty' he was right at the top of my 'most wanted' list! As I peered in the net I instantly recognised the 'stubby dorsal' as belonging to the fish that had rolled at the end of my last session, what a result!

I phoned around and summoned a photographer, as this one really did warrant a proper picture and we weighed him in at a very respectable 33lb before sliding him back into the rain lashed lake. This time I really had made my mind up, Sonning had been more than kind to me and this was a fitting end to my campaign, I packed away and bid the lake farewell for the very last time.

A great change was due to come over Sonning during the following

year and the very landscape of the lake would be changed forever, the future of the fishing and even the fish became uncertain.

In the previous Summer of 2000, Keith and I had sat on the banks of Sonning listening to Steve Redgrave and Mathew Pincent winning a gold medal for England and, as Keith in his usual overly patriotic style leapt up and down in joy, we had no idea then of the consequence of the event that was happening on the other side of the world.

Who would have thought that two of the people that would ultimately be most directly affected by that fateful result were actually Keith and I!

In fact, to be more precise, it was Keith who would be most buffeted by the spreading ripples as they charged back across the globe and washed up on the shores of Sonning. You see, the owners of Sonning pit actually sponsor our intrepid gold medalist rowers and the upshot of the whole event was that a new and splendid rowing course, stretching for some 2200 meters and fully equipped with stadium and all facilities, would be built on the strength of it.

The project would be backed by lottery funding and the whole thing would be started forthwith, and the venue? Well, the venue was underneath our rod tips as we sat and listened to the little transistorized circuits announcing the result, Sonning was for the chop!

Luckily for me, my result came along just in time but poor old Keith was left to struggle, not only against all the normal odds involved in targeting one fish from an ocean like Sonning, but against a clock that was ticking away the very moments that Sonning had left as a viable fishing lake at all!

The plans turned up for the new project about the time that I was bidding the lake farewell and were soon well under way.

A 'Bund' or 'divide' was put right through the center of the lake; to act as a roadway and viewing area for the course. This involved the removal of whole islands and tons and tons of infill being used to literally fill up a great big strip through the lake until it sat proud of the surface.

It stretched from one end of the main lake to the other and split the lake in two, the out of bounds side was being divided further into three separate lakes.

These lakes will be used for various 'other' water pursuits.

This would have only left a strip about 1000 meters long but the second stage of the plan was to remove the top bank (Kit Kats) from Sonning and join the lake to the nearby marina.

This effectively doubled the length of the lake and provided the necessary 2200 meters that a rowing course demands.

Obviously, these changes had a massive effect on Sonning over the following couple of years and, despite the best efforts possible, Keith never did manage to track down the Eye, although this may have been down to more than just the changing topography.

After my capture of the Eye, Keith obviously stayed on and angled hard in his pursuit of the great fish, he was also joined over the remaining and following season by anglers such as Terry Hearn, Ricky Blakelock, Bernie Loftus and others who, although very successful, wish to remain anonymous.

During the spring, when I took those stunning photos of the bigger

fish in the snags, the carp were very visible and easily identified, as indeed they were the following year. The only difference on the following years was the noticeable absence of the 'Big Girl' herself; in fact the mighty fish has not been caught or even seen since (although I believe Terry did see it roll once in the summer, shortly after I had stopped fishing there).

At first there were rumours of it being moved but, to move a fish, you first have to catch it and after speaking to everybody in the know, I do not believe that this is so.

There is, unfortunately, another possibility for the disappearance; apart from, of course, the fact that it may just be keeping a low profile and that is an accident involving a speedboat.

During a routine 'belt' about the lake by the water-skiers a very large fish was hit, just outside the ski club near to where I caught my first Sonning carp.

Keith subsequently spoke to the driver of the boat who confirmed that he had indeed hit a big fish and turned back to see if he could find it but saw no further sign, the driver seemed very convinced that it was a big pike and I really hope that he was right. Not that I have anything against pike, of course.

Personally I tend to think that a carp is more likely to be basking on the surface than a pike and less likely to get out the way in time should a speedboat happen by. It's a horrible thing to imagine but, unfortunately, it is a possibility and the more time that goes by without a reliable sighting of the 'Eye' then the more worried for its welfare I become.

Hopefully, it's just hiding behind an island somewhere and keeping out the way of speedboats, gravel barges, diggers, dumpers and Steve Redgrave!

As for the future of Sonning, well we will just have to wait and see but I would be lying if I said that I was hopeful that it will all turn out all right in the end, I tend to think of the coming of the diggers as the end of an era, but only time will tell.

# Chapter 10

# *Paradise Found*

"*I had often heard Phil talk about the Fiords and Meadows lakes in St Ives. He had fished there years before and had told me that, if I should ever need a challenge, then to take a look as they were mysterious, low stocked, under fished and beautiful".*

It was getting too late in the year for a return to the Mere so, faced with prospect of having nowhere particular to fish, I decided to take a trip up to Cambridgeshire for a little look.

I made my way up the M11 clutching a sketchy little map on a scrap of paper in search of the promised refuge from circuit waters, anglers and probably carp! It was just a reconnaissance trip but as soon as I set foot on the place I knew I was hooked, I didn't care if there weren't any carp in there, I loved it.

It so reminded me of Wraysbury in the early days as there was water everywhere and little points and channels dividing it all up, I was actually physically unable to figure out what bits joined to where and every turned corner presented me with yet another beautiful bay or chain of overhung islands.

I wanted to fish everywhere all at once so, like a kid in a sweet shop, I spent the rest of the day bouncing from one treat to another, unable to stop long enough to savour any of them.

I hadn't seen any fish, but I'd seen enough to know that I wanted to try, and the final assurance came as I finally made it back to the car and prepared to leave for home.

I stopped for one last wee up against an old ash tree before setting off on the long drive and there, in a deep back bay, I saw the sign I had been waiting for as a great big, round brown mirror came sliding up out of the depths to wave goodbye. Not once, but four times, showing me every profile, before disappearing back into the depths from whence he came.

He was an incredible looking beast with high shoulders and a deep brown frame, a real old gravel pit warrior, that was good enough for me, I was back a few days later with my new permit tucked in my back pocket and a whole world of opportunities before me, literally anything was possible for who knew what could be lurking in about one hundred acres of wild and twisted waterways.

Lakes joining other lakes with bays and islands and spits of land, all co-joined to one large and windswept sailing pit, carp fishing heaven!

I immediately made my way around to the Ash tree swim in the steak pit (this was the name of the Back Bay apparently) and staked my claim by putting up a brolly under the tree, although, quite who I was staking my claim against I wasn't sure as there was not another angler in sight.

After this I decided to go for a little walk around the whole pit, just to find out what was what and where exactly it all sat in relation to everything else.

That first day I walked for a total of six full hours and I was absolutely amazed at everything I saw. There were secret hidden swims, fantastic bays with huge gravel bars running in parallel about ten yards apart, which bore testament to the old style of drag lined pits.

Other larger bars bore the marks of deeper bars as the margins had long shallow slopes in one part and deep silty parts only a few yards away. There were beds of lilies, overhanging trees, totally impenetrable sections and then, stitched on the end, was the big square sailing pit where even the slightest wind would howl across the surface whipping it up into a foam.

The dividing spits of land had originally been banks and there must have been four different pits at one time, but the higher water levels had now created one super pit.

The spits were all fishable as well but there was precious little room for bivvies and the like as they were only about six feet wide in most places, but I knew I'd be trying my luck on them in the near future. I wanted it all at once, and it all looked fantastic, the only thing I hadn't seen on my travels was any sign of carp so I set up in the Ash tree for the night, hoping the big brown mirror was still about.

I tried to stay up as late as possible to savour as much of the ambience of the lake as I could. I had some dinner and the best part of a bottle of red wine and was just sitting there staring out into the darkness when one of the buzzers started going, slowly at first and then the bobbin smacked against the rod.

I almost slipped straight down the steep margins in my panic to get to the rod, surely I hadn't caught one already?

The rod hooped over into a healthy bend and for a minute I could hardly breathe with excitement but, then, a strange ziz-zagging motion coming up the line told me it might not be quite what I was after.

In the light of my head torch I could see a great big silvery snake-like creature thrashing on the surface as it tried swimming backwards and then contorting itself into a tight ball.

With one great big heave, I hoisted a massive eel up onto the bank where, before I could grab him, he shot off across the damp grass and disappeared behind the umbrella.

Following the line, I chased him around the bank for a bit, praying he would somehow unhook himself but it was not to be, and eventually, after a lot of struggling and swearing, I caught up with the bugger and wrestled the hook out before pushing him down the steep slope and back into the lake.

I was covered in slime and smelt disgusting and the rig was tied up like a cats cradle, he was a bloody great thing and I really hoped he was the only one out there, knowing of course that he wouldn't be.

I woke early the next morning, all fired up with the excitement of a new lake and started walking circuits of the Steak pit, checking the little baited spots I'd set up the evening before and, at every one, I expected to see the Round brown one feeding happily on the baits, but it was not to be.

From what I could glean at the tackle shop, where I bought my permit, and from the few anglers I'd phoned during the week who knew anything at all about the lake, there were not a great many fish in the place, probably between twenty and thirty of any size and they were very rarely, if ever caught.

There had been a fish of around thirty seven pounds caught on a floater a few years previously, by a guy I sort of knew a bit and I'd spoken to him at length about the lake.

He assured me that the biggest fish he'd ever seen in the UK used to live there and was regularly seen during the spring in the Fiords section, but he'd not seen it for at least three years and wasn't sure if it still lived.

Nevertheless, if it was still there it could be huge and even if it wasn't, there could well be others of the same stamp lurking out there somewhere in the many hidden areas of water, islands, and bays etc.

Just around the corner from the Steak pit, if you walked past the Ash tree and the point that formed the entrance to the Back bay itself, was another large bay that looked so 'carpy' it was unreal. The water was very clear in here and the bottom was made of a mixture of silt and shingle, like tiny little stones that glowed silver as they extended down the marginal shelf into the depths below.

There were also many small, visible humps as the bottom rose and fell like the inside of an egg carton. This, coupled with the snags and large reed bed at the entrance of the bay, made it a sure fire bet that the carp would get in there at some stage of the proceedings, and although they were blatantly not there on that particular morning, I still baited up a few spots just in case.

I was quickly coming to realise that to bait all the best looking spots once or twice a week was going to take an awful lot of bait and I decided to concentrate mainly on where I'd seen the fish, until the fish themselves showed me otherwise.

Returning past the point into the Steak Pit I suddenly had a stroke of genius; if I parked the car on the grass at the top of the pit I could stand on the roof and look down into the clear water and probably see most of the Back Bay.

The car park end of the lake was a lot higher than the other banks and from this elevated position I had a terrific view of anything silly enough to swim past me.

Unfortunately for me, though, I was just about to suffer a very severe set back to my carefully laid plans, as heaven was just about to be invaded!

As I wobbled about on the roof, trying desperately to keep my feet on the roof rack and not the rusty shell itself, I heard a distant clanking from the big gates from the lane on the other side of the field.

I suppose it was about a third of a mile back to the track across a bumpy but grassy field that was permanently covered in about a thousand Canadian Geese.

As I turned to see who was approaching I was just in time to spot the bolt croppers disappearing back into the side door of a white transit and I watched in horror as a whole procession of mercs and big silver Caravans filled up the field as quickly as they possibly could.

Within ten minutes there were Pikeys everywhere, Lurchers and cross breed mongrels were running around yapping at each other, ginger haired kids were un-strapping trials bikes from the back of pick ups, and a beaten up little red fiesta with no licence plates was already bouncing through the startled geese and heading towards the lakes!

I knew, instantly, that that was the end of any chance of a fish as I'd have to spend the whole time running between car and tackle to make sure neither just miraculously disappeared into thin air.

I have fished, in the past, near Pikey camps and quite simply it's a bloody nightmare. You can't relax for one minute and the associated junk, scrap metal, old sofas and human toilets that appear in and around the bushes make it really not worth the effort it needs to survive.

I could have packed up and moved to the other end of the complex but I knew it was pointless, I needed the freedom to leave my swim and tackle unattended for hours each day and walk around looking for signs of fish so, with my tail firmly between my legs, I packed up as quickly as I could and drove through the camp, noticing the chain and padlock lying useless on the floor as I passed through the gates for the last time that year.

By the time the owners had managed to get a court order and evict them, I knew it would too late in the season to start a campaign on such a big pit and I had no intention of doing the winter on there.

Regardless of the set back, though, I was still quite buoyant on the way home, knowing that the lake and the fish would still be there the following spring and I could plan the downfall of it's elusive residents in fine detail throughout the winter, it was just a case of where would I fish while I did so?

# Chapter 11

# Dinton Pastures

"*I was sitting at home chatting on the phone to Keith, telling him my tales of woe about the invasion of the Pikeys at my new found nirvana and thinking out loud about where I could fish now. He was still all tied up with Sonning and would stay that way until the day the big fella rolled into his net, I hoped it was soon*".

One water that we had heard a lot about during our time at Sonning was Dinton Pastures, which was situated only a few miles up the road from Sonning Eye.

We had regularly chatted about the lake with Dean Fletcher, one of the Dinton Regulars, as he walked his crazy dog around Sonning.

Sharing both a love of dogs and carp, Dean and I had soon become friends and I had got to hear quiet a few stories about the inhabitants of Dinton and they sounded almost too good to be true.

The only real down side was the night fishing, as it was run on a syndicate basis and the waiting list was about ten years, but the days, however, could be fished on a council day ticket for the princely sum of £4 from dawn till dusk, so all was not entirely lost.

As I had to travel quite a way to the lake, it would still be awkward, but there was also the opportunity to do occasional 'guest nights' at an extra charge of about £15 to the controlling council.

Although not a permanent replacement water for me it could serve perfectly as an autumn and maybe even winter stop gap until the spring, when I could return to Cambridge.

In fact I could plan my coming year perfectly with Dinton to start, the Fiords for the Spring and then maybe a return to the Mere in June, as I knew I'd have to go back there eventually, and keep going back, as the Black Mirror was never going to be crossed off my list, not in a thousand years. One day that fish would definitely be a photo in my album, no matter what it took to achieve it.

Dinton is about 24 acres in size and shaped a bit like a Wellington boot I suppose. The stock level really is something special, though, and the fish have been nurtured and grown on under the watchful eye of Simon, the head ranger.

Various holding lakes have been used to rear stock fish and the balance of existing stock in the main lake has been kept at a constant, with home grown thoroughbred English carp.

At that time there were about 180 fish in the lake, with 20 over 35lb and about half a dozen over 40lb, depending on the time of year.

The quality of the carp really is stunning and the different strains and types of fish make it even more exciting and some of the bigger fish are among the best lookers in the country.

When I first decided to have a look at Dinton I was amazed at just how easy the fish were to locate and, stupidly, thought that it looked like a dead cert for a couple of 'quick fish', I soon learned differently.

The fish in Dinton have seen everything thrown at them over the years and, as a consequence, they have wised up to the ways of anglers to a very frustrating degree.

Somehow, the fish there seem to discern between one bait and another at first glance, and stick with their decision for good. It's almost as if they carry around a checklist of all the things that they won't or can't eat and will not stray from the list no matter what you dress it up in, a bit like trying to feed kids something other than sausage and chips really!

During my first few trips I tried everything in an attempt to find the magic bait, and all the usual levellers were dragged out of the bag; sweet corn-the forgotten wonder bait, pints and pints of maggots-balled up with 'sticky mag powder' and fed at range, and obviously the entire Mainline catalogue of boilies. Pellets in bags with black pellet hook baits even failed to get me a bite, despite being on fish nearly every single day!

The lack of night fishing availability didn't really worry me in the slightest and, to be honest, I sometimes felt that I was at a big advantage rather than a disadvantage by fishing Dinton on a day only basis.

Apart from the travelling and early starts, I was starting each day from scratch with my gear on the barrow ready to move onto anything that showed. Far better than being tied to a swim full of bait and a mountain of tackle, I was up and ready to move in no time.

A day spent being mobile like this seems like a long time and I would usually fish a few different swims, most of the time getting on fish, in fact the only thing I couldn't seem to do was get a bloody bite.

Another day-angler who had started on Dinton about the same time as me, and was to become a firm friend over the coming months, was Clive Percival. He, unlike me, had got straight to grips with the Dinton carp and their fussy dietary requirements.

As it turned out, we held a whole list of mutual friends that went back years and it was unbelievable that we had not met before. Clive was good friends with a bunch of lads that I knew from Taplow Lake, and it was they who were probably the most successful group of 'baiters' on the lake, so I just assumed he was on their bait.

It transpired, some months later, that he had been on a separate bait altogether but obviously one that the carp found acceptable as he took a string of captures in quick succession.

The closest I came to banking a carp was one sunny afternoon in early October; I had just completed another circuit of the lake and settled in at the top of a tall tree in the corner of the 'heel' section of the Welly boot. From my lofty perch I could see out across the lake and right down to the shallows at the other end.

As I looked out across the calm and tranquil surface I could just make out two shadows below the surface, about one hundred and fifty yards away, and they looked distinctly 'carp shaped'.

As I watched, they started to crease the surface as their backs lifted higher in the water, whilst they cruised down towards my end of the lake. It was almost as if they had spotted me as well, and were coming over for a closer look, as they accelerated and made a course straight for me; on and on they came until, incredibly, they disappeared into the branches below my feet!

I shuffled down the tree until I was just a few yards above them and watched as they both circled a small sandy patch on the bottom before moving off along the margins. No sooner had they left than they were back again, only this time with a third friend in tow.

The clear patch was blatant and glowed like a beacon but, as is often the way, it didn't seem to be the actual feeding spot. One by one they all dropped down and sort of rubbed or 'grazed' across the spot and then the last fish tilted up and fed briefly in a tiny hole just to the right of the main spot. I watched for a further ten minutes and, in that time, every fish had tilted up on the same, small spot!

The time was ripe for a bit of bait, but what bait to try? After much deliberation I crept back to the barrow and dug out a can of corn and, when the fish weren't looking, I sprinkled a few grains on their dinner table.

As luck would have it they hoovered them up on the very next visit and my confidence soared as I quietly 'fell' from the tree and scrambled back for a rod. I knew that this was my best chance so far and I tried my hardest to stay calm and composed but, as always, I failed miserably!

My heart was pounding and I was shaking so much that I spilt about half a can of 'jolly green giant' into the grass, while trying to get two pieces onto the hair. The hardest part of the operation is always getting the bait in position without spooking the fish, the main problem being that you can't see what's happening from the ground. Many, many times in the past I have resorted to taking a rod actually up a tree and lowering a bait from above, this way you can hit the spot first time and make sure that the carp aren't already feeding on it when you cast.

In fact, I caught Mary from Wraysbury in exactly the same way from a tree in Sunnymeads corner, and a couple more of the lakes finest jewels as well, all from 'tree casts', so I knew that it could work.

I stood hidden behind the trees considerable trunk and passed the rod up into the branches, butt first, hanging the reel on the highest branch I could reach. I then shinned up the tree, retrieved the rod and set about weaving the tip through the branches into position.

Of the three fish under the tree at Dinton that afternoon, one of them was a very big fish indeed and had a pronounced lump on one side, grey in colour and extremely deep bodied, he seemed to be around forty pounds from where I was looking so you can imagine how intimidating the whole procedure was becoming.

As soon as I got the chance, I gently lowered the rig onto the small spot to the right where I had seen them feed and then, with the bail arm open, I threw the rod down into the bushes below.

I should point out, at this stage, that I have actually snapped the handles on two reels doing this in the past so it's a method that's not without the odd sacrifice!

Back on the ground I set the rod on the rests, turned on the alarm, and sat way back from the waters edge, almost bursting with anticipation. Sweat was dripping down my face and I took off my Polaroids, put them beside me on the grass, and wiped the salty water from my eyes as I waited for the inevitable to happen.

After a minor eternity, and just as I was giving up all hope of a take, the alarm piped up and the bait runner roared as a very surprised carp left the area at high speed.

I leaped into the margins, up to my thighs, to give me room under the tree to strike and leant into a fish that, hardly even slowing down, proceeded to beat me up something rotten!

The first run stripped fifty yards of line from the reel and as he stopped he boiled on the surface. I looked around for the net, not that I was ready for it but I wanted to make sure I had it when the time came.

A passing dog walker and his family had stopped to watch the action and he kindly passed me my landing net as he could see I was struggling to get it into position in the water next to me.

The fish was just wallowing on the top now, unwilling to be led any closer and just deciding what to try next. All the line from the tip to the hook was out of the lake and I have found this, in the past, to be a most dangerous position to be in as the strain on the hook seems magnified, somehow, without the cushioning effect of the water. Just as these thoughts ran through my head the bloody rod sprang back and he was gone. I hurled down the lifeless, useless, piece of carbon into the lake and swore out loud, which instantly dispersed the onlookers and I was left alone to sulk.

Sitting on the grass, head in hands, I looked down and saw my new Polaroids smashed into pieces on the ground where the dog walker had accidentally trodden on them, bloody typical, it never rains but it pours!

After a few weeks of chasing the carp around for no further action, and with the weather ever changing further towards winter mode, I decided that I needed to get something established a bit quick if I was to have any chance of a bite once the fish stopped showing.

As I have done so many times before when I have been at a loss on the bait front in winter, I turned my attentions back toward the 'original Grange'. This was Mainlines first bait and has always been a winter favourite of mine, I also had it in my head that the Dinton carp were not keen on high attractor levels and the Grange is a subtle bait that uses only the smells inherent in the ingredients as attractors.

I looked long and hard at the lake and picked an area that would offer me the most scope and greatest range of vision before deciding where to bait. On the inside bend of the 'foot section' of the lake I reasoned that I could bait one swim in the car park bay and two or three swims in the main section and, by walking up and down my 'beat', I could keep an eye on a large area of water in two different 'sections', and easily move from one to the other should the need arise.

I put the plan into effect immediately, as the nights were drawing in and the temperatures were starting to plummet. I baited heavily with ten and fourteen mil Grange baits in my four new swims and moved freely between them, always baiting heaviest at the end of the day, and especially on the last day that I would be there on any particular week.

After only three baitings I had my first result and it coincided with the first proper frost of the year, in fact it was bloody freezing!

As the lake had quietened right down by then, and there were next to no anglers around, I had been offered the odd 'guest night' with people I had got to know over the preceding weeks and it was on one of these rare nocturnal visits that I had first spotted fish on one of my areas.

There had been a bitterly cold wind blowing since darkness had fallen and I had been huddled up under the brolly for hours, and I suppose it was about ten pm when the wind suddenly decided to drop off and the lake fell calm. I was set up in the small swim at the mouth of the bay and decided to take the opportunity to check the other couple of spots while the wind held off.

Within minutes of looking I saw a fish go over on the surface, big silver rings in the moonlight gave its location away and then, immediately afterwards, another one, closer in and right on one of my spots.

Despite the late hour, and the beginnings of a frost, I legged it back and dragged all my gear around to a swim known as 'The beach', where the second fish had shown. No sooner had I flicked two baits out than the wind was back with a vengeance and I had to fight to get the brolly back up. Eventually, I clambered into the warmth of the sleeping bag, just as the closest rod burst into life and had me diving back out again.

I had the fight all planned out before hand and the waders were laid out in anticipation to help me get past the marginal lily pads and into netting range. In the dark, however, I misjudged the drop off and ended up with a wader full of ice cold water, but it was well worth the agony, though, as a lively common of twenty-six pounds rolled into the net.

There is always something magical about the first one from any water and it seems to break the spell somehow, it's as if once you know they are catchable you look at everything differently and the next one is never far behind.

The next morning dawned under a white carpet of thick frost and I nearly froze my hands off holding up my prize for the cameras, but I still managed to smile, of course!

The very next week and I was back for a short day session in the same

swim when, as is often the way at Dinton, another angler turned up to pre-bait just along the bank from me.

As a result, the water only twenty yards to the right of my baits was suddenly being pounded by spods full of maize by an angler who wasn't even fishing for another three days! He never even came over and asked where I was fishing or if I'd caught anything, just filled it in and buggered off again! I couldn't sit there with any confidence after that, so I just took the rods and tea kit and moved up a couple of swims to the corner.

No sooner had I put the baits out than I saw a small ring appear in my other swim, just into the bay. It was right where I had baited and, although only the tiniest of movements, I felt sure that it was a carp so, winding in one rod, I plopped a hook bait straight on target. It was a bit of a tricky flick from where I was, but I was happy with the other rod so I didn't particularly want to move next door.

Well, the bait could have barely hit the bottom before the line tightened up again and I was in!

I was so shocked at the instantaneous result that I didn't really expect a carp to be the culprit but, sure enough, a healthy bend in the rod said differently.

Staying deep he chugged about in front of me for a few minutes before allowing me to lead him up from the deep margins. The water at this time was crystal clear and I could plainly see a big old mirror twisting and turning his way up the marginal shelf, it was all very scary indeed! I kept thinking that he would drop off at any second but, fortunately, my fears were unfounded and he slid straight into the mesh at the first attempt.

I'd just voiced my approval with the customary "Light my Fire" battle cry when two other anglers, who had just arrived at the lake, wandered into the swim to see what all the fuss was about. It was well handy, really, as I would have had no one to do the photos otherwise. Leroy and Jason helped me weigh the big mirror at just over forty pounds and then took some lovely shots against an autumnal backdrop for me.

It was to be my last fish of the season from Dinton as the weather soon deteriorated and it was time to move on again for the winter. Although it had started off as a bit of a struggle, I'd ended up with two good fish for my efforts and, despite an incident in the car park, where I lost a stereo system and a side window, I had thoroughly enjoyed the couple of months I'd spent on Dinton Pastures.

I did actually return for a few more sessions in February with Clive, as he had assured me that the lake usually throws up a few whackers near to the end of the season, and he certainly wasn't wrong.

I think I fished four guest nights and a couple of day sessions without so much as a sniff of a bite, but I was fortunate enough to witness Clive in full swing, one bitterly cold February evening.

We had just sat down to a veritable feast of Chinese food, there was a mountain of the stuff on our plates and, just as Clive lifted the first forkful to his mouth, his buzzer sounded in the swim next door.

It was only a stuttery take and he shot off expecting to find a tufted duck hanging on the end, I on the other hand already had plenty of duck on my plate, of the crispy aromatic variety so I was going nowhere.

The wind had got up a bit and, even though Clive was only next door, it took three attempts to get me to hear his shouts for help. At least that was my story afterwards, in reality I was forcing down my dinner like a tramp let loose in Harrods food hall, no way I was stopping to unhook a water chicken!

Eventually I realised he sounded serious and I trotted round just in time to help net Forty Five pounds of mirror carp!!

The biggest known carp in the lake, Bruno, had chosen that

inopportune moment to join us for dinner and suddenly Clive didn't seem that worried about eating cold food anymore.

The next day Clive had to leave and it would have been rude of me not to move in after him, as I had my final night on the water booked in. After this, the guest tickets would run out for the last two weeks of the season.

I set up full of confidence, but the weather had turned from merely blustery to near gale force.

I only had an Oval umbrella with me so I lashed it to a wooden post that stuck from the ground with a big number five emblazoned on it to mark the swim.

I had to bodge it up a bit by using all the available cords and ropes and bits of string that I could find before settling in for the night.

At some time during the wee small hours I was awoken by the distinct feeling that I was wetter than I should have been.

The rain was torrential and the wind roared like a banshee, and as I opened my eyes I was greeted with the sight of a screwed up Oval umbrella whirling around four feet above my head, tethered only to the ground by the twisted ropes and wooden post.

It was as if it was filled with helium and, by the state of the many small pieces of ribs sticking out the sides, I knew there was no way I could repair it in the dark in those conditions.

I had to settle for just re-pegging the bits that were left and wrapped my arms through the remaining spokes until dawn.

For some strange reason, the fish didn't seem too interested in feeding either that night so I packed up, sodden, broken and fishless.

If all this wasn't bad enough I returned to the car park to find all four tyres on my van had been slashed!

I couldn't believe my eyes, I only had two hours to get home, get changed and pick up my son Conor from junior school and here I was, looking at a van with square bloody wheels, what sort of a moron could get any pleasure out of that?

Needless to say I didn't make it and my wife had to take time off work to get Conor home safely, while I spent the whole afternoon sorting out the van.

Over the next weeks I heard many different rumours of who and why and when my van met such a pathetic fate but, in the end, the strongest ones pointed to a jealous angler who thought he had more right to catching fish than I did, if this is even halfway true then what a truly sad man he must have been!

# Chapter 12

# *Paradise re-visited*

"*B*umping back up the
dusty old gravel workings
lane, I looked to my left
and the vast expanse of the
Meadows sailing lake
spread out before me, its
rippled surface pushing up
towards the far entrance to the large Fiords and
ultimately the Steak Pit that lay beyond".

I was tempted to stop straight away on the Meadows and start my crusade there, but the wind direction drove me onwards towards the big gates at the end of the track which would, hopefully, be equipped with a new padlock and no sign of a single caravan, flea ridden lurcher, or old abandoned sofa, and so it was.

The gates were repaired, the field had been restored to its original state and all was well with the world, I was back in paradise!

The Steak pit was a bit more sparsely decorated by nature than it had been the previous autumn but it still looked glorious, even if the lilies had yet to struggle to the surface and the flowering shrubs and trees were only just in bud.

I was surprised though, to see another two cars already there at the end of the muddy track but, I need not have worried, as they were only day anglers on the little triangular lake next door. I had recently learnt that there were a few carp in that lake as well, and it was included on my club ticket, so that was going to be added to the already challenging circuit I intended walking every day.

I parked my new, and most impressive car so far, under a big tree at the head of the pit and rummaged around behind the seats for some binoculars, glasses, and the lucozade and crisps I'd purchased en route, from the garage in the village.

The new car was a two and half litre Vauxhall Omega with a BMW engine in it. This, to me constituted a massive leap forward in automotive transportation and, although far from new, it was like a Rolls Royce compared with everything else that had had the misfortune to be owned by me in the past.

I was so proud of it when I first bought it that I had actually fitted a waste paper bin in the passenger foot well, although, to be honest, it had been full for some time and the surrounding overspill of discarded crisp and drink packaging had already reached halfway up the sides, but it was in there none the less, somewhere.

I only managed half a circuit of the lake that first day as the causeways were all still flooded from the extra water of winter and a lot of places were unreachable without the waders, which were lying safely in the back of my car, half an hours walk away.

Also, the weakening spring sunshine was so low on the horizon I knew I would struggle to see anything much at that time of day so I opted to wander back and set up right next to the car at the head of the Steak Pit, from where I could keep a good eye on everything around me.

Every year I seem to fall for springs clever façade and let her trick me with her bright sunny days and promises of summer nights. Consequently, by midnight, I was nearly frozen to death in my pathetic little three season sleeping bag and t-shirt and still wide awake, shivering. In the end, I had to get up and wrap the bag and bed in my unhooking mat and a piece of old carpet off the floor of the car just to get warm enough to get to sleep, and the morning eventually dawned with a white and crispy coating over everything, including me!

Why didn't I just get in the car and sleep with the heater on?

Because I'm a stubborn idiot and it just wouldn't count as fishing, would it, and who knows, I might just have missed the sound of a carp jumping?

As the sun heated the ground and melted the frost it was all soon forgotten and, after a quick breakfast of a bag of crisps and a cup of tea, I set off with a pair of waders in hand to explore the lands beyond the gaps and flooded causeways.

I had been walking for hours, wading across the flooded sections of

path that formed the entrance to the bays, totally alone and loving every minute of it.

I sort of lost track of time a bit and the day was actually quite warm by the time I rounded the last corner into the smallest Fiords bay and saw two fish, one a common and the other a small mirror, cruising around on the surface. They looked to be as alone as I was, so I decided they needed a bit of company.

They weren't too far from the car, as I'd nearly completed my circuit, so I ran back for some gear and spent a frustrating few hours pestering them with surface baits, but they had other ideas and eventually swam off through the gap into oblivion.

I comforted myself with the fact that I'd actually seen fish this time, and I planned and re-planned my attack during the drive home that evening. In fact, I thought of very little apart from the lake for weeks, it was as if all other lakes and people had just faded into the corners of my vision, still there somewhere but blurred out of focus by my new found obsession, I just couldn't get enough of the place.

Even when, a couple of weeks later, I managed to ram a great big shard of ancient and filthy wood under my finger nail while clearing out my garden, I refused to go the hospital to have it pulled out as I was due to go to the lake as soon as I'd finished and couldn't possibly face any delays.

I had Kev Knight on the phone, telling me horror stories about his friends similar incident and the resulting blood poisoning, but this only made me pack a first aid kit as a precaution and, an hour later, I was flying up the M11 with a big red throbbing finger and an ominous looking black line that reached right below the bottom of my nail.

After the customary long walk I actually managed to find three fish, only small ones but it was definitely a start.

I had found a tall tree in the small fiords that overlooked the shallowest part of the pit and this was now part of the planned route for every walk. From the top branches I could see right along the front of a large reedbed that grew out of a shallow sandy section, which probably used to be a gravel washing area when the pit was being worked, it certainly held all the signs of being so anyway.

There, on the fringes of the reeds, in only a foot or two of water were three commons, all about twenty pounds and just milling about in the sunshine.

I couldn't actually get to the bit they were in with a rod, but I figured that there must be other fish around and, if they came in or out of this small section of the Fiords, then they would have to swim through a tiny gap in the flooded spit that separated it from the main sailing lake.

By wading across the gap with all my gear I could save a walk of about half a mile and set up on the causeway itself, this way I could actually fish in three different sections of the lake at once.

It was a bit of a treacherous route, as the under water boulders I had to balance on were as slippery as hell, and I had to hold each item of tackle above my head like a Sherpa as I waded across, one slip and I would have been sitting in five feet of water with my bedchair or rucksack soaked right through on top of me!

It took about three or four trips across but I was soon setting out my traps and figuring out exactly how I was going to bivvy up on a six foot wide path, surrounded on all sides by water.

It only made matters worse that the path was still a bit flooded and very muddy and as a result, my poor finger was covered in grime and black ooze and had started to swell up even bigger. By the time it got dark I had one rod out into the big sailing lake, just in front of the gap, and the other two were in the small Fiords, each one on the end of respective bars that both led down towards the shallows. I decided to ignore the large Fiords behind me as I'd seen no signs of fish in there, and there were enough spots in front of me for about twenty rods as it was.

There was no room for a bivvy so I just set up the bed in the trees on the highest and driest piece of ground I could find.

I sat there, as the sun sank over the sailing club, imagining great big mirror carp queuing up to move into the shallows and falling foul of my carefully laid traps as they drifted through the gap.

About midnight, just as I was finally drifting off to sleep, the rod in the sailing lake bleeped a couple of times and then slowly but surely trundled off.

This was more like it, I flew out of bed and then realised I couldn't see a thing, as a curtain of cloud had blocked out all available sky light.

I hadn't been prepared enough for a head torch so I just blindly ran towards the glowing light of the LED and promptly collided with a tree branch, neatly splitting my nose open as I did so!

As if to add insult to injury, the culprit of the bite turned out to be another bloody eel!

So now I had a finger like a balloon and blood pouring down my face from a gash on my nose, and this was supposed to be fun!

Rather than risk further injury, I dug the torch and secateurs out of the rucksack and cleared all the offending branches from the swim, before recasting and climbing back into the meagre accommodation I called home.

I remembered, although a bit too late, Chilly telling me something about an army procedure of clearing all 'eye level hazards' when setting up a night camp in case of just such an emergency that now had my nose throbbing harder than my finger.

In the clear light of morning I could see that my swim wasn't as good as I'd first imagined. After all, if something was passing through the tiny gap then that was exactly what they would be doing, passing through, and not stopping in an obvious trap area to feed, so I upped sticks and moved, only this time I took the long route, conscious that bad things often happen in threes!

The small commons were still on the shallows, only now there were four of them and, right on the edge of my vision, I could just make out a fifth, only this one was a lot lighter and was probably a mirror.

I decided to settle into a swim just to the right of the reed bed and wade my baits along the shallow margin to reach the fish, but first I had to perform a bit of DIY surgery involving a baiting needle and a now puss filled finger, that was going a horrible purple colour!

I won't go into gory details, but let's just say the first aid kit came in very handy, however, the feeling of absolute relief, as a mouldy old piece of wood and what seemed like quarter of a pint of various fluids shot out from under my nail was indescribably good.

Once soaked in anti-septic cream and wrapped in plasters it felt so much better, so I started the long and slightly dodgy task of wading two rods along fifty yards of very soft margins.

The actual area where the fish were was hard sand, but the bit between my swim and there was thick black ooze that bubbled up with a smelly methane type gas as soon as you trod on it, and it stunk to high heaven.

It was awkward fishing but I knew I was getting closer to my first capture and I was fairly sure I'd found the spot that they would gather before spawning as well.

The rest of the session only produced a few line bites but, as I packed up the next morning, I could see that the numbers had grown by at least another two.

I couldn't wait to get back down and I just hoped that the temperature didn't rise too quickly and lead to spawning, which would mean it would all be over before I arrived.

I'd be lying if I pretended to remember what happened in between my driving home and my next visit, as all I could think about then was getting back again, and all I can recall now was that the barometer had gone through the roof by the time I got back to the tall tree in the Fiords.

Just as I'd expected it to be, the bay was full of fish, and not just the small ones either, because I could see fish of all shapes and sizes belting about on the shallows.

The big round brown one was there and she looked to be one of the bigger ones, but alongside her was one of the darkest coloured mirrors I've ever seen, it was practically black. There were a few other good sized fish mixed in with the pack of smaller commons and mirrors, and they all looked like they were just about to spawn.

Leaving the rods in the motor, I pulled on a set of waders and made my way around to the swim past the reeds for a closer look.

There, in the margins right in front of me were two fish of around twenty five pounds in size, rubbing up against each other and flicking their dorsals on the surface. I knew I'd missed the boat as far as fishing was concerned, as they were right on the brink of spawning and, within an hour of my arrival, the bay erupted with a frenzy of fish flesh and thrashing tails as they started in earnest.

From where I was standing I could only glimpse what was out there and from up the tree it was impossible to gauge the size of any of them. Knowing that they would hardly even notice my presence, I waded along the margin and hid myself up against the reedbed and watched in awe as they charged past, only a few feet in front of me.

God knows how long I stood there, spellbound, but it was definitely measurable in hours rather than minutes.

At one stage the Round Brown fish came past and, right on her tail, the really black mirror lifted half of his body out of the water as he chased her across the sand. There was actually more of him out of the water than in it and, by holding my arms out in front of me, I could see exactly how big he was going to look if the day ever came when I managed to catch him.

He was so black it was incredible and an old saying sprung to mind, 'as black as Black Jack Shellack', and so he was named from that day on.

The spectacle went on for most of the day until, eventually, I realised I hadn't eaten or drunk for hours, let alone sat down. My feet were rotting away in the waders, so I quietly made my way back to shore and found somewhere comfortable to set up camp for the night.

Once the brolly and bed were suitably situated I went for a drive into the local town and sussed out a few of the more useable amenities, as I knew I'd be spending a bit of time in and around St Ives over the next months.

I tried a pint of Guinness in the local pub, stocked up with cold lager from the off licence and then gave the directions to the lake to the pizza delivery place for future reference, before setting off back with a pepperoni special and some liquid refreshment to await the dawn and see how the land lay for the day ahead.

During the night the weather cooled considerably and, compared to the recent mid summer like conditions, it was almost chilly as the dew settled in the early hours.

Throughout the morning I saw the return of a handful of the fish but, with the sudden weather change, they looked more interested in feeding than spawning any more, so I set up a stalking rod and kept an eye out for an opportunity to arise.

By midday I had found one spot, a tiny clear patch of sand in about two feet of water where the fish looked more interested than anywhere else.

Black Jack was there but the big brown female had totally disappeared, in fact it seemed as if only the males had returned, which would indicate that they had finished spawning altogether.

I carefully and slowly crept through the shallow margins with a single tiger nut dangling from the rod tip, having elected to place the bait by wading as I couldn't see anything from ground level and I knew it had to be exactly right.

The spot was about twenty yards away, on a diagonal along the margins, and ten yards out. With only a few yards to go I froze on the spot as Jack and two of his smaller mates (both commons) appeared to my right and circled the clear spot, before making off again.

If I could put a hook in that black beast I knew it would mean more to me than anything that I'd ever done and I'm surprised the sound of my heart hammering in my chest didn't scare off every living thing for miles around. With the nut in place I started to creep back towards the bank, sinking the line as I went when suddenly and without warning the line shot out of the water as tight as cheese wire!

I was taken completely by surprise, as I was still ten yards out in the lake and, like a complete Pratt, hadn't even set up a bloody landing net yet.

I had to stop the carp from reaching the gap into the adjoining lake, and with it almost definite freedom, while at the same time struggling to reach shore and then set up the net with the other hand. Had it been the black beast himself then I would have been really up against it and I dread to think what the result may have been but, as it happened, I could tell from the lack of any solid resistance that wasn't the case.

Sure enough, but still by some minor miracle, I managed to scoop one very indignant and totally surprised little common into the net. Everything was soaked, and plastered in mud and weed, and there on the mat lay a little wildie shaped common carp of about twelve pounds, and I was over the bloody moon!

Had I caught 'Black Jack' I think I might have had heart failure as this little chap had me shaking like a leaf as it was.

Obviously, I have caught hundreds of fish just like him over the years, but not many from an unknown quantity such as this and it made me realise that I was doing the right thing fishing for these carp, whatever the size.

It's only occasionally that something so all consuming comes along and really lights your fire in that way, but this lake had got me hooked fair and square and, at that moment, I was prepared to give whatever it took to come to grips with it.

It was a tough couple of months that followed the departure of the carp from the spawning bay and out into the wilderness beyond, but I made every conceivable effort to narrow the gap between me and them.

I did see the odd fish over this period, but the water quality was very poor with the ever increasing algae blooms and location was becoming a nightmare.

I still loved the place though and every new swim I fished brought with it a renewed vigour and excitement.

I particularly loved a little hidden swim on the end of the centre spit that you had to wade to reach, as the spit had now become an island, stuck in the middle of nowhere and never bothered by anyone.

In the few sessions I had spent on there I'd not seen a single soul apart from the resident Goose that, I must admit, I'd struck up quite a friendship with.

There were a couple of tench anglers that I used to bump into fairly regularly on the bigger sailing lake and we would swap stories of what we'd seen and trade off information on location of our given quarry.

I actually used to see some incredible tench and, on the odd occasion, a display of big dish shaped bream rolling on dusk.

Unfortunately, the return flow of information was not so encouraging but those wily old carp didn't give too much away to anyone.

One night I'd set up in the small Fiords after seeing a small common cross the bar in the gap and, come the morning, the entire silty end of the gulley I was fishing was alive with bubbling and fizzing.

By mid morning I was just beginning to doubt the effectiveness of my rigs when the tip whipped around toward the margin placed bait and my buzzer let out its first howl for months.

At first I was convinced it was a carp, albeit a small one, but the frantic and determined see-sawing that came back up the line convinced me otherwise.

Now I've caught a fair few big tench in my time, as have most carp anglers, but I'd never seen a male fish anywhere near the size of the one I steered into the net that afternoon.

Usually I wouldn't bother, but he was straight up on the scales and at nine and half pounds it's still by far the biggest male tench I've ever seen, and probably ever will!

One bit of feed back information that was very interesting came from a couple of bream anglers I met at the beginning of my weekly visit in the car park, one afternoon.

I was standing there plastered in mud, having just had to push my new motor out of thick ooze in the car park, with the help of a brick on the accelerator, when a couple of old guys appeared with their gear after a day session on the cut tree point.

Apparently they had seen no fewer than about twenty fish show near the gap to the Meadows.

Now, normally I would have written this off as pure fantasy as there are only about twenty fish in the whole lake but, the more I listened, the more I believed it.

They could obviously tell one fish from another as they reckoned it was probably about three different fish and even described one of them and he sounded just like the round brown one!

I had heard a similar thing a few weeks previously from a pleasure angler that had seen fish in this area and I was starting to think I was seriously missing out on something.

The best place to fish the area from was my favourite secret spit swim, which involved wading wherever I approached from, so not wanting to risk getting the motor stuck again, I decided on the slightly longer option of carrying the gear from where I was, in the Steak pit, and wading across the very rocky and slippery large gap at the back of the big Fiords.

It seemed to take for ever to get everything around to the gap, and I was tempted to fish from the spit side, but I knew that it would be worth the extra effort to wade it all across the underwater bar, at least then my gear would be totally safe if I wanted to just leave it and go wandering the next day.

I had couple of hairy moments as I stumbled on the underwater boulders and then, on the final crossing, with just a few bits of bait and food left, I tripped on a rock and ended up sitting on the bottom of the lake up to my neck in water with buckets and bags bobbing around beside me.

The worst was still to come, though, as I realised I'd still got my mobile phone in my back pocket!

Why I didn't leave it in the swim after the first successful crossing I don't know but now it was full of water and totally buggered!

I ended up stripping it down and putting it on the car dashboard in the sun to try and dry it out but it was a bit beyond repair.

The thing was, I was down for three days so I was practically on the missing persons list by the time I returned to civilization, lost presumed drowned I think.

The even more annoying thing was that I only saw one small mirror as he swam along the gap one morning, but no sign of the leaping fish and definitely no sign of anything feeding.

Fishing on the point was really awkward, and the water level was still high, so most of the time even a brolly wasn't an option. Also, the rods had to be waded out and set on long bank sticks at various stages of the flooded causeway to fish effectively, it really was a bizarre set up.

I was getting on quite well with the goose by now and we had a mutual agreement, if I waded along the margins rather than disturb her from her nesting duties, by using the bit of path she had set up home on, then she, in return, would refrain from chasing me back to my swim every time I got up for a walk around the causeway, it really worked quite well!

Something that didn't work quite so well, though, was my phone and no amount of drying and hitting it had any effect so, once back in Crawley, I took it back to the Carphone warehouse to complain that a slightly damp morning dew had penetrated the casing, but I think they sussed me out when they took it apart and found extensive water damage and a couple of tadpoles living inside the circuit board!

They gave me a temporary shop replacement and ordered me a new phone, and I promised them faithfully that I'd look after the temporary one a bit better and would take it nowhere near water.

I lied!

The next week I was back on the point, wading across the gap to go and top up with supplies when I slipped on the same rock as last time. I stumbled about for a bit trying desperately not to fall in but gravity had other ideas and under I went.

All I had on was a pair of shorts, so I that didn't matter, but I had my wallet and phone in my pockets.

With an amazing show of quick thinking, I whipped out the phone as I slid into the water on the side of the bar and held it up above my head like the sword Excalibur poking out from the surface of the lake and, despite gashing my knee open on the rocks and being soaked right through, the phone was completely and utterly dry.

At the end of the spit lies another carp lake where they do water skiing and suchlike, it was on the same ticket but I'd never actually fished it. What I used to do was walk along one bank of it on my way back to the car and then cross the river on an old rickety footbridge that brought me back onto the Steak pit.

This avoided getting ripped to shreds by the brambles and stinging nettles at the back of the large Fiords and, at the same time, gave me something different to look at.

As I rounded the corner onto the Ski Lake I bumped into Mickey, the bailiff's son, and I felt I had to tell him the phone story to explain why I was dripping wet from head to toe.

I was so proud of the way I'd saved the replacement phone, with no regard for personal safety at all, and it was better to have a little bit of blood loss than have to go back, a week later, to the shop with yet another destroyed piece of equipment.

We chatted for a while and then I wandered off toward the car. As I approached the bridge, which really was on it's last legs, I noticed that one plank in the centre had disappeared, probably rotted away and fallen in the boggy, muddy trickle below that was once a river. I looked at the gap and told myself to be careful as the phone had made it this far and I was nearly at the safety of the motor.

What happened next was like a script from a Laurel and Hardy movie. I stepped on the first plank, which snapped clean in half, throwing me forward and landing me with a thump on the bridge. As my knee cracked into the wood I clenched my hands in pain and the phone shot out of my fist like a slippery bar of soap. I lay there and watched in horror as it somersaulted, in slow motion, through the air and disappeared perfectly through the gap where the missing plank had been!

It didn't even clip the sides as it went through, and there was a dull, soggy 'plop' as it landed in the liquid ooze in the bottom of the stinky old river bed.

I couldn't just leave it down there, so I clambered under the bridge and fished around in the goo until my fingers closed around what was left of the phone and, amazingly, after I scraped off the worst of the mud the bloody thing still worked, sort of.

It was a bit erratic and only showed half the numbers on the screen but it still had some life in it, and after a good drying out on the car heater, I even managed to send a text.

I suppose the mud was thick enough not to totally short circuit the thing, but it stank and looked a bit sorry for itself, all the same as, the screen had totally misted up and you couldn't read anything on it.

On the fishing front, the whole session was just as unproductive as the previous week had been and I started to wonder if all this extra effort was actually worth it. Wouldn't it just be easier to go back to the Mere for the summer, return in the spring and wait for them in the Little Fiords again?

The more I thought about it the more sense it made, after all I couldn't fish the Mere in the spring and I couldn't catch them from the Fiords any other time by the look of it.

I hadn't been to the Mere for a while and it was starting to call to me again and, once I'd sewn the little seed in the back of my mind, it only took a few days to sprout and flower into a great raging monster.

Needless to say, that was to be my last trip on the M11 for a few months, I was in Mere mode once again and I couldn't wait.

# Chapter 13

# Back to Nature

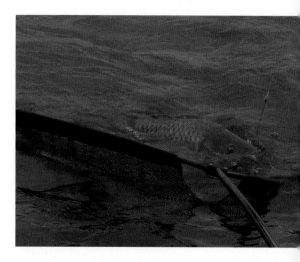

"*K*eith and Chilly were off to the 'Carp World Cup' in Romania and somehow I had been elected as chauffer, not all the way to Romania I hasten to add, but as far as Heathrow departures lounge".

It meant getting up at the crack of dawn and loading up Keith and his gear in Crawley, before driving over to Aldershot for Chilly and then up the motorway to reach Heathrow by about 8am. I didn't really mind, as it was nice to get all whipped up in the fervour of pre-match enthusiasm, and there was certainly plenty of that flying about!

The 'get up' that the pair of them were garbed in had to be seen to be believed, they had enough visible Union Jacks to put a Brighton pier souvenir shop to shame, and that's not counting the inevitable 'jingoistic' underpants!

I mean, the British abroad are bad enough anyway and Keith and Chilly are probably worse than most but, when you add the small matter of representing your country in a multi-national competition, then the sublime really does become the ridiculous.

At least they were happy anyway, even if they did walk through the departures gate looking more like the Pearly King and Queen than a couple of carp anglers.

After they had disappeared off to the airside bar, to drink lager and sing 'Ere We Go' at the top of their voices, I found myself at a bit of a loose end.

It was bang on the rush hour time so the M25 was totally out of the question, for a couple of hours at least, and not being overly keen on plane spotting either I decided to take the back roads over to the 'Mere' and have a little look around.

I parked the van up in the old spot in the lay-by and dug out a set of rip-proof trousers and jacket from behind the seat.

Unless something radical had happened to transform the landscape since my last visit, I was certainly going to need them!

It was weird going back to the Mere again, after such a long break, but the old place had hardly changed at all, apart from being even more overgrown than usual, although quite how that's possible I'm not sure, but I swear that it was.

I started off by sitting up on the high bank and taking it all in for a while, hoping to see one of those old warriors leap out from the pond and wave 'hello', I suppose. After a while, and with no sightings of over enthusiastic or over friendly carp, I decided to 'bite the bullet' and attempt to walk a circuit.

All my senses screamed at me not to do it, and all too vivid memories of pain and blood loss flooded back to warn me of the dangers but, I steadfastly refused to acknowledge them as I marched straight into the undergrowth on the first leg of my journey.

Within two or three hundred yards of nettle and bramble infested terrain I was forced to crawl on my hands and knees, as the matted blackberry and hawthorn bushes had formed an impenetrable wall. Luckily, I knew from experience that it would open out a bit as I reached the snaggy point on the west side. I always used to call this bit the murder mile and it certainly hadn't improved with age, it was as if nobody had walked it for years and, at one stage, even the ground level path disappeared and I was blindly pushing my way forward on my belly into solid brambles!

After a while, the feeling of claustrophobia began to become too much to bear and the hood of my Gortex jacket had been pulled free of my head, leaving my neck exposed to the millions of nettle leaves and insects that were in frantic competition to destroy as much eagerly awaited flesh as possible.

I was soaked to the skin in sweat and ripped across the face by thorns and brambles, now I remembered what the 'Mere' was really like; it's funny how time can dull the memory!

Eventually, being able to take no more, I wrapped my hands around my face and forced myself upright, even though my clothes were determined to stay on ground level among the barbed wire terrain.

Even standing bolt upright, only my head was clear of the undergrowth, my back was covered in nettle leaves that had fallen down my shirt and stuck to the sheen of cold sweat that covered me, my arms were unfortunately pinned to my sides by the wrapping effect of the vines of thorn that seemed to be actually thickening around me as I stood, a bit like that man eating plant in 'The Little Shop of Horrors' I half expected them to scream out "Feed me now" as they dragged me down into oblivion!

All around I could see a wall of thicket and not even a glimpse of the lake, it was impossible to walk over or through it, so I just had to drop back down and crawl. Luckily, I picked up the old path again, which was now no bigger than a rabbit run, and I knew how Alice in Wonderland must have felt!

Eventually I broke free into the sunlight, fifty yards short of the snaggy point, and then made my way out onto what we used to call 'the lawn' at the back of the swim. Unfortunately the lawn, and the swim, had totally been reclaimed by the living entity that is 'The Mere' and the only free space was a small circle of about four feet in diameter that stood at the end of the point.

I was 'buzzing' all over from nettle rash and soaked to the skin; I just had to get out of the Gortex clothes and feel a bit of fresh air against my skin.

Laying myself at the mercy of the legendary mosquito population, I stripped down to my pants and stood there like a semi-naked lunatic, drinking in the cool breeze as it drifted in from the lake. Imagine what it's like with a rucksack on your back and rods and a bed chair strapped around your shoulders and you can see why the 'Mere' is never likely to become a circuit water!

I consoled myself with the fact that I'd already come about halfway and, on the second half, there were spots where I could actually reach the waters edge and look for fish. I was obviously reluctant to leave 'snag point' but I knew that it was only a short battle to my own favourite little swim beneath the canopy tree.

Hardly anybody ever fished this spot and it was the first one I'd ever made so, therefore, I'd sort of adopted it as mine.

The hideous path that the mystery menace had hacked into the back of the swim, a few years earlier had healed beyond recognition and it was back to the old method of crawling along the waters edge for thirty yards, one foot in the margins and trying not to slide down the steep shelf into eight feet of water, before hoisting yourself up the steep bank ten yards short of the swim and disappearing under the thick trailing canopy.

It was as if I had never left, hanging in the inner branches was the remains of my old camo net and a dropped tent peg still lay on the ground where my bivvy once stood; the only new addition to the swim was a hideous smell of rats piss, the whole tree seemed to be soaked in it and hanging from the branches was the reason why.

In my haste to leave, at the end of my last stint, I must have left an air dry bag full of bait tied to a branch, and now there was just a ragged up piece of material swinging there, absolutely soaked in the vile smelling acids that rats somehow think it is necessary to spray all over their dinner.

I crept to the front of the swim and looked over the bushes in the edge, down into the deep, clear, margins and bugger me if there weren't a couple of carp down there!

As I watched, two more fish joined them and the four commons circled lazily around the roots of the snag tree, no more than ten feet away from my face.

All of them seemed a lot smaller than anything I ever remember seeing in the Mere back in the 'old days', and I realised that these must be some of the 'natural stockies' that arrived with the floods.

Two of them had obviously been bought and paid for by somebody at some stage in their lives as they were high backed 'stock fish' like the ones that went into Wraysbury while I was on there. The other two looked like typical, old fashioned English wildie/commons that probably would never grow very big at all.

As I watched them weave their way around the branches, a fifth and bigger common appeared from behind the tree, this one was blatantly an original 'Mere' fish and looked to be around thirty pounds.

Interesting that they had integrated in this way, it got me thinking that a baiting campaign might tempt the smaller fish into a response and thereby break down the defences of the big originals by way of competitive feeding, a situation that had never existed at the Mere before.

I found myself making plans and hatching plots and, before I knew what had hit me the Mere was once more coursing through my veins, forgotten were the acres of bloodthirsty brambles and dog rose, I had carp in my sights once more.

I didn't even notice the second half of the trek back to the car, as I was lost in a brave new world with a population of two, The Black Mirror and Me!

The hunt was on once again; only this time I had a plan!

By the next afternoon I had deposited the first five-kilo's of the new

Maple-8 boilies into the swim, I had only just received my first batch as they were just out for testing but I loved the smell and I was sure that the Mere carp would too.

I baited all around the tree and also fired in a big bed of them to an area near the middle, I had seen carp there in the past and I was confident that those little stockies would find it wherever I put it in.

My intentions were to bait for a few weeks and get them really 'having it' before moving in and reaping the benefits but, as is usually the way, it didn't quite turn out like that.

If the old saying is true and patience really is a virtue then it's certainly not one I possess. All I could think about was the Mere, even the old dreams had started again and every night I'd be creeping around in the undergrowth somewhere looking for the Black Mirror, paranoid that someone would beat me to it. Sometimes it would be a tiny little pond or on other occasions the Mere had been opened into a busy public park, sometimes it was even a field full of grass without any water in sight but, in my tortured dreams, it was always The Mere.

The three days following my first baiting up session were spent spraying up the gear, once again, with Halfords finest green and brown aerosols. I sorted out a new boat and sprayed that as well, as there was no way I could possibly carry my gear around the lake this year!

The paths were so overgrown that it created a perfect environment for what I had in mind, I was planning a single swim assault, boat the gear in and leave it there until I'd either caught the bugger or the lake had beaten me back once again. With no access to the swim, my tackle would be safe and, if I kept my head down, so would I.

I'd decided on the Canopy for obvious reasons and within a week of those first sightings I was back, loaded gear with for everything I would need for a full on assault.

Setting up the camp was a doddle really, particularly in comparison to most of the other swims, and I soon had the house concealed beneath the trailing branches, with the repaired camo net screen at the front, set up so that I could pull it back like a curtain as soon as night fell.

The rods are always the hardest part, as there is no real swim at lake level, and just a small gap by an old tree root has to house three rods and a net, leaving no real room to even balance yourself next to them, let alone cast.

One bait only needed swinging out a few feet to the spot where I'd seen the commons, but the other two were being fished out in front, about fifty yards, in the deeper water where I'd put the bulk of the bait. Even with waders on it was tricky but, with a wide sweeping sideways cast, I somehow managed to get them both pretty much on target before settling in to await the cover of darkness.

I'd had the foresight to bring a book with me on this occasion and I settled in my little hide to read a few chapters, but the Mere is far too interesting to ignore for long so I ended up spending most of the afternoon perched right at the top of the tree, looking out over the Mere and the surrounding areas. The view from there was massive and I could see for miles.

As darkness fell I started to get a few liners on the long rod and, about midnight, one of these liners suddenly turned into a full blown run, on my first night back as well!

I was as nervous as hell playing that first fish in, but I could tell it

wasn't one of the much sort after prizes by the lack of any real resistance, and as it turned over into the net it was a bit bizarre to be landing an upper double common from a lake that previously never held anything anywhere near that small.

Two hours later and a repeat performance on the other long rod came up with the same result, only that one may have scraped about twenty pounds.

It was certainly novel getting takes but I worried how much damage it would do to the swim, after all, those big old Mere warriors were anything but stupid and they'd soon cotton on to the fact they were being fished for if it was going to be like that all the time.

About five in the morning, and still in the pitch black, the close in rod tore off as well. This surprised me a bit because all the margin disturbance with the other two should have put paid to that rod. I should have known by the take that it was something more substantial as it was a complete one toner as the alarm threatened to go into meltdown and, the eventual strike, after nearly killing myself getting down the slope, resulted in the rod being pulled flat and line being ripped from a tight clutch.

This was more like it, the fish raged away for a while and tried to gain sanctuary in the snags to my left a couple of times before I managed to bundle him into the net, while standing nearly up to my waist on the dangerously steep, sloping margins.

There, in the bottom of the net lay one of the lakes glorious thirty pound commons, the first one I'd ever managed to catch and I was over the bloody moon with him.

Digging out a big sack, I slipped him into the deepest bit of margin on a long cord and sat there drinking tea until it was light enough to take some very bad quality self take photo's, in the incredibly confined space behind the rods. It was a great feeling having finally tricked one of the 'proper' fish into picking up a baits and I was absolutely buzzing with excitement for the coming weeks. It seemed as if I had the place fairly well to myself, although I had heard that another angler I knew, Kenny, was doing the odd session on there. Quite where, I didn't know, but I'd seen no signs of path damage, so I assumed he was using a boat and, later that night, I found this to be the case when I nearly scared him to death as he rowed through the swim.

It was about midnight, I suppose, and I was sitting on the high ground in front of the bivvy with the camo net behind me. From here I could see through the gap in the tree branches and watch the long spot from where I'd had the two smaller fish.

I was sipping a nice hot cup of tea and taking everything in when I heard a distant, but rhythmic, splashing that could only be a set of oars. It was coming from the big lake behind and heading straight for the causeway, about sixty yards along to my right. Sure enough, after some sounds of scraping and swearing as the boat was hoisted across, the splashing continued to grow closer.

I had no idea who, or what, was coming so I kept stock still in the shadows and waited. As he came around the corner, keeping tight to the bank, he passed clean over my submerged rod tips and then ended up no more than ten feet from where I sat.

Seeing it was another angler, I simply said 'Good Evening', in my best jovial voice, and the poor bloke nearly threw himself out of the boat in shock!

The last thing you expect when you're out on the Mere in a boat, in the

middle of the night, is a voice a few feet from your ear, asking how you're doing.

Once he'd calmed down, we had a little chat for a bit and he was most apologetic for practically cracking the rods with his oar, it turned out he had some plans for a camp on snag point so, I wished him good luck and off he went.

The snags were far enough away for it to be of little consequence to me, or my fishing, so I wasn't particularly worried to have another angler about.

In retrospect, I had a perfect situation in the Canopy Tree that year and, had I stuck at it, then the book may well have ended here but, somehow, a few weeks later I got waylaid once again.

# Chapter 14

# Bruno and Friends

"*While I was sat in the Canopy Tree swim one afternoon, I had a call from Clive at Dinton; he had just bagged Brian, the same forty pounder that I had captured the year before. Clive seemed to have got the measure of Dinton and, although like me, he was also only on a day ticket, he was making the most of any opportunity that arose*".

He was trying to get me to go over there with him and, after another success call a couple of days later, I was beginning to crack.

He was getting amongst them most trips and the lake was fishing well, I hadn't had anymore action from the Canopy but I was sure that I would, as I was hearing them most nights as they crashed out in the open water where I'd been baiting.

Fishing two different lakes at the same time is not something I have ever really been able to get my head around, as I like to get in touch with the fish and their behaviour and focus all my attentions on where and how they may be moving, their reaction to different changes in the weather, favourite snags and weed beds etc. Jumping from one to another just fries my brain, adding extra distractions to an already mighty task.

However, there was no getting away from it, the fishing at Dinton did sound alluring, and I had a feature for a magazine booked the next week

and nowhere in mind to do it on, so it looked like another visit to Reading would be on the cards after all.

I had arranged for the photographer to arrive about 8am, so I met Clive in the Dinton car park around six-ish, this would give me a chance to get set up and get fishing before having to do the photo's.

The article was about various Mainline Baits products so I was laden down with packets of boilies, buckets of pellets, crumballs, flavours, dips and pop-ups, which was far from my usual lightweight day fishing kit.

What I also had, though, was the new Maple bait that we were just starting to put through its paces, it smelt delicious and I had further fortified the smell by soaking my hook baits in the liquid attractor to really boost the signal. It was to be launched as Active Maple-8, and I'd already bagged the three fish from the Mere on it, so it was showing early signs of being a little bit special.

The fish at Dinton always seem to favour the weedier areas and the layout this year had changed a little from the previous season. Whereas, before the weed had petered out in front of peg no8 and the lake had been practically devoid of greenery over the majority of areas, this year it had spread considerably further up the lake. Clive had taken his fish from a

swim known as the 'Oak' and it was here that the weed started to peter out a little. Due to the fact that he was only down for a few hours, combined with the fact that he is too generous for his own good, he let me start off in the Oak while he opted for a smaller swim called the Secret, which is right next-door. We were both fishing out into small holes in the thick carpet of weed that covered most of the lakebed in front of us. Exact pinpointing of areas had been a crucial factor at Dinton the previous year; in fact I am not sure that I've ever fished a lake where such a minute difference in bait placement can make such a vast difference to your catch rate.

After a few chucks about from the Oak, I found what I was looking for, a small clean area, only a few feet wide and surrounded by thick weed in all directions, the perfect spot for one bait. The other was cast further over, into a clear strip where Clive had had his fish a week or so previously. With both traps set, it was time for tea and a chat before Patrick turned up to photograph all the Mainline paraphernalia. Tea however was a very short-lived affair before I'd even had a chance to dig out the chocolate 'Hob Nob's', the rod in the small hole was away!

I had only been at the lake for less than an hour and I had a fish on already, I couldn't believe my luck, the smelly old Maple had done the trick in double quick time. As I bullied the fish out from the weed beds we saw it roll on the surface and the golden flanks of a common were clearly visible. Now I don't mean to sound either unappreciative or blasé in any way, but my heart always sinks a little when I know it's a common on the end, I love all carp and especially from tricky venues such as this, but a common usually dictates that it will be a smaller fish and not one of the real 'characters' that you remember for ever.

As Clive waded out to net the fish, though, it rolled again and I could see that this was far from a 'little' common, in fact as it went in the net I started thinking that it could be my biggest ever! On the scales it almost made it as well, but stopped just a few ounces short at thirty-three pounds four ounces, a real cracker as well, and perfectly timed for the feature as Patrick had just pulled into the car park.

Later in the day I went for a little walk around and found a couple of fish in a small corner up against some reeds, it was not an overly popular swim either, as a park bench sits right in the middle of it, and this obviously attracts herds of people and dogs to the area.

The fish looked relaxed and happy in the weedy environment, though, and from atop the small tree in the corner I could see a couple of classic little feeding spots glowing yellow on the bottom where all the silt had been displaced.

Despite my results in the Oak, I ran back and grabbed my rods, finishing the day in the bench swim. The fish slowly melted away throughout the afternoon and I piled in the rest of my Maple-8 baits before making my way home, after a very successful first day back.

I was really in a dilemma now, as I knew I should return to the Mere, at the same time all I could think about were those Dinton mirrors scoffing all that free bait I had deposited in the corner. The next day was Saturday and I knew that the lake would be packed out, so I could forget about it for the weekend and make up my mind by Monday morning, when I had my next free day. Needless to say but by 6am on Monday I was pushing my barrow along the path from Dinton car park with my £4 day ticket in my pocket, and praying that the 'Oak' was free. I arrived at exactly the same time as another angler was also considering moving in but, luckily for me, he opted for a swim further up the lake on the shallows.

There was an angler in the secret swim next door and, apparently, the 'Oak' had also been permanently occupied since my departure, but this is always the way at Dinton over the weekends. Normally I wouldn't feel confident moving straight in after another angler but, as I have already said, it seems to be down to the exact placement of baits and I was well confident of one particular spot and soon had a bait bang on the money. My second spot seemed to have closed up or drifting weed had obscured it, so I carefully plopped this bait on the edge of the original clear hole as well.

I only intended fishing the Oak for a couple of hours, before moving off into the bench swim, and I wanted to keep any disturbance to a minimum. After switching on the alarms I wandered next door to ponce a cup of tea but I had hardly even set foot in the swim than I heard a series of bleeps from my rods. Running back I could see I'd had a drop back on the right hand rod, so I struck, but felt no resistance and then I noticed the other tip was bouncing and realised I'd hit the wrong rod!

I am still unsure as to what happened and I can only assume that being so close together he had fouled the other line as he shot into the weed after feeling the hook. The fish had used the moments of confusion to bury himself deep into the weed but, as I heaved, I could see the tell tale sheets of bubbles as the roots started to pull free of the silt.

The surface of the water bulged, as a great big weed bed lifted up, and I slowly pumped the whole lot towards me. As it neared the bank I could clearly see a big old tail sticking out from the back and I knew I was still in business.

The angler next door had wandered around to see what all the fuss was

about and he was even more surprised than me at how quickly I'd received the take, especially as he'd been fishing his bait only a few feet away all weekend! He held the net for me as I steered a mountain of weed and buried carp into the mesh.

It was a bit of a job to tell what I'd caught at first, as there was so much Canadian pondweed in the net that I couldn't even see the fish at all. As I pulled the weed away from his flanks I caught sight of the unmistakable scaling of one of Dinton's finest, the big mirror known as 'Bruno', and, as is customary on such an occasion, I let out the old 'BRUNO, BRUNO' cry and pretty soon two more very bemused looking anglers arrived in the swim to witness the event.

After stripping away about fifty pounds of weed, I was left with forty-one pounds and ten ounces of beautiful mirror carp to hold up for the camera.

I'd been trying out my new pop-up rig, which looked a bit radical compared to most presentations, but I'd caught fish from a few local waters on it and now I'd bagged a big Dinton fish on it so things were looking up. It also seemed to have caught the attention of the few guys standing in the swim because, when I looked behind me as I swung the lead back for the re-cast, I don't know how I avoided hooking three or four sets of nostrils they were standing so close to it!

I couldn't stop smiling all morning and I think I was probably in a bit of a state of shock really, I'm not overly sure that everybody else was quite as happy about it, though, but what the hell eh?

I'd paid my four quid and had a bit of pay back for the four slashed tyres the previous season, it can't all be bad luck can it. As it happened my luck held out all day because later in the afternoon I moved up to the bench swim and managed to winkle one out of there as well.

I'd taken the rod up to the top of the tree, so as I could see properly to lower the bait on one of the small clear spots, and from here it was easy to sprinkle a few loose baits around the perfectly placed hook bait.

It was then that it became a bit of a complicated affair that involved dropping the rod down into the reed bed below, and then wading along the margins to retrieve it, laying the line out in front of marginal weed as I did so. Afterwards I had to then re-climb the tree and check that the slack line was laying tight to the bottom and wasn't hung up on any weed and obvious to the fish as they entered the swim.

With the rod set, I sat back on the bench, fending off any over zealous dogs, but eventually, the temptation to climb back up and check had become too much to bear.

As I peered down from the branches I saw a fish creeping along the reeds towards my bait, he obviously knew it was there as the water was crystal clear, but he acted as if he could neither see, nor smell it. Oblivious to the feast, he drifted around the area, passing within inches of the bait but never even so much as looking at it, but his circuit was definitely getting more and more localised.

After a period of about fifteen minutes and, I assume, when he had decided that nobody was watching, he suddenly dropped down and started eating everything in sight. It took me totally by surprise and, before I could even start to climb back down, I saw the hook bait disappear into his mouth and all his fins bristled as he realised his mistake.

That was the last thing I saw before throwing myself out of the branches into the brambles below, to the accompanying sound of the bite alarm howling.

Luckily, down was a lot quicker than up, and I managed to stop him before he'd got up any speed and steer him away from the weed beds out in front. When you know that it's only a small fish you tend to take a few more liberties and I soon had him ready for the net, the carp had other ideas, though, and absolutely soaked me as I bundled him into the mesh!

Luckily, a old couple who were walking their dog happened by at that precise moment and, enthralled with the whole proceedings, they agreed to take a couple of photos for me.

After I had returned the nineteen pound common they couldn't stop thanking me for letting them see such a monstrous fish, they found it hard to believe that freshwater fish grew that big!

I certainly drove home like the proverbial Cheshire cat that day I can tell you, all this in only two short day sessions. All thoughts of the Mere were put firmly to the back of my mind and I looked forward to a few more Dinton carp before the approaching winter arrived.

I suppose that I really should have known better, nothing is easy for long and the next session ended in disaster when I lost a fish in the Oak after about an hour of fishing and then, after another move to the bench the next day, I nearly broke my wrist falling out of the tree as I lost another good fish from there!

The Oak fish came adrift as soon as I hooked it, and there was not a lot I could do about it, but the fish from the bench really pissed me off.

I had baited heavily before I left the previous week, putting about three kilos of bait on an area of clear in the weed bed in front, at about ten yards range. I'd arrived back and lost the fish in the Oak in the morning and then spent the afternoon up the tree in the bench swim. I hadn't fished, but just watched as a very large common kept visiting the area. This fish was definitely a personal best and could have weighed as much as forty pounds!

He never really came close to feeding there, but it was compelling viewing all the same. I spent a few hours sat behind my rods, with baits on the pre-baited patch, but most of the time I just watched from the tree.

I couldn't wangle a guest ticket that night, as the quota of two per night had been booked already, so I filled in the spot with another two kilos of bait and made my way around to the river bank, intending to spend a night barbel fishing instead.

I'd never really tried my hand at it before but Paul Shields, one of the Dinton regulars, used to catch loads and he had invited me on there for the evening.

I didn't really know what I was doing, and I spent the first hour or so buggering about with maggots and hemp, without any action at all.

In the end I went for the easy option and hair rigged a boilie against the far bank, setting the rod up with the tip poking in the air, and sat back with a can of beer waiting for something to occur.

Now, I know this doesn't sound very 'Chris Yates', and a barbel specialist might think it's a bit of a heathen approach, but the eleven pound Barbel that nearly tore the rod from the rests five minutes later didn't seem to notice my lack of etiquette!

I was convinced I'd hooked a river carp at first because I didn't realise quite how hard barbel fought, it was amazing really and I was well chuffed.

I ended up sleeping the night just in the open, on a bedchair, without any rods out and, by daybreak the next morning, I was making my way hurriedly back to the bench swim. I knew there would be nobody in there, as it was a very unpopular swim, and sure enough it was empty and there was even some pinprick bubbling over the spot.

I rigged up a single pop-up and swung it out into position below the bubbles. The second rod was fished on the close in clear mark where I bagged the small common and, although I cast it from the ground, I still had to quickly climb the tree to check the line wasn't sitting up proud on top of the weed, like a warning beacon.

I only needed thirty seconds in the branches to peer down and check the line angle and I could have been back behind the rods, but sod's law struck, and that was the exact moment that a fish picked up the ten yard bait.

It had only been in the pond for a few moments and it was over the top of all that bait from the night before, but I just wasn't expecting action so quickly.

In retrospect, the fish had probably polished off all the freebies and just grabbed the hook bait as soon as it saw it, hence the lightning fast take.

I tried jumping from the tree again, as I had with the small common, but this time I caught my wrist in the crook of a branch and my leg in another and ended up hanging upside down, with my head about a foot from the ground, watching the spool spinning in front of my eyes. I was only a yard or two from the rod and, with a quick wriggle, and a severely bent wrist, I was deposited unceremoniously on the deck next to the rod.

As I struck I saw a big old mirror roll on top of the weed, but he was already under full steam and my pathetic attempt to stop him just ended up with the hook pulling free, as he buried himself in the jungle of Canadian pondweed. I was so annoyed with myself, if only I'd cast the other rod first and waited until I was down before I'd put out the rod over the bubbler, but at the time I just assumed that I'd have to wait at least a few minutes for a take.

It was a schoolboy error on my part and one that I'd just have to live with, but at least I knew that it wasn't the massive common I'd seen the previous day. Whatever I had lost must have communicated with the others, though, as my little corner died a death after that session and I never saw the big common there again.

The fall from the tree hadn't exactly done my back any good either, and I had to part with thirty five quid at the Chiropractors to get it put back into line again.

The last thing I needed was to put any strain on it, so I decided I deserved a few days off from Artexing, and a nice relaxing session at Dinton Pastures was just what the doctor ordered.

Unfortunately, it wasn't to turn out quite as relaxing as planned and I arrived at the gate to find it still firmly locked and, as only the syndicate members had keys, I'd just have to wait for one to either leave or arrive, unlocking the gate as they did so.

I waited for about twenty minutes and then decided to drive up the other lane to the parks visitor centre and walk from there instead.

I didn't actually know the way but I figured it couldn't be far as the park is not that big, however I failed to take into account the fact that I was trussed up like a chicken in a big body belt and could hardly even walk properly, let alone push a wheelbarrow full of tackle.

It seemed to take forever to reach water and, when I eventually did, it was only the wrong bloody lake!

I was in complete agony by then and could only manage little pigeon steps, resting every few yards from the increasing pains in my lower back.

I wasn't sure quite where I had ended up but figured I must be on 'Black Swan Lake' which is the larger, no-fishing lake, where families go to feed the ducks.

It was too early to ask anyone as nobody was about and anyway, I'd have felt a right bloody idiot, pushing a big barrow full of fishing tackle and asking if anyone knew where the lake was!

By the time I, eventually, did find the right lake I was in so much pain that I just laid the unhooking mat in the first swim I came to, and lowered myself carefully down on my hands and knees with my head resting on the mat, trying to take the weight off my back.

God knows what the early morning walkers thought when they saw some bloke praying to Allah on a padded green prayer mat, but I didn't care about anything by then, I couldn't have got up again if I tried.

The whole session, which included a guest ticket for the night, was spent in a haze of painkillers and, thankfully, no fish to try and hold up.

I did manage to totter back to the visitor centre the next day and move my van to the closer car park, but even this ended in disaster, as some thieving git nicked my stereo and half the wiring loom from the dashboard in his bodged attempt to unplug it!

Oh well, I hadn't really intended to return at all but I'd had a right result really, and all for a few quid spent on day tickets and a crappy old stereo!

As the year was getting late anyway, and the captures of Dinton fish had all but faded away, I decided to call it a day once more and move on to my winter water a bit earlier than planned.

# Chapter 15

# A Frozen Adventure

"*I don't know what it is about Oxfordshire but it seems to have a certain appeal as soon as the temperatures drop, and most of the more comfort minded anglers hang up their rods for the winter*".

We have spent many a winter at Oxford, mainly on Linear Fisheries various waters, and I quite fancied taking a look at some of the other lakes on offer in the area, particularly the Lynch Hill complex, which I had only visited half a dozen or so times before.

There are three lakes on the site, varying in size, but all holding a good head of carp. The one that appealed to me was Christchurch Lake, the furthest from the car park and, I suppose, the smallest of the three lakes.

It had one very big fish known as Petals, which had become a very well known and, also, fairly well caught fish over the years.

Apart from this jewel, which weighed around forty five pounds, there were quite a few thirties of all sizes and a back up head of beautiful scaley twenties.

My first trip of the year was just after the New Year and I arrived to find a deserted car park and an equally deserted lake. It was hardly surprising really as, during my journey over to Oxford, I'd driven past field after field of frozen wastelands. The nearby river Thames had first burst its banks, and then, temperatures of minus six degrees at night had transformed the landscape into one gigantic skating rink. Luckily, though, I met Derek the owner at the fishery gates and he informed me that that the lake was still totally ice free, even with the hideously low night time temperatures. He did warn me, though, that the predicted temps for that night were about two degrees lower still, so I was in for a cold one!

I dragged all my new thermal gear from the van and started to wrap up in layer after layer of warm kit. I had hooded fleece tops and a two piece insulated winter suit, so at least I would be staying warm if nothing else, or at least that's what I thought until I went to put my boots on!

When you arrive at a lake 120 miles from home, in polar ice cap conditions, it's a really bad time to remember that your big furry boots are still sitting in the airing cupboard at home and all you have with you is a pair of trainers! Usually I have at least some form of spare footwear but all I had extra, on this occasion, was a cheap pair of rubber waders, which didn't seem that appealing really, but I threw them on the barrow anyway.

Luckily I had also signed a deal with JRC at the start of the year and this session was to be the testing ground for a mega new sleeping bag and thermal, fleece lined cover, so at least I had the option of staying in bed for two days if the old tootsies got too cold.

There was just one angler on the entire day ticket side of the road, which comprises of two lakes, and I think there may have been a couple of guys on the syndicate lake, fishing for the big roach. Even more fortunately, the one angler who was there and had been fishing on Christchurch was just packing up anyway, so the entire lake would be mine to do with as I pleased.

In the far corner of the lake was an inlet pump, not connected at the moment but it had, apparently, been running recently and during this period the lake had fished very well, especially the swim where the water had been coming in.

Regardless of the time of year, or even the temperature of the incoming water, I am always drawn to any form of inlet pipe or influx of water of any description. Over the years I have scored well from many various pits by fishing tight up against a new flow of water. According to the departing angler it was due back on again any day, so I took a gamble and set up in the 'pump corner' to start with, knowing that I could easily cast to anything that showed anywhere else from here anyway.

I had a bit of a bad start when I realised I'd left all my bivvy pegs at home in the garage, it's rare that I don't forget at least one important item, I even forgot to take the rods one week!

The ground was frozen solid, so the normal method of cutting bits of stick to the right length was not going to work too well, but a quick stroll

around the bushes surrounding the lake soon sorted out the problem.

I'm not sure how professional the finished bivvy looked with three teaspoons, two forks, one bent peg and the inner section of an old bankstick holding it together, but it worked, and that's the main thing.

Unfortunately, although the pump was started later on that day, the pipe ran straight past Christchurch and poured thousands of gallons of lovely chocolate coloured water into 'Stone acres' next door, so I'd just have to hope for a sighting or two to guide me instead.

I'd brought along three pints of white and red maggots for the trip and a selection of small baits, 10mm boilies, pellets, and plastic corn and maggot hook baits. Christchurch fish can be very fussy creatures, especially in the winter, and I didn't really want to offer them too much of any substance as they can take a while to get on it and I wasn't intending hanging around for days on end in this weather.

I set the traps in the edge, near the recent pumping area, and sparingly spread a few maggots and pellets around the whole area. As the Evening drew in (about three pm) the temperatures started to plummet at an alarming rate and the allure of the new bag soon became too much to ignore, consequently, by about six pm in the pitch black Oxfordshire night I was all tucked up and snoring like a pig!

My new sleeping arrangement passed the test with flying colours and I was genuinely surprised to find that the entire vista (excluding the lake) was frozen solid on my emergence back into the real world, the next morning. The bivvy was like an igloo and the ground resembled white concrete more than the usual Christchurch mud, at least I was nice and warm but I didn't hold out much hope for my feet throughout the coming day.

During the morning I spoke to the foreman of the workings next door; he was in charge of a big excavation of gravel and, of course, the water pump that had drawn me to the corner in the first place. As far as he knew there were no plans to shift the hoses into Christchurch for at least the next few days so I decided that a change of plan was needed.

I was sorely tempted to pack up and high tail it back home again as the conditions were appalling for a bite, high pressure and mega-low temperature is not considered conducive to winter feeding, although, to be honest, I have often found it to be alright at the Oxford venues in the past. I think that if you hit it right then the fish can often go on a last feeding spree before the lake freezes up. With this in mind, I decided to up sticks and move swims to the middle of the lake, often the best place in these conditions.

Before tackling the frozen bivvy I walked along the thirty or so yards with rods and marker, spod rod and maggots. My plan was simple, three baits all spaced out over the middle area and two small spods of maggots over each one. The thinking being that, in the high pressure, the fish in Christchurch often spend a lot of the daytime in the layers of the upper water, regardless of temperature. Small, bright and attractive baits on the bottom may attract the odd one but a trickle of maggots, slowly sinking through the shoal, would be more likely to draw the fish down toward the hook baits.

The plan was to regularly top up the swim with a handful of maggots every hour or so. All three rods were positioned using a marker rod with a large, big-gripper lead and braid to locate the gravel areas that run through the centre of the lake. One rod out in front and one further around to the right and left in front of the swims next door, as I was the only angler on the lake I had plenty of scope to choose from.

Dragging the still frozen bivvy up the bank was the worst job as my hands were like blocks of ice; mind you the air temperature was still only minus three degrees!

It's at times like this that you seriously have to question your sanity but, to be honest, it was easier to move swim and just go back to bed with a bottle of wine, than it was to pack down a frozen bivvy and rods and then walk for half a mile back to the van (which probably wouldn't start anyway) and then drive all the way home again!

Just as I was sticking in the last of the teaspoons in my new swim, I received a savage drop back on my left hand rod and, to be totally honest, I was convinced it would turn out to be a tuftie or coot of some sort but no, it was a carp!

After a lively little scrap in the margins I netted a cracking looking scaly mirror of just under twenty pounds, he looked fantastic in all his winter colours, all orange and red with big golden scales.

As quickly as possible I cast another bait out on the spot and dropped a spod full of maggots over the top, feeding times in the winter are usually painfully short but they can often produce more than one take, especially on heavily stocked waters where there are probably a large number of fish in a very tight shoal. This was to be no exception either as, about twenty minutes later, the same rod was away again. This time a long leathery fish of nearly twenty-five pounds was the culprit, and to be totally honest I found it hard to believe that it was really happening!

Two fish in minus three degrees and, with the ground and margins all frozen solid, it was a right result and I was so glad I'd decided on a move rather than buggering off home. I made a few phone calls (how did we manage before mobiles?) and pretty soon I had Marc Coulson wandering

up the bank to take a few photos for me. Both fish were mint conditioned and he was as amazed as I was, especially given the conditions.

As if catching two fish in sub-zero temperatures was not enough on it's own, what happened next belied belief. During the photo's we were interrupted twice more by a further two takes, both mirrors and weighing twenty-one and twenty three pounds respectively. Luckily, Marc still had my camera in his hands at the time and got some rare shots of me playing a fish in January. The only down side was that I had to put on the waders to get past some frozen marginal reeds and a large area of cat-ice, the thin rubber did precious little to keep out the temperature as it was but, when I accidentally over stepped the mark while returning one of the fish, it was akin to having my toes amputated with a rusty knife! The pain as that ice cold water flooded in and soaked one foot right through had to be experienced to be believed; at least I had a nice warm pair of summer trainers to change back into!

It was about this time that I noticed the great big thermal boots that Marc had on his feet and, needless to say, with a bit of gentle persuasion, his boots stayed for a lot longer than he did. Once he had gone trotting off in his new trainers, and darkness was once more wrapped around the

frozen Oxfordshire landscape, I had a chance to reflect on the madness that carp fishing could be at times. I would not have bet a penny on anybody catching a fish that day and yet I'd had four of the buggers in a few hours, I couldn't wait until the next day-god only knows what might happen.

That night was even colder than the previous one and, by about seven pm, I was wrapped around the exhaust pipe of the nearby generator that ran the water pump.

It was topped up with diesel in the afternoon and scheduled to run all night and the heat that came out from the grid on the end was wonderful. The exhaust stack on top spewing out hot air and I capped it off with my soaking wet sock, which dried in no time at all (although it was so black with soot that I had to chuck it away in the end).

I spent most of the evening traipsing back and forward through the big ditch, over the fence and off to the pump for a much-needed warm up, and I couldn't believe that the lake was still wobbly; after all it was at least minus-eight degrees!

Every time I got back to the swim and settled down to read I could feel the heat pouring out of me as the freezing wind cut through everything in

its path, including my new thermal jacket. It was too much to resist, knowing I could be warm again even if it meant stinking of diesel and looking like one of the black and white minstrels, with soot plastered all over my face!

The next day dawned to another thick frost and even heavier cat ice but the bite time came and went without so much as a bleep for my efforts, I kept a constant supply of maggots trickling through the swim all day but the only thing to show an interest was the Robins.

If anybody ever tells you that Robins are so fiercely territorial that they kill any other Robin that strays into their patch then, take it from, me they've never been to Lynch Hill. With all other food supplies frozen solid I had at least four robins at any one time all hassling me for food, they

were actually sitting in the bait box and eating as many maggots as they could in as short a time as possible. I managed to get a photo with one sitting on my kettle scrounging while three others leapt on and off the rods behind him grabbing anything that wriggled.

Eventually, I had to brave the frozen canvas and wrap up my house, leaving the cooker until last, as my hands needed constant thawing along the way. As predicted, the bloody van wouldn't start and I had to jump start it on my own across a totally flat car-park, which nearly killed me in the process but, eventually, I was under way and headed off back to Crawley.

What a way to start a winter campaign, four fish

in such hideous conditions certainly gave me all the confidence I needed and I couldn't wait to get back for another go.

As it turned out, the constant bombardment of sub-zero temperatures eventually took their toll that very evening and, as I was soaking at home in a nice hot bath, the lake was finally freezing over. I could have returned about five days later for another go but it would be nearer to two weeks before the thaw came and I could cast another line into Lynch Hill.

After the brief and extreme freeze up that had swept through the nation, calling a halt to most Stillwater carp fishing by turning the surface of every lake, pond and ditch to stone, I couldn't wait to get back out there and re-acquaint myself with the Lynch Hill carp population. I was so impatient to go fishing again, especially after my early successes, that I found myself driving along a motorway flanked by many still frozen or half thawed lakes.

I had phoned ahead and spoken to Derek, who had informed me that there was one small section of ice-free water, but the wind was quickly working the rest loose and chopping it back into the lake to melt.

It's a ridiculous time to fish really as the water temperature is low enough as it is, and still falling further with every pound of ice that dissolves back into it but, 'where there's a will there's a boilie' or in the case of Christchurch lake 'a piece of plastic corn and a few maggots!'

The surrounding fields were still pure white when I arrived, but that's not unusual for Oxfordshire as it seems to have it's own micro climate and is regularly three or four degrees colder than any surrounding areas. Pushing the barrow down to the lake before starting is always the worst bit as, by the time you get there, you are sweating like mad in all that thermal gear and stripping off the layers to cool down only results in you freezing half to death ten minutes later. Mind you, there was always the exhaust pipe of the generator again if I got too cold!

I'd actually managed to remember my thermal boots this time, and a few extra layers of clothing as well, not to mention the bivvy pegs, extra hot curry and mulled wine!

Even with the extra kit, after standing there in the freezing wind for two hours waiting for the ice to abate far enough to allow me a clear cast into the small amount of 'wobbly' water, I was begging not to lose all feeling in my hands and feet. I really, seriously began to question the sanity levels that a lifetime of carp fishing had left me with!

Surely this wasn't normal behaviour but then, as if to quell my feelings of doubt, two other hopeful lunatics arrived and set up on the bank opposite me, so at least I wouldn't freeze to death alone!

I wasn't really expecting to receive any action at all on this first trip after the thaw, but it would be a good measure of things to come, and even a sighting of a carp in these conditions would be a good sign for the coming weeks.

As the main bite time on my last session had been between eleven and twelve o'clock I made sure I was up and sitting next to the rods by ten in the morning. As before, I put out the odd mini-spod full of maggots over the area where my hook-bait lay, hoping to drag any mid water cruisers down to the bottom, and once again I was practically mugged by a gang of robins as I did so.

The carp in Lynch Hill are very cute creatures indeed, and I am surprised that they stick to such exact feeding times in the winter as, if utilised to the full, it can be used as a chink in their ever present amour.

I suppose more factors than just choice conspire to create these winter 'slots' of feeding activity. I have long been of the opinion that it might be somehow uncomfortable in some way for fish to feed on the bottom, or indeed, even for them to be down there at certain times of the day. Maybe it causes them discomfort in some way, at times other than those of the obvious feeding activity, to stay at the required depths. If you think about the many effects of water pressure and temperature and how the oxygen levels can change many times in a twenty four hour period, then it can be safe to assume that the pressure on a carp, or the ready supply of oxygen at any given level, must also change throughout the day. If fish are in your swim for days on end, as is often the case, why then can the bite times often be limited to two exact feeding slots, of less than one hour each, in any twenty four hour period?

I can only assume that it is within these short feeding times that the fish feel 'comfortable' enough to drop down and feed, and often the entire lake will 'switch on' at the same time so it's not a case of the carp only visiting your swim during this period. Whatever the reason I always make sure that I am extra vigilant during the 'hot time' and this morning was no exception. Even the merest lift of the bobbin at Lynch can be, and often is, a sign that your hook-bait has been inspected as these fish learn at an amazing rate.

I have heard so many anglers moaning that their rigs were tangled when they wound in, and some report that a braided link was practically 'spun' into a ball. I am convinced that the massive majority of these occurrences are carp 'getting away with it' and quite often they have been hooked for some time without bolting, before expertly shedding the hook and swimming off. I was determined to stay 'on the ball' throughout my entire time at Lynch, and to keep tweaking rigs in an effort to convert as many pick ups as possible into fish on the bank.

At about ten past eleven that first morning, a small drop back of an inch or so had me striking into my first fish of the session, plastic corn did the deed again, over a small scattering of maggots. Unfortunately, the fish came adrift after only a few moments of battle, probably very lightly hooked due to their finicky nature.

Although no more runs came that session, I was well pleased to even get one pick up in those conditions and, by now, I had total faith in the methods I was using, although I was determined to keep an open mind and change rigs at the slightest sign of trouble.

Shortly before I left I saw my first fish show, he was a bit further up the bank in a swim that usually gets overlooked, even in the warmer months when the lake is very busy. I plumbed around the entire area before leaving and found the perfect feature for winter angling. It was a nice fresh looking weed-bed on the nearside of the area with a clear, silty run along the far edge. Further investigation with just a lead on a braided mainline showed that another weed-bed, further out, made this area into a clear channel that terminated in a dead end just to the left of the swim, where the weed joined together in a wall. The fish had shown in this channel and I hoped they were using it as a sheltered sanctuary from cold water flows, especially as it faced the rising sun and would receive maximum sunlight hours. A perfect spot to lay up in and also there seemed to be a certain amount of natural food in the thick onion weed that bordered the area; all in all I could not have scripted a better spot. I deposited the rest of my maggots and chopped up Maple-8 boilies over the area and headed off back to the car park.

As expected, the bloody van refused to start again, it was becoming commonplace now and the cold weather was just making it worse. Like a prat I forgot to check if it would start before loading all my kit up so, once again, I had to bump start the damn thing with a full load across a flat parking lot on my own. In reality, it probably only needed a new starter motor but I tend to push my motors to their absolute limit before getting involved in any of that maintenance malarkey.

On the journey home I reflected on the session and, although I was a bit upset that my only chance had come adrift, nobody else had received any action at all so I had at least been doing something right and, if all went well, my little bit of preparation in the weed-bed could pay dividends over the coming weeks as well.

My next trip started encouragingly enough and I was not to be disappointed in the new swim as my very first morning in the weed produced a typical Lynch Hill scaley double.

My next three or four visits were all spent in the new swim, fishing the slot in the weed and the surrounding areas. Throughout this period the temperatures were all over the place, heavy frosts some nights would threaten to re-freeze the lake while, occasionally, total thaws during the day would turn the surrounding bank-sides into a muddy swamp. The thick, cloying mud at Lynch Hill is legendary, and the paths, and swims, can resemble a scene from the battle of the Somme at times. Luckily, this particular year, the owners had been thoughtful enough to deposit an entire tractor trailer full of bales of straw at the entrance to the lake and, whenever you needed it, you could barrow one to your swim and spread it all over the ground, creating a nice thick and dry carpet to set up on.

Due to the varying temperatures, condensation, and the sudden cold snaps, I even had to resort to using a proper bivvy dome in the end, just to stay warm and dry enough to keep it all bearable. I usually push my luck with the brolly and sides as long as possible but, especially if I know I'll be plotted up in one swim, I eventually succumb to the sheer decadence of a twin skinned shelter!

I had two nights a week at my disposal, and I suppose I could have stretched it to three, but it's a long slog at that time of year, on your own in the dark for hours and hours on end. The daylight hours are so short that two days is really about all I can handle anyway (even with the bivvy). The results, though, were well worth the effort and I took a string of fish from the little slot in the weed over a period of a few weeks.

I was using plastic hook baits on two rods and a small pellet Maple-8 on the third and baiting very sparingly indeed. Accuracy was the key factor and although the spot was only twenty-five yards out I would cast and cast again until I was absolutely sure it was 'on the money'.

Every day at about ten thirty in the morning I would scatter maggots over the area as quietly as possible, using a tiny little pocket rocket type spod and gently touching it down on the surface. Each rod would be cast, attached to a tiny round PVA bag and filled with caster and ground bait; the bag would be no more than 30mm in diameter.

Due to the exact and pinpoint nature of the feeding spot I could only make two rods produce, there was no room for a third and, no matter where I tried to place the other, I couldn't find another feeding area.

By fishing on a Monday and Tuesday night I managed to have the lake practically to myself for a lot of the time and, on the odd occasion that there were other anglers present, they never set up in the 'apparently' sad little swim that I'd adopted as my own.

The inlet pump from the new excavations next door never once even looked like being moved back into Christchurch, although I did keep a good eye on it and regularly used the generator for a little warm up in the middle of a particularly cold night.

I would always ask any workers that I came across in the daytimes, when they were planning to move the pipes back into Christchurch, knowing that they would have to eventually, as the water levels of the lake were actually plummeting due to the leak off through the gravel sides into the massive hole they were digging only a few dozen yards away. I just hoped that, when they did eventually switch them over, it fell on a Monday or a Tuesday, and that I was the first to get in there and fish next to it. Even in the depths of winter there are few carp that can resist the allure of an inlet pipe.

During that whole month I only saw about three fish roll on the entire lake but, by fishing in my little weed bed, I still caught an average of one or two carp per visit, every one of them came from an area no more than ten feet by fifteen and all bar two of them picked up the bait between 10.30 and 11.30 am.

The bite time was so precise it was incredible, although I knew that the fish were there at other times, as I would receive the odd line bite. All of the fish were between nineteen pounds and twenty seven which, for Christchurch, is a fairly low average but I was far from complaining. There had only been about ten fish landed so far that year and somehow I had managed to catch all of them; when the weather is that extreme you have to be thankful for a fish of any size.

The two fish that I caught outside of the normal 11am feeding spell both came around four thirty in the afternoon, shortly before dusk; a lovely low twenty pound linear and a small common. Neither of these fish came from the close in hot spot and that led me to start moving two rods out of the area during the 'slow time' and searching the further marks for a bite, although during 'golden time' I would often try and squeeze all three in and around the hot spot.

One particular session, in mid February marked the change of things to come, as a natural phenomenon of some description stirred the fish from their winter lethargy and opened up new possibilities for me as an angler. Quite what occurred below the crystal clear waters I don't know, but I would suspect that light levels, moon phases or some such natural trigger persuaded the lakes natural larder of hibernating creepy crawlies to start making an appearance. This, in turn, persuaded the carp to move about a bit more freely in search of an easy meal.

I had seen next to nothing jump up until this session but the change was evident from the start and as soon as I set my tackle down on the now familiar piece of straw covered ground, a fish stuck it's head and shoulders out as if to greet me.

Ten minutes later and another fish, quite a big one as well, left the pond at a range of about seventy yards, toppling back in with a resounding crash. Luckily they had both been well and truly within the bounds of my swim so I could plug away with the close, hot spot, and still fish two rods on the newly showing carp.

With the rods not in position until midday I had missed the morning spell by setting up right in the middle of it, but I still had two mornings ahead of me, although I need not have worried as the afternoon spell was just about to get a lot better.

At 4.15pm that afternoon one of the long rods gave a couple of forward beeps followed by one drop-back bleep, which, at Lynch Hill, is practically a screamer!

I watched the line at the point of entry just to check it wasn't a line bite and as soon as I saw it tremble on the surface I struck into a solid resistance. Straight away the fish started to tear line from the clutch and I knew that it was a fair bit better than the normal doubles and low twenties I had been getting up until now.

Whether it was a result of its size, or of the sudden wake up call they had undergone, I don't know but that fish fought like a tiger and even thrashed about in the folds of the net once it was all over. He was a cracking looking linear that pulled the scales around to twenty-eight and a half pounds and my biggest fish of the winter so far.

Things were looking good, as I had only been there a few hours and I'd had one already. I wasted no time in getting the rod back out there on the same mark just in case there were more of them about, and they were still feeling a bit peckish!

It was a good decision as, about half an hour later, in the last rays of light as the sun settled into it's final descent behind the trees, the same rod was away again. As soon as I set the hook the rod was nearly torn from

my grasp as an angry old carp charged off down the lake. This one also felt like a big fish and I got all the confirmation I needed when a great big back broke the surface about twenty yards out and sent up a spray as he charged around in the margins, fighting just under the surface the whole time. At one stage, as he surfaced near the net I began to wonder if I'd hooked the famous 'Petals' as there was a great big chunk of back sticking out above the surface. When he rolled again, however, I could see that it wasn't him, but a big old orange mirror and obviously a winter thirty.

Once beaten, and up on the scales, he went thirty three pounds exactly, a right result for this time of year and I just managed to get the photo's done before the last of the light disappeared altogether and another freezing night began.

Fully fired up by the change in the lakes mood, I was up around dawn, sitting there watching the skyline crack open another beautiful Oxfordshire day, and the chance of yet more winter jewels.

Around nine o'clock a fish crashed out in between my two areas at about fifty yards, shortly followed by another about ten minutes later. They were obviously on the move but I resisted abandoning the old margin spot to cast at them and instead recast all three rods to cover as much activity as possible. The close rod went back in 'the zone', with a top up of maggots and a small Maple-8 pellet on the hook, even though that area now seemed dead in comparison to the main body of water in front of me.

Eleven thirty on the dot and my perseverance was rewarded with a short, stuttery, take on the close rod, which resulted in a slow plodding resistance being transmitted up the line. Twisting and turning below the surface, pinging the line across his fins and trying all the tricks in the book to shed the hook, a big golden common eventually hove into view through the crystal clear margins. As he plodded around the net cord I started to think that I had attached myself to a new personal best common, one that could better the thirty four pounder I had captured from Sonning eye a couple of years previously. I knew there were commons over this weight in Christchurch but, as it turned out, I just missed the mark with this one but at thirty-three pounds he was still a very impressive beast indeed, and looked glorious in the low rays of the winter sun.

I stayed on for another night, hoping for even more of the same or, ultimately, the appearance of the big fella himself, after all they were obviously on the munch and a big old carp like 'Petals' would have to feed at least as hard as the others, if not harder, to sustain his considerable weight.

Whatever mysterious switch had been thrown to trigger the upsurge in

activity was just as mysteriously switched off again that night, however, as the next day dawned over a decidedly 'dead' looking lake and the indicators stayed glued to the spot until it was once again time to do battle with the old Astra van!

Even with a minor back injury from pushing half a ton of scrap around the car park, the 125 mile journey home was the best yet, two winter thirties and an upper twenty to back them up was a blinding February session by any measure and I was grinning like a Cheshire cat all the way back to Crawley.

Being the Middle of February, I figured that I only had two or three weeks left on Lynch before the crowds re-appeared and there was no way I was going to fish it when that happened. At the moment I was still only seeing a maximum of three other anglers at once and still, occasionally, I would be all alone which suited me just fine, but I knew it would not last. I would just have to make the most of the time I had and give it a final effort to find that big old mirror and, even if I didn't, I had already had my best winter for years!

Although I was still fishing mid week sessions, I knew that sooner or later the crowds would arrive back at Lynch Hill and, to a certain extent, I was partly responsible myself for any early interest. To fish at a commercial venue like Christchurch on the Lynch hill complex I am usually faced with two options, either pay the full wack and have no obligation to publish anything or strike up a little deal with the owners regarding a bit of publicity. Now, me being a tight git I obviously went for the latter option and, as a result, I had been writing regular articles about my winter results on the lake, whilst Derek also, had obviously been telling people of my results. I think they call it cutting your own nose off to spite your face or something like that!

Anyway, my sessions were starting to get more and more populated by other anglers, not that I mind that at all, but I had got used to being there on my own and the lake definitely doesn't respond well to pressure, especially when the fish don't really want to feed that hard anyway.

January is always the quietest month on any water but I've always found that it can be quite productive if you have a method they want, and you know exactly what area the fish have picked to hold up, it's just the never ending nights that get to you, and sometimes I find myself all tucked in bed by six in the evening!

I had a couple of mates come along on guest sessions during February which made life a bit more bearable, a couple of bottles of wine, a curry and a chat make the evenings last a bit longer, sometimes we stayed up until at least ten o'clock!

Even though there were now a few more people about, my little area that I regularly fished and baited was being left free, as it was one of the least favoured swims on the lake; most anglers seeming to prefer chucking their baits straight out into the middle for some reason. The fish were starting to show a bit now as well and, although I was getting most of the action from a gently, gently approach in the weed, the odd fish was starting to get caught from other areas. It all meant that, before long, the lake would be rammed out once more.

My mate Clive, who I had fished with at Dinton had been over for a one-nighter earlier in the month but we'd both blanked on that occasion so I'd arranged to meet him on the last Monday in February for another go. The bloody van had still been playing up, in fact it was so bad now with the dodgy starter motor that it was a guaranteed bump start every time. I had to get into the habit of only ever parking on a hill! Obviously, there comes a time when even I can't put off essential repairs any longer so I'd also arranged for a local angler/mechanic to take it away during my session and, hopefully, return it fully repaired in time for my journey home. You'll notice that I managed not to get involved in the slightest bit in the entire mechanical operation, apart from handing over the keys when I arrived!

I'd arrived a night earlier than Clive and set up in the first main swim to the right of my normal area, this way I could still fish my hot spot with one rod but also save some room for Clive, as nobody would take 'my' little swim as a first option but the one I'd set up in was very popular. I realised already that I was now fishing as much against the anglers as the fish!

Clive arrived early morning, in plenty of time for the eleven am feeding slot, and the lake was already quite busy. Being the kind hearted chap I am, I wound in my left hand rod so Clive could move in next door as it looked to be the best option and so it turned out to be as well, only ten minutes later!

I had literally just wound in to make room when Clive plopped a bait out there, bang on the money and away it went, just like that.

I stood next to him as he played it with my scissors at the ready, one sign of 'Petals' chugging up from the depths and I was snipping! He kept reminding me how he'd surrendered a swim to me at Dinton under similar circumstances the previous year and I'd caught a thirty three pound common just as quickly, but the scissors stayed out just in case.

As it turned out, it was an immaculate twenty plus common that rolled into the net so we were all happy. It made it all the more worth while really as I'd already had a few fish over the winter and it was nice to see a mate get one (especially a small one!).

The only result I had that session was the van getting fixed and delivered back in plenty of time for the hideous 120 mile return trip, but at least I didn't have to bump start it this time.

I decided on the way home that the next session would be my last, as the lake was getting far too busy for my liking, and I didn't want to get myself into a frame of mind where I was on a 'Petals Hunt', as that was not the reason for going there in the first place.

It is, however, a fantastic incentive to know that there may be a chance of a fish of that size in the winter, but I didn't want to get tied down to a witch hunt on a busy water like that.

The final session arrived and I had three nights ahead of me. There were only a couple of other anglers on the lake and they were both on the far bank in the usual 'middle' swims, so that left me plenty of room to manoeuvre, although, one of them informed me that the lake had been totally rammed out at the weekend and everybody had blanked!

Behind me, further along the bank, Richard (one of the bailiffs) and a young lad called Ben (on work experience from Sparsholt College) were

clearing some bushes and building up a bonfire. There is something about the allure of fire in the open that is very hard to resist and I was soon lending a hand and teasing the flames up as high as possible, it was also a good way of warming up as the temperatures were still painfully low.

About half an hour before dark they had called out good night and set off home, planning to return the next day and burn the rest of the timber. Needless to say, but by the time they returned the next morning there was not a single twig left on the bank and the pile of embers I'd created were glowing orange like the inside of a volcano. It was the warmest winter's night I've ever spent!

During the next morning, the other two anglers started to pack up and leave and I started looking for a change of swim as I'd seen nothing in my usual spots. While I was wandering around looking for inspiration I saw a couple of workman up on the gravel at the end of the lake and it looked to me like they were actually setting up the infamous pump at last. All winter I'd waited for this pump to arrive and now, bang on cue during my final session, it was finally happening.

I absolutely love fishing inlet pipes and I've had countless results from a fresh influx of water, regardless of the time of year, so I grabbed my rods and was in there like a shot, pushing in the bank sticks as the generator kicked into life and the pump started running!

Clouds of coloured water spewed out into the lake as the pressure of the incoming flow stripped the silt and sand from the bottom and started to dig itself a 'plunge pool', directly below the pipe. The sheer force of water from these big industrial pumps is awesome and the pipe bucked and jumped about as if it were alive. Before long there was a tantalising trail of 'new' cloudy water stretching out into the pit and every time it looked as if it would run clear I threw a bucket full of sand and mud into the flow to keep it coloured up. I also started introducing a few Maple-8 pellets and I even poured some of the liquid attractor into the flow as well!

Later in the evening I even tried lifting the pipe into a new position, a few yards further along the bank, to instigate another mud cloud. It's amazing just how much pressure comes out of the pipe, and I found this out by ending up flat on my arse trying to hold on to a boa constrictor-like piece of pipe, thrashing and twisting in my arms and jetting water everywhere!

There was no way that the fish were going to ignore this, and I positioned the rods with total confidence that a few bites were imminent, especially as I was the only angler left on the lake.

I was massively confident as night fell and, before long, the liners started as one by one the fish drifted into the area. I was fishing one rod right in the turbulent water at the base of the pipe and the other two at ten-yard intervals along the muddy flow. How the hell I didn't get a pick up that night I'll never know as the bobbins never stayed still from the liners for the entire time. But as soon as it started to get light, the fish started to show, rolling and jumping all over the swim.

Figuring that maybe the hookbaits were buried under the settling sand, I wound in the 'pump rod' attached a fresh Maple-8 boilie pellet and flicked it back into the flow. I repeated the procedure for each rod but there really was no better position for them so they all went back in the same spots while the fish continued to show.

Then, suddenly, somebody somewhere must have thrown a switch.

First the rod next to the pipe burst into action and I struck into a right scrapper of a carp that tore around in the muddy water. After a decent battle I slipped the net under a mid twenty mirror and, thinking there was another chance straight away, I recast while the fish was still in the net at my feet. Amazingly, while the rig was still in the air, and with line still pouring from the spool, the next rod in line also ripped off. There was nothing for it but to simply let go of rod number one and let it 'cast itself' while I struck the second rod! I wasn't too worried as the fish in the net was quite relaxed and I had two landing nets set up, which is a habit I got into some years ago, leaving one at each side of the swim just in case!

This second fish was really going hell for leather and it was all I could do to stop him taking line, then suddenly I heard a rustling sound at my feet and when I looked down I could hardly believe my eyes. The rod that I had dropped on the floor, mid-cast, was being shaken around as line was pouring from the open bail arm; I'd got another take!

This was ridiculous, talk about 'like buses', I'd waited all night for a take and then three had come at once!

I quickly put the bait runner on the rod I was playing and placed it in the rests while I shut the bail arm and struck the third fish, before putting the rod up on the rests and let it just run off a light clutch, while I returned my attention to the second fish again. All the time I was playing him, the third rod was absolutely tearing off and I was just praying that the fish didn't find any snags (luckily there are next to none in Christchurch). Somehow, and after an arm aching half an hour I was ready to net the third fish, having secured the first two in a net apiece but how? Both nets were full and I was still all alone so I just had to quickly dip the net and scoop up carp number three, hoping that the other one didn't pick that second to make a break for freedom.

Luckily, I managed to get all three safely in and I sacked them up for a few minutes while I sorted my life out a bit. I phoned around and managed to get somebody over to do the photos for me (once again it was Mark although this time he made sure to wear trainers!). All the carp were between twenty five and twenty seven pounds in weight and all stunning examples of Oxfordshire beauties and, as is often the way in that neck of the woods, they all had totally different scale patterns.

There were lines and rods all over the bloody place, but three full sacks in the margins made for a very happy angler, I knew the pump would pay off in the end!

Ben, the lad from Sparsholt College, came down to see me during the morning and I arranged that he go in to the pump swim after me as he'd never caught a twenty pound fish before, and the chances were obviously massive of him achieving that in there. I had one more night to go before leaving the lake for the winter and the steady stream of anglers that had passed me already that morning did little to dissuade me.

On my final morning, as if to say farewell, a last minute mirror of twenty-four pounds came along and pulled my string, rounding off the session nicely.

I handed over the swim to a very eager Ben and also left him a couple of my rigs to try out, as the fish in Christchurch are just so riggy it's unbelievable.

The next morning at work, I couldn't wait to see if Ben had caught his first twenty or not so I sent a text to Derek to find out. Unfortunately he had blanked, and I could only think that the fish had moved off altogether, I was gutted as I really thought he'd get one. He was only fishing the nights, as he obviously was there to work in the day but the next morning I got the text I was waiting for; Ben had bagged a twenty-five pound mirror on one of my rigs from the pipe swim. Hurrah!

I was glad that I'd made the decision to travel all the way up to Oxfordshire for the winter, as I'd had an excellent time and caught some lovely looking fish, despite hideously cold conditions.

I am sure that there can't be that many lakes that were producing regular carp throughout the January and February of 2003, as it really was one of the coldest winters we've had in this country for many years.

# Chapter 16

# One Step Behind

"*As soon as spring had sprung its way across the country, I found myself back on the M11, Cambridgeshire bound, and very excited about re-acquainting myself with those elusive carp in the Meadows and Fiords lakes*".

I was positive that they would follow the same routine as the previous year, which in the end, just went to show how little I really knew about them!

As always, I started far too early in the year, and I had to suffer a few cold and fishless nights before the spring really kicked in and the carp started to move about the lake once more.

My first real sightings came on the end of the long point in the big fiords, there are a number of cut down trees sticking out of the water here and I'd sort of named it 'cut tree point' for my own reference. It's funny but I always name areas and swims even if there is no one else to relate them to, it just helps me keep track of it all, particularly on a water of this size.

Cut Tree Point forms the entrance to Shingle Bay, a beautiful little area that lays at the intersection of the main paths around the many different bits of water.

I was up in the branches of the tallest tree on the point and looking out towards a tiny island near the far bank, when I caught sight of three large

*Mouth of shingle bay*

grey shadows, working there way along the far margin and then cutting out to circle the island. As they came closer, so they grew substantially in size, until I could see the unmistakeable forms of Black Jack, The Round Brown one and another fish that I didn't recognise, although, had I seen it on its own I would have been convinced it was the Brown one.

From the corner of my eye I spotted another long fish coming in from the main body of water, but I was so engrossed in the trio in front of me that I didn't get a good look until it was almost too late. I wished I'd given it a bit more attention though, as I am sure, looking back, that it was a common, and of quite large proportions. Unfortunately, he sank down deep as he passed and I never got another decent look at him.

The original trio milled around for a bit and then drifted further into Shingle Bay, down towards the little bridge at the bottom, so I shinned down the tree and ran around the bay to try and get in position before they arrived.

As I came charging around the bushes at the bottom of the bay, splashing through the flooded causeway, I was stopped in my tracks by the sight of not one, but two, bivvies set up in the swim nearest the bridge. At this point of the lake it was possible to face both ways and, either fish into Shingle Bay, or fish the Lagoon Lake next door. The causeway is only a few yards wide here and luckily both anglers seemed more interested in the Lagoon, but I didn't want to attract any attention to the three huge fish that, by now, were cruising in only a few yards away from the back of their bivvies.

I tried nonchalantly to have a little chat with these two new anglers, all the while I could see the three fish over their shoulders, just milling about a few feet from the bank.

I decided to leg it back to the motor and grab some rods so that I could stake a claim before one of them stood up and accidentally stumbled upon them.

Trying not to look too keen or excited while running at full pelt through bushes, floods, and stinging nettles is not the easiest thing in the world and, as it turned out, it was all in vain. I returned to find them both stood on the little bridge pointing into the bay and making Ooing and Wowing noises! Apparently one of the guys had stood up to go for a wee or something and practically tripped over the fish as he did so, the game was up, and I had to go back to Cut tree point and hope they left using the same route as they had when they arrived.

With my baits in position I sat up the tree and waited for them to come, and waited, and then waited some more until, just before dusk, I made out the shape of three carp re-tracing their path back along the far margins towards the island. Two of them broke off and headed off through a swamp of reeds and shallow water that separated the island from the bank, the other one came around the front totally ignoring my first bait as he did so. As he reached the little sandy, shallow bar on the far side of the island, where my second bait was waiting, he dipped down and rubbed his flank along the bar, cleaning his sides only a few feet from my hook. I opted to stay up the tree and watch, planning to jump if he even looked like feeding, but it was not an option I needed to take as he righted himself in the water and drifted off to join the other two as they emerged from the reeds. All three of the grey ghosts just slowly melted from view as they entered the open water and went off somewhere else to spend the night.

I was sure that they would return the next day, after all there was no reason for them not to as the weather was forecast to stay the same and

they hadn't been in the slightest bit bothered about my presence on the point.

Cut Tree Point, like so many other areas on the Fiords, has next to no room for a brolly, let alone a bivvy, so I had to make do with cramming what shelter I could behind a tree and leaving the rest of the gear in the small copse of trees on top of the little hill that formed the entrance to the swim.

It would have been a fairly comfortable night, spent waiting, after all I had beer and curry to pass away the hours with and the bedchair was almost level enough to be comfortable. What I hadn't bargained for was the owls, they seemed to be everywhere, and they spent the entire night

Twit-Twooing at each other. At one stage there was one perched in the tree, right above my head, and I swear he had the owl equivalent of a megaphone and in the end I had to beat the tree with my landing net pole to scare him off but, even then, he only went about twenty feet away and started all over again!

By the time it got light I was absolutely knackered and it was all I could do to clamber back up the tree and settle in for a long and, as it turned out, totally fruitless wait.

The fish did re-appear but they didn't hang about for long once they reached the bridge, I would imagine that the other lads had laid traps of some sort and about ten minutes after drifting happily past my baits they came bolting back out, not looking too impressed with whatever it was they'd just encountered.

Later that afternoon I went round to the little bridge myself, where the two other lads were just packing the last of there stuff away, I had a better chat with them now that the fish had gone and I was not in such a blind panic. They introduced themselves as Mick and Dave and, apparently, it was there first year on the complex and they also fancied the

Fiords now, which wasn't surprising considering the fish they'd just seen on their first visit.

I had the option of another night at the lake and, considering these lads were just off home, I made a gamble and brought my gear round to the bridge, hoping to get it set up as subtly as I could, and ready in case the fish came back for a third day in the bay.

The bridge swim was not really a swim at all; in fact there was a small wire fence about a foot high that ran along the path, stopping you setting up the rods near the waters edge. The actual swim was designed for the Lagoon behind but I set up in it anyway and just poked rods through any available gap in the fence, with the rod butts sticking out over the path to stop anybody blundering too close to my perfect little traps.

I had tiger nuts on two rods and a small chopped boilie on the other one and I'd staggered them along the margins, but none of them were fished out more than about three feet from the bank, exactly where I'd seen the fish patrolling the first day.

It's a long old wait when you are fishing for carp that you know for sure aren't even turning up for another twelve hours or more and I spent most of it with the rigs in the butt rings while I wandered around the lake, listening and watching for some sort of signs as to where they disappear to every night.

As soon as it was light enough to see the bottom in the edge I set all three traps, taking care to bury the line and even push the leads out of sight using a landing net handle, if they came back I was going to be ready for them.

It seemed to take for ever for the sun to reach a high enough point in the sky to start warming the margins with its rays but, eventually, the fish decided it was time and I could just make out a pair of bow waves, creasing the lakes surface, as a couple of carp made their way around the little island and down into the bay.

I made myself as comfortable as was possible up the tiny, spindly tree, by the bridge, and watched as they rounded the corner and cruised to a halt over the shiny shingle stones that made up the marginal shelf.

I was expecting to see the same fish as before but the first two to arrive were different, one was a common of high twenties and the other fish was a big mirror, obviously holding a fair bit of spawn already, as its sides were bulging.

Both fish passed straight over the baits without so much as a glance, even though the water was only a couple of feet deep on the shelf. At one stage the big mirror just floated above one bait for ages, blocking the rig from my view with its bulk.

After a while they moved off and another three fish moved straight in, these were the more familiar group but they, just like the first pair, showed no interest whatsoever in the bait.

I waited patiently until they also left and quickly wound one rod in, there had to be a way to get a bite as it was all so perfect with the fish having no idea that I was there.

I thought for a bit and then came up with the perfect plan, mussels, what fish could resist a hair full of crushed zebra mussels?

I grabbed the landing net and went off 'scooping' in the margins, well away from where I was fishing; returning in no time with enough Zebra's to fill a hair, and a little pile of pea mussels. I dropped the pea mussels into a PVA bag, clipped it to the hook and quickly lowered the lot onto the gravel before the moisture in the mussels melted the bag.

From up the tree I continued to watch and wait, all I could see of the

mussel rig was one stone the wrong colour and that was the lead, even this was a camouflaged version and it almost blended in perfectly, if anything it was a little dark but, compared to a normal carp trap, the whole set up was perfect.

The first fish to return was the common and he glided up the marginal shelf and stopped six inches from the rig, stock still, totally and completely motionless, staring straight at the bait. For what seemed like an eternity he eye-balled the mussels and only the occasional puff of his gills gave away the fact that he was still alive. Without spooking, or visibly reacting badly in any way, he dropped one pectoral fin, like a submarine changing course and, with a flick of the tail, glided back the way he'd come, just like that, a flat refusal of the best I had to offer!

I spent the rest of the day up the tree with a camera, if I couldn't catch the buggers with rod and line at least I could capture them on film, it was a poor second but, for the time being, I was totally out of other ideas.

For three weeks they kept on visiting Shingle Bay and, during my time in there, I never saw them eat once.

It all ended one day when I turned up to find Dave and Mick set up in a camp at the bottom of the bay, they had cut a new swim and bait boated a pile of particles out under the tree next to the bridge.

If those carp wouldn't eat a small pile of naturals and had ignored the maggots, casters and hemp I had carefully laid before them over the last weeks, then they were never gonna eat half a kilo of carp food dumped in front of them and, consequently, they moved out.

I don't blame the lads for trying, after all it might have worked and I couldn't catch them anyway, they really were the most indifferent natured carp I'd ever seen.

A week or so later I found a pair of fish in the big Fiords, sunbathing in an area where I'd not seen a fish before.

I was just strolling along a causeway and, as I came to an intersection, there they were, no more than three feet from the edge.

Luckily, I saw them before they saw me and I quietly melted into the bushes to watch from a position of concealment, I was determined not to muck it up this time. For about ten minutes I watched from behind the tree, trying to figure out a plan of attack. The fish were quite happy to just lie there, facing the reeds on the bank and occasionally lifting up their heads until a small dimple would appear on the surface above them.

Although I'd never seen the Meadows fish eat floaters, I knew they had in the past, and this pair looked to be bang up for a little bit of floating crust.

I crept back around to the other side of the lake and worked out the wind direction into the corner where the fish were, I wanted to drift baits right across the lake rather than risk spooking them by firing them out too close to the fish.

I had all day in front of me to try and trap one of these elusive beasts and I was going to try as hard as I could to make it happen. To start with I didn't even get a rod out, just a couple of small pieces of crust flicked out on the back of the wind and sent sailing like little white boats, bobbing on the ripples and making their way towards the far corner.

Because the corner was so exposed at ground level, with only two feet high reeds to hide behind, I cut myself a 'bouquet' of reeds to hold in front of my face as I crawled on all fours along the path and into position.

There was no hurry, as I could still see the two little white boats bobbing their way across, and they looked to be bang on target as well. If time is an option and you have a bit of camouflage at hand it's amazing how close you can actually get to the fish without them seeing you. I ended up no more than four feet away from the bigger of the two and, if not for the bouquet of reeds I held in front of me, we would have literally been staring into each others eyes, I could see every movement of his gills and lips as he breathed slowly and contentedly.

The two crusts were just entering the back of the swim and to be honest, I could not have driven them more accurately by remote control. The first crust passed over the bigger of the two fish, working it's way up from his tail and appearing right in his line of vision, unfettered, safe, and begging to be eaten, at least that's what it looked like to me.

The fish dropped a bit lower in the water as it passed and turned, slowly, just like they do before they rise up and slurp down a floater but, instead, he nudged his companion in the side and they both swam away!

One stupid little bit of bread, without even a rod in sight, let alone a hook, and it had been to much for them. I knew they hadn't seen me, no way, so what the hell was going on?

I couldn't believe it, I had stalked as well as anyone possibly ever could and I couldn't even get them to eat a free offering, there was only one thing for it now, and they sold it at Threshers in St Ives!

I stomped off along the path, making as much noise as possible, and then drove to the Off Licence where I bought a massive crate of industrial strength lager and a bag of ice, no fishing for me that night I was gonna drown my sorrows and drink away my ineptitude!

I suppose it was fortunate that I bumped into Dave and Mick on my return to the lake as I would have felt even worse in the morning if I hadn't had someone to help me drink it all, as it was I was bad enough anyway. They were set up on the base of Cut Tree Point on a nice comfy little lawn and I think they were a bit shocked when I marched up to them, dumped down a crate of cold beer and said, right, let's get wasted!

Up until then we had only sort of bumped into each other as I went about my business and they must have thought I was a lot more professional than I looked that afternoon, and far more professional than I looked by the end of the night!

We had a right old hoot on the little bit of lawn that night and I can't actually remember where I slept but, one things for sure, the rods stayed locked in the back of the motor, as I needed another plan.

Even with a rotten hangover, the journey home was full of plotting and scheming for the next trip, I ran through everything I'd learnt about those fish in my time on the lake, and it didn't exactly amount to much!

I knew that I'd only ever seen them eat in one location and that was the small fiords, where I'd caught the little common from.

I also knew that the only bait I'd seen them show the slightest interest in was tiger nuts, so at least I had something to go on, however vague.

The next week I turned up armed with a small jar of crushed and whole Tiger nuts and spent most of the time up the trees in and around the small fiords, it was all I had to work with and I was praying to see at least some signs of carp.

Around mid morning my prayers were finally answered while I hung out of the branches of one of my favourite spotting trees on the shallows. It was situated at the intersection where the three channels between the islands all come together as they meet the long bar at the bottom of the bay. Any fish taking this route across the Fiords bay would have to cross the bar and be on full view as they did so.

I was just staring down at the silkweed covered bar and imagining a big old mirror waddling along the side of it when, bingo, one appeared! I'd never seen the fish before, at least not that I could remember, he had huge pectoral fins that he used to keep himself on an even keel as he picked through the short weed.

At last I had a chance of a bite, as this fish was behaving like a normal carp, grubbing around in the silkweed and looking for bits of food. To reach the bar with a rig was easy enough from the adjacent bank but to accurately hit one of the tiny holes in the silkweed was another matter entirely so I hatched a cunning plan. By attaching mini-marker floats to the hooks I cast two rigs over the lake onto the shallowest spot on the bar and then walked back around to the base of the climbing tree. I had a quick shin up the branches to make sure the carp wasn't there as I didn't want to spook him off now, not after all the planning and hard work. Luckily he was off on another circuit of the bay, so I took off my shoes and

waded along the bar to find the floats. At first I thought I'd blown my chances as a fish spooked from under my feet but I just caught sight of a confused looking tench scuttling off across the bar. With the floats located I retrieved the rigs, removed the floats, and placed the baits by hand onto two tiny clearings on the side of the bar, scattering a few chopped nuts around it. Both traps looked perfect and everything bar the bait was hidden from view, it just had to work.

Back in the swim all I had to do was wait and resist the temptation to climb any trees as the bar I was fishing was also the entrance to the other section of lake and, should I hook one, I had to keep it on my side at all costs.

How I stayed on the ground for five hours I'll never know but my patience was rewarded when a massive swirl erupted over one of the baits. At first I thought the fish had just spooked off the rig but a single bleep, and a bounce on the tip, told another story. The fish shot straight up onto the top of the bar, with his back sticking out the shallow water. I grabbed the rod and heaved him backwards as hard as I dared, there was a moment or two of total stalemate as he teetered on the bar more of him out of the water than in. He knew he had to get over the bar to reach safety but there was no way on earth I was letting that happen and he thrashed on the surface as I piled on the pressure and, eventually, won the first stage of the battle. With the fish in the near side channel it was just a case of playing it cool and tiring him out in the comparative safety of the deeper, silty water. Unfortunately my cool had long since departed and it was a terrifying experience as he did everything he could think of to avoid the net. There was no way that I was going to loose that carp, even if I had to leap in and wrestle him to the bank with my bare hands.

Luckily that wasn't necessary and after a few sphincter-twitching moments on the net cord he rolled into the folds.

If you'd have heard the scream, the release of pressure mixed with the flood of adrenalin as I finally saw a big brown mirror carp roll into the net, you'd have thought I'd broken the British record!

The mirror was, without doubt, the one I had watched earlier, his fins were as huge on the bank as they had looked in the water.

I have never, ever, been so happy to see a twenty-six pound carp in all my life, the photo still has pride of place next to my computer and is one of only two carp photos on show in my house, the other one has my dear old dog, Fat Sam in it.

I'd just bought myself a new camera that had a self take facility on it, which was just as well as there wasn't another soul in sight. I set up the tripod on the grassy area between the lakes and clicked away, all the while laughing at my good fortune, now I had a method all I needed was to find the others, and things were going to change.

Well, things changed alright, the entire lake was struck down with an algae bloom and within two weeks of my meeting with the big finned mirror the water resembled cold pea soup, with a mouldy blue scum around the edges. It was a disaster and I couldn't see anything through the surface. Not wanting to waste my time and effort chasing shadows I decided to take a little trip back down to the Mere, I hadn't seen it for a while and I was starting to miss it.

It's always exciting, the first walk back through the tunnel of trees that leads to the Mere, not knowing who or what may lay at the other end. Part of it is the expectation and part is the fear that something may be wrong, changed for the worse, fenced off or worse still, opened up for all to see. I need not have worried, though, it was all exactly as I had left it, bramble hung, nettle and hawthorn enveloped and stunningly beautiful. The early morning mist was still rolling off the surface, like a slowly discarded duvet, as the Mere stirred itself back into life, ready for the day ahead, but was it ready for me?

I walked along the footpath bank first, breaking myself in slowly and straight away noticed the odd, turned back branch and slightly worn path to the usual climbing trees, a sure sign that someone had been here fairly recently, looking into the margins for signs of fish.

I hoisted myself up the first big tree on the path and was a little disappointed to see that the water quality was not too great and the same algae that had effected the Meadows and Fiords was also spreading quickly over the Mere.

I made my way along the dog walkers path until it led me out onto the Reedy point. Climbing the little spindly tree on the side of the point I looked out across the mottled green surface of the lake and, almost straight away, spotted two dark shapes, milling about over a small gravel hump that rose above the weed about ten yards out from the bank.

Even through the green water I could still make out a dull yellow glow on the apex of the bar, evidence of recent feeding activity and an obvious spot to place a bait.

I had everything that I needed to fish with, laying under a bush at the beginning of the track, so, I set off like a jack rabbit, trying to run through bushes without making a sound!

Sneaking back into the swim, with a baited rod and a net, I first climbed the tree to check what was what and, after seeing the coast was clear, I threaded the rod up, through the branches, and actually cast from up the tree to ensure I hit the mark. By some small miracle, I saw the stream of bubbles from the lead arc down and hit the yellow area first time, bang in the middle, perfect.

Not wanting to risk a disaster, after such a good start, I decided one rod was enough so I set it up on a buzzer in the reeds below and shinned back up the tree to watch.

Because of the murky water I couldn't make out very much at all below the surface, just a little glimpse of the weed, occasionally, as the light breeze shifted the floating scum about and opened random windows into the world below.

As I hung there from the branches, I was fairly sure I could see a couple of dark shadows mooching about over the weed, just a few yards from the bait. I couldn't be positive at first but then they split up, and one swam directly towards me, taking my eye off the bait for a moment. As I watched him come closer, I saw a brief flash of gold from the corner of my eye, right over the spot, immediately followed by the flashing green of branches whizzing by, as I threw myself out of the tree to the accompaniment of a howling buzzer!

I couldn't believe my luck, not only had I got a take within minutes but, by pure luck, I'd landed right next to the rod in the reeds, and not on top of the bloody thing, which would have been a proper disaster. Because of the overhanging branches and the speed of the first run, I waded straight out onto the marginal slope and piled on the pressure from there, turning the fish just under the branches of a big willow. There was an almighty boil on the surface as he swung out and around, moving across in front of me as he did, taken totally off guard, and heading away from the worst of the danger. Even though I could tell he wasn't one of the real monsters, my legs were still shaking like jelly, as I struggled to pull the net through the bushes, and into position. With the mesh in the water, and the handle resting on the bushes, I steered him away from one weed bed after another until, with a final big pull, I dragged him over the cord and into the net.

Straight away I recognised him by his small, slightly twisted mouth; he was the same common I'd caught on a floater on my first trip, although he'd definitely put on a bit of weight since then.

Because I'd had him before and, more importantly, my camera was still in the car, I weighed him and then slipped him straight back into the lake but, at twenty six pounds I was still well chuffed with my result, especially as I'd only been on the lake about an hour.

Strangely enough, Martin, one of the other Mere regulars turned up shortly afterwards, so I could have actually got a photo of the fish, although I didn't really mind that much, I'd had a big slice of luck, a nice

fish, and I had already got a photo of him at home from our last meeting.

Martin and I got chatting for a while, and it turned out that it had been him that had created the little foot trails through the trees, he'd been there a lot that year and had seen fish regularly, but the algae had made it more difficult over the previous few days to see anything at all. The algae blooms at the Mere tend to appear very quickly and, when they do, it spreads like wildfire, turning the entire lake into green mush in a matter of days.

I knew I wouldn't get many more, decent, sessions on there and this was confirmed my very next trip a week later. As soon as I turned up and

looked at the bay beside The Beach swim, I knew I'd left it too late, as huge clumps of the green stuff were floating around on the surface, and the water underneath was also tinted so badly that I could only see a foot below the surface.

Fishing in zero visibility at the Mere, or anywhere else come to that, is a waste of time for me as I just don't have what it takes to sit there, day after day, waiting, with only blind faith for company.

I stayed on for a bit but it had changed so much in just a few days that I knew, realistically, I had to move on again and return when the algae had run its course. Either that or plan a more concerted effort for the following season, starting a bit earlier when the water was its normal crystal clear colour.

# Chapter 17

# The Fat lady Sings

"*I was struggling to come to grips with exactly where I wanted to fish now; I was happy with my results so far that season. After all one fish from the Mere and one from The Meadows was, in my book, a right result, regardless of the size of them; it still meant the world to me*".

I seemed to have both lakes totally under my skin but I knew, realistically I couldn't effectively target either if I didn't have a decent level of visibility. Due to the unbelievable weather we had in England that summer, most of the other lakes that I fancied were also either choked with weed or the colour of pea soup due to the algae blooms that had swept the country, fuelled by the high temperatures and lack of rainfall

The Meadows and the Mere would both still be there for me the next season, and the one after that, so I decided to look around for another 'interim' challenge.

Not far from the Meadows was another, slightly smaller, gravel pit that had held at least one big carp that I knew of.

It was at least a mid-forty on most occasions and known as 'The Fat Lady' and although the area was still shrouded in secrecy at that time I had heard rumour of a couple of other good fish that also inhabited its depths.

At about thirty acres in size it wasn't anywhere near as daunting as some of the other lakes in the area, and the addition of a couple of well positioned islands helped to break it down even further into manageable chunks.

Although the water was far from clear at the time of my first visit, it still looked to be quite healthy, especially when compared to most of the surrounding pits and the visibility was still about four feet, which was exceptional for most places at the time.

I'd travelled up to Cambridge with the intention of fishing the big pit again but the weed and algae put me off and it was more desperation than anything that drove me to take a look at all.

I had another new water lined up for the coming winter and it was a lot closer to home as well, the ticket for there was due to start on the first of October.

It was to be a much-anticipated chance to fish, once again, with my old mate Keith Jenkins, as we had not angled together since our time on Sonning a few years previously.

This only left me a total of eight possible sessions, totalling a maximum of sixteen nights, not long at all to get to grips with a new lake.

Also I knew that realistically, I would not do even that many nights angling as I had various other engagements lined up that clashed with my normal fishing nights, like seeing the 'Red Hot Chili Peppers' in concert at Hyde Park for one thing. Some things just can't be put off on account of a fish!

I had been more enthused by the look of the lake than I'd anticipated, though, and as a result I couldn't wait to start my mini-campaign.

The very next Monday saw me rolling down the lane, fully equipped for my first two-night session. I had actually fished there before on two single night sessions the previous year but I still knew very little about the place.

I arrived to find the wind was blowing steadily into a little, lily infested, corner so at least I knew just where to start looking.

On that first session I never actually made it any further than that windy little corner as I instantly found three fish feeding on the shallow silt beside the pads.

For two days I hid and slept beneath a set of bushes, hidden from view behind a bed of reeds, in the hope of fooling one of them into taking a bait.

Despite seeing them in the vicinity a few times over the forty eight hours they seemed very reluctant to feed so I eventually packed up and left them in peace to do whatever it was that was so much more interesting than eating my bait.

They hadn't been particularly big fish by any means but not catching them had fired me up to try even harder on the next attempt and the journey home was spent hatching plots to outwit myself a carp or two.

By my next visit the wind had abated but the country was still held in the grip of the hottest summer on record. The surface of the lake was only slightly agitated by the mere breath of wind that trickled in from the North West and in the oppressive heat it could have been mistaken for being devoid of all life. No other anglers sat patiently beside its banks on the scorched earth and it was looking as if I may well have the entire lake to myself.

A large point or peninsula jutted out into the lake, half way along the western bank and marked the start of a serious weed bed where, under close scrutiny, the odd dorsal fin could be seen clipping the surface.

Just as I started to unload the van, another angler, Gordon, arrived for an overnight session.

I had met him before as a visitor on the big pit and I hoped that he was not also headed for the peninsula and the adjacent weed bed. My fears were unfounded, as he continued along the bank, setting up some one hundred yards further up, on the other side of the weed and well away from the few carp I had seen to my left in the slightly shallower water.

On investigation with a lead and a braided line I found that the entire area was incredibly weedy and the visible weed was just the tip of a big green iceberg!

I was in a bit of a quandary what to do as I didn't want to risk spooking everything in sight by thrashing the water to a lather looking for clear spots in the weed, on the other hand I wasn't willing to just hurl them into a forest either.

Quite often on lakes that receive a bit of pressure, the better spots are created over a period of time by the introduction of bait.

The cycle is instigated by bait on the bottom producing a fish and then getting re-baited and re-fished. More fish get caught and more people bait that particular spot, the more the fish feed there the more that the bottom of the lake gets eroded away and the silt layer removed, which results in less weed growth.

Eventually, if a spot is fished regularly enough it will stay reasonably clear even when the weed really takes a hold in late summer. If you stand in a popular swim (as I was) and look along the horizon you can usually make a pretty good guess as to where the regular spots might be as, we as carp anglers, are creatures of habit and usually pick the most obvious land mark to fish towards.

It's a sensible move really as it makes it so much easier to re-cast and bait at night but if you ever want to keep a spot hidden from others then create it on the most boring backdrop imaginable!

There in front of me was a visible church spire and a couple of obvious tall trees, all spread evenly across the horizon; it was just a matter of range really. A good place to start is always maximum catapult range with multiple boilies (about fifty yards) and it was exactly there that I got my first 'donk' onto a clear bottom.

The second rod was a lot harder to position as the weed had almost covered what was obviously a spot earlier in the year. It was straight at the spire but totally surrounded by dense weed that came within inches of the surface. The only way to accurately drop into the hole was to overcast against the line clip and skim the lead back across the top before dropping it down quickly into the hole. Baiting was also a nightmare but I opted to fill it in with 16mm maple-8's and just hope that some of them made it to the bottom!

With two rods in holes in the weed and the other chucked out into open water I sat back with a nice bottle of wine to take in my new surroundings, it really was quite a nice little lake really.

Just before dusk I caught sight of a strange occurrence, a large tail fin appeared in front of me and, with a very erratic, jerky, nature, proceeded to zig-zag its way around the swim. I watched it for ages, long after dark, and it seemed to be attached to quite a big fish but I was puzzled by its strange behaviour.

Eventually, I grew tired of watching him, and anyway the wine had run out, so I retired to bed to dream of naked carp and big fat women (or something like that).

The sun was up a damn sight earlier than I was in the morning, which is always a sign of a good wine, this summer of ours seemed absolutely relentless in its enthusiasm. The lake was looking well and truly 'cooked' and it was only seven o'clock in the morning!

With a cup of tea in hand I sat and looked out at my spot, watching the coots feeding happily on the 'shallow' baits that had stuck in the weed. As I watched, a great big bow wave appeared over the bait, and I mean big as well, it was more like a super surge of water as a very big fish pushed itself through the upper layers.

My hands flew instinctively to the rods, expecting one of them to tear off as the line tightened behind the rapidly exiting fish but it was not to be.

I swear I saw the same great big tail fin disappear beneath the surface as it sank out of sight, like the last sighting of a submarine fin as the U-boat just makes it back below the waves on a tacky old British war film.

It was such an intense display that I was sure that one of the biggest fish in the lake had just spooked from the swim, but I didn't know why.

My only consolation was that if it had been the biggie I watched the previous night then it had been acting very strangely anyway; surely they couldn't be thinking of spawning again so late in the year?

Within half an hour of the strange bow wave incident there had been the odd appearance of dorsal fins on the surface, mainly in the exact location of my middle rod, over the tiny hole in the weed. I was happy about my location but it looked more promising for a chum mixer than a boilie fished on the bottom so I rigged up a light spodding outfit to deposit a few mixers out in the swim.

It could not have been better conditions really for surface fishing as a very light breeze was now blowing directly at me and any bait I put out would end up in my own margin, keeping any interested fish in the area rather than drifting them off across the lake.

Just as the first spod full of mixers was launched and making full steam ahead towards the back of the swim, so the rod fishing on the bottom gave a few bleeps and then stuttered into life.

The spod was still in flight as I dropped the spodding outfit and struck the rod into a fish. Needlessly to say the now falling braid on the spod rod managed to wind itself around the taught line on the other rod but, luckily, it came off again just as easily.

Although I could tell from the start that I was attached to a carp, the fight was a dour old affair and, to be honest, 'fight' is far too strong a word to describe the pathetic attempt to free himself that he made on the way to the net. Within seconds it was all over and, as I drew him across the cord, I was amazed at how big he looked compared to the impression he had given me so far.

On the mat I recognised him instantly, which was bizarre in itself, as I had only ever seen pictures of two of the carp in the lake before!

Sure enough though, second only to the 'Fat Lady' herself, the next biggest fish in the pond lay before me, a deep-bodied mirror of thirty-six and a half pounds that had the unfortunate moniker of 'The Black Pig'.

Neither was he black nor indeed did he resemble a pig, although he did appear like a fish that certainly liked his boilies, he put me in mind of the old Longfield and Horton warrior, 'Jack the Net Ripper', now there's a proper name for a carp if ever I've heard one!

This was indeed a fine start to my campaign, only three nights in and the second biggest one in the bag already, I was beginning to like it even more.

Its funny how quickly you come to expect things as I was quite disappointed not to get another one the next morning as well, but I can assure you I wasn't complaining too loudly, it was a terrific start and I couldn't wait to get back for another go.

On my next trip I made that age-old mistake of charging straight back into the same spot without even looking and suffered a well deserved blank as a result, although I did spot the 'Tail Fin' again, cruising over the weed.

My next trip down was delayed due to the afore mentioned Chili Peppers gig and, due to various other circumstances as well, it was a couple of weeks before I angled at all.

I'd decided to start looking at the far end of the lake as the point swim was obviously very popular and I'd been told that it had been fished pretty much solidly during my absence. The far end was a lot deeper but sported some lovely little features, including quite a long, diagonal bar that ran from the distant island almost into a small reedy bay in the far corner of the lake.

I fished in this general area, moving twice within the bay but,

unfortunately, I could only manage a one-night trip, although I did actually see a good fish lunk out in the morning shortly before I left, which obviously filled me with confidence.

Once again the following weeks were full of events that seemed to conspire against me, and I had only managed to add one more 'single night session' to my tally by mid September. Again it had been fishless but I was confident that the top end would produce as soon as the conditions were favourable.

Remember that we were still locked in the everlasting summer at this stage and anglers all over the country were praying for a big low-pressure system to arrive and whip the carp into a feeding frenzy.

Eventually, all our prayers were answered and, on the eve of my next, and probably to be my last, two night session the barometer plummeted and the big winds came in earnest.

It was, as expected, a Southerly that finally usurped the high pressure system that had been throttling us for months and I raced through it along the motorway, watching trees straining to bear the brunt of its onslaught along the way.

I knew exactly where I wanted to be and I was praying that nobody else had beaten me to it.

On the very end of a southerly wind lays the Reedy bay I had favoured on the last two visits and a large point of land that cuts it from the main body of water. Either would do, although the point would offer far, far, more water to fish to and a lot more options than the little bay, but the bay would be the ultimate 'end' of the wind.

All the way along the motorway I could think of nothing other than that area and the dubious likelihood of it still being un-occupied.

The trees that flanked the road were bending to their limits in the big Southerly wind; ideal conditions which made the 130 mile journey seem to last forever.

Half way along the lane to the lake is a small gate that opens out on a dirt track across some fields and, ultimately, ends up directly behind the swims in question.

Anglers are not usually allowed to go in this way but, due to some adverse attention to cars left in the car park recently by the local Pikey community, the management had allowed anglers to park behind the swims in safety.

Unbelievably, an artic driver had picked this particular day to abandon his truck right across the gateway, blocking any entrance or exit and pissing me right off at the same time.

The walk from the other end was not so long as to be out of the question but I was frantic and needed to be in the swim right that second, or at least know if it was still free.

A few hundred yards further along the lane I found another gateway. The actual gate had long since been torn from its hinges and two large mounds of earth had been deposited there by a digger instead, obviously to stop the caravan and transit brigade from moving in.

Well, it may have been enough to stop a transit but it stood no chance against a manically possessed carp angler in charge of a battered old Astra van, no chance whatsoever!

After a big run up and a chassis grinding crescendo at the apex, the van crashed down the other side of the mound and into the field, dropping bits of rusty metal everywhere as it did so, I could just make out two cars already parked up behind the trees and my heart sank.

I bounced my way across the field and was gob smacked to see Terry Hearn's black BMW parked directly behind the point; I didn't even know he had a bloody ticket!

Sure enough, though, as I walked onto the point, there was Terry staring out into the waves, although no tackle was visible and the bay was still empty so I wasn't totally despondent.

It turned out that he had just joined and this was his first trip, unfortunately for me he'd just seen a fish in the open water in front of the point and was about to move in there.

The wind was absolutely piling into that corner and the bay was the obvious next choice which made me wonder how on earth the only other angler on the lake had decided to set up on the far bank, on the back of the first decent wind for about three months!

After chatting about the lake for a while, Terry offered to make the tea and, just as he turned his back from the lake, the most enormous carp rolled in the waves to the right of the swim. It was in the mouth of the tiny, reedy bay, and obviously following the wind that was steaming in there, almost flattening the reeds in its intensity.

Usually when a fish rolls it's practically impossible not to shout 'there's one' or 'did you see that' at the top of your voice, but time is a good teacher and I knew from experience that some things are best left unspoken, especially when it's blatantly obvious that the biggest fish in the lake is involved.

Besides that, I suddenly had a vision of a little yellow pop-up floating away from a rig and thought now was the perfect opportunity to even the score!

It was more like a wallow than a roll and three times she went over in quick succession, on the third time I looked straight along her back and it put me in mind of a lorry tire bobbing about in the waves. The 'Fat Lady' was in the house!

As nonchalantly as I possibly could, I expressed a vague interest in the tiny swim in the bay and, with feigned indifference, I started flicking about with a marker before the tea bag had even hit the bushes.

Knowing that the big girl herself was in the swim, and that Terry was next door, I wanted to ensure that she stayed there and as a result I scattered about two kilos of bait around the area, making sure that wherever she turned she would find the magical Maple-8 waiting for her attention.

My rigs were based around 12mm pop-ups on large hooks and short links, a devastating method for fishing over baited areas.

With the wind increasing even more in strength I could barely sit still and when the same fish rolled again right over my left hand rod, I was fit to burst into flames!

As I sat there rubbing my hands together and waiting for the inevitable take, I noticed the trees doing a weird dance, as if suffering the effects of two opposing forces. There on the horizon to my right, and moving at an incredible rate of knots, was the weather front from hell but, somehow, it was moving against the wind. Before I had a chance to realise what was occurring the beautiful big Southerly wind that had brought the fish to my feet, like lambs to the slaughter, was flattened by a northerly gale that lashed the surface of the lake with torrents of rain and tore the upper layer of water back down the lake in the opposite direction.

The brolly rocked and bucked in the wind and I had to zip on the front and put down the door to ensure it stayed fixed to the ground.

I was suddenly sat on the back of a hooligan and my confidence plummeted.

Knackered from the drive, I stretched out on the bed and had a kip, hoping to wake up and find everything back to normal, but it was not to be. The wind stayed in the North and both Terry and myself suffered a very frustrating blank nights fishing.

The next day dawned dry but still windy and we went on our separate searches for the carp that we had been so close to only a few hours previously, but the windy end of the lake was freezing and did little to enthuse me to move. Terry decided to relocate to the opposite side, still off the wind but he'd seen a few bubblers and that was good enough.

I still couldn't get the sight of that big mirror out of my mind, why would it want to bugger off on such a cold wind, after all, my little corner was now the hottest part of the lake.

I decided to sit and watch for the afternoon and, despite it being the 'Autumn Equinox' official first day of autumn, I was shirtless by mid afternoon.

The wind still raged but the trees in the bay kept it sheltered and the ripples did not start until the open water off to my left.

The sky, however, had cleared to a brilliant blue and I even suffered a bit of sunburn on my nose, if I were a carp I knew where I'd want to be and it wasn't down the other end in a big cold wind!

After a few hours in the sun looking, hoping, and even praying, I eventually saw what I was after when a fish stuck it's head and shoulders out in the corner of the bay. It was so deep into the bay that I decided, rather than move out, I was actually going to move further in. There was only one more swim in the reeds and it was even smaller than the one I had been fishing but it had carp in it and that was good enough for me.

Shortly after setting up I had a further confirmation as a massive patch of bubbles hit the surface in front of me as a fish rolled on the silty bottom.

I had a good feel about with a marker rod and braid and found a few interesting features in this little corner, things were looking better all the time!

A small bed of silt at close range gave away its presence by sending up a sheet of bubbles every time the lead came into contact with it and a long bar that stretched out into the lake seemed to terminate about fifty yards out, straight in front of me.

I baited up again, running a line of Maple-8 boilies between the bar and the silt patch and spacing three rods out along it, concentrating most of the bait at either end of the line.

As dusk fell over the lake, things started to liven up a bit. Out in front of me, just behind the furthest rod, two fish rolled in quick succession and a bit later on I heard another couple as well, further out into the lake and hidden in the gloom of early evening.

Somehow I managed to drift off to sleep about midnight but I was rudely awakened about an hour later when my furthest cast rod burst into life. By the severity of the run and the sheer determination of the fight I was expecting something larger to greet me as I peered into the net, but I was still well happy with the most beautiful little mirror of nineteen pounds that lay in the bottom of the mesh. For some reason I couldn't find my unhooking mat anywhere and assumed I'd left it in the previous swim. As carefully as I could I sacked the fish while it was still in the net, bobbing about in the margins, and then secured him in a deep corner beneath a big over hanging tree.

After that carpy interlude I found it totally impossible to get back to sleep, I lay there looking out over the reeds for hours, listening to the odd fish roll out there in the darkness. Looking upwards at the stars, I spotted a group of three satellites arcing there way across the night sky and I made a brew while I watched their progress, imagining they may be the first of an alien armada come to rape and pillage the earth.

Maybe they were, as I have never before or since seen three satellites together, let alone flying in such perfect formation, they probably looked down, saw me sitting there like an idiot trying to catch a fish and thought we weren't worth the bother!

By three thirty in the morning I was starting to realise that I had to get some sleep as I was due home the next day, in fact this was probably going

to be my last visit, although I may have been able to squeeze in one more before my winter ticket kicked off, if the conditions looked right that is.

Just as I climbed back into the bag a massive explosion of water in the margins had me jumping back out again. There, straight in front of me at only twenty-five yards range, the water was rocking from the re-entry of a big old kipper and I just had to put a bait on it.

Although it had jumped only ten yards from my closest rig I couldn't resist being bang on the money so I re-positioned the bait and then buried my head under the covers to get some kip.

As the sun woke me up, about seven, I was amazed that I hadn't caught another one, although when I got out of bed I was equally amazed to find a frost covering the grass and the landing net that lay on the reeds beside me.

The first frost of the year, the Autumnal equinox and the first big winds all in one session, surely this was the much-awaited breaking of the eternal summer and the cue for a big feed up in the carp kingdom.

I was torn as to what to do over the next few weeks as I really felt that it was too early to be pulling off and starting a winter venture, although I was looking forward to the social scene with Keith, but I was getting action on here and the sight of that great big back in the waves was haunting.

As I sat and pondered my situation I received a single bleep to the re-cast close rod and the tip bounced into the air, the way it does when a kingfisher accidentally clips the line as it flies by. I stood next to the rod to check and it did it again, only this time more savagely and I saw the line shoot out tight and then fall slack. Sweeping the rod up off the rests I felt a solid resistance but not the usual carpy one at all. The rod was wrenched downwards but then pinged up straight almost, immediately, time and time again the process was repeated as if I was attached to an underwater kangaroo!

The bizarre fight only lasted a short while, during which, I sort of figured it all out as I drew it nearer and nearer the net. If the big buoyant fish with the tail sticking out the pond the previous month was the biggun, and the strange wallowing fish the day before had also been her then it was odds on that this bizarre fight was also the big girl herself.

Obviously, she had a strange way of swimming and an even stranger way of fighting, as such it was no great surprise when the 'Fat Lady' herself popped to the surface at my feet. I had waded out to get a better netting depth and now found myself face to face with an enormous great carp.

One careful pull more and I could keep that social appointment with the Jenks after all!

As she slid into the net I was astounded by the size of her, admittedly I had been expecting a mid-forty but this fish was far bigger than that.

Having no unhooking mat handy I simply dragged the bed chair out from under the brolly and laid the great fish on that instead. Luckily for me, the angler who had moved in next door, after Terry had moved out, was a friendly native and he came round to help in the weighing and stuff.

It turned out that I had left the mat and all my spare sacks at home anyway (that's why I couldn't find them in the night) so I had to borrow everything from my neighbour who, unlike me, was not surprised at all by the size of the fish.

Apparently she had been steadily growing for years and had already been caught over fifty pounds earlier in the year.

Even so, as we weighed her at a new biggest weight of fifty-two pounds we were both still suitably impressed. What a terrific looking fish as well, I could hardly believe it was all really happening.

I phoned over to Terry who came round to help with photos, I was pleased about this as it's nice to have someone you know is good with a camera when you catch a biggun like that. As it turned out, though, all the photos were blinding on both cameras and I had a whole host of good shots to choose from.

As I waded out and released her back into the water, behind the weed, I knew instantly that I had been right in my earlier assumptions, the unmistakable tail lobe protruded from the surface like a sail as she waddled awkwardly away, eventually forcing herself down through the water and out from sight.

So it was her that had been circling my swim for two days on only my second trip, maybe she had been stalking me!

So much in this game relies on luck but sometimes it's as if you are just destined to catch a particular fish.

Usually I struggle to get to grips with the bigguns and I never manage to get a quick result, all my previous biggies have come as a result of at

least two seasons of bloody hard work, so for everything to fall into place so quickly was a welcome change.

It was still a strange feeling, though, driving back across the field and knowing that I wouldn't be back again, especially as I'd only spent a total of ten nights on the lake, it was a shame really as I was just getting to like the place.

They say that the opera ain't over till the fat lady sings, well, if that's true, then I must have just been a part of the world's shortest performance!

# Chapter 18

# *Black Jack Shellack*

"*A*fter a most enjoyable winter spent on a pit near to home called Sandy Lane, with plenty of big carp and even more plentiful curry and wine evenings with Keith, I was ready for a return to the big pit in Cambridgeshire once more".

Maybe this would be my year to make the acquaintance of 'Black Jack' or the big 'Round Brown' carp that always swims by his side. The fishing in Surrey had been good but, if I'm honest about it, I hadn't really got the buzz from it that you would imagine a winter full of thirty pounders should give you.

I suppose that I was getting used to the challenge of low stocked waters and had come to appreciate that style of fishing a lot more, the winter had hardly been challenging as far as getting bites had been concerned but, good fun all the same.

Now, however, it was time to return to the wilds and pit my wits against those extremely elusive Cambridgeshire mirrors, and I couldn't wait.

My first trip was in horrendous conditions, strong winds and driving rain is hardly conducive to finding a handful of carp in an inland sea but, regardless of this, the lake still looked as appealing as ever. Unfortunately, during the winter, the sailing club had decided to chop down the trees on the causeway between the big lake and the adjoining smaller sections and this had destroyed one of my favourite little hidden swims, throwing it open to the elements and leaving it exposed to fish and anglers alike.

Apparently they do this to increase the flow of wind for sailing, as if they needed any more wind on a great big open expanse of over eighty acres!

Walking and looking was once again the main approach for the spring, although it was getting easier every year as I learned more and more about where to look. The large section of the pit, which is used for sailing, is extremely open and fairly featureless and, because of the thick reeds that surround it, it is very hard to search for carp.

One area of the large lake however, that lays in the Southwest corner, has a large climbing tree in it and I had seen the fish there in previous years so I always included this in my walks. In previous years a typical circuit had also included wading through chest high water through a three hundred yard reed bed, hoping to see a fish bolt from the stems or cruise along the edge. In three years of looking I had never seen a single sighting along this section so, although I am sure they do use it, I decide to scrap this from my circuits this season, concentrating more on the areas where I had seen them in the past.

On the whole, though, I was trying to find them in the three smaller lakes that adjoin the big lake via two small, shallow, channels as, it is in these more intricate areas that you can get a closer look at the fish and hopefully tempt them into feeding for a while. The main problem is that the carp are naturally more cautious when they enter these confined areas and very seldom have I seen them feeding on anything, even natural food stuffs such as mussels or snails.

Every tree and bush had become familiar to me over the years, as had most of the fish, but there will always be surprises and that of course is the whole appeal of these sort of waters. There was one particular afternoon that I was sitting up in the branches of a tall tree, looking down through gin clear water at a small shoal of bream, when I noticed three bow waves moving in from a bay to my right. As I strained for a better view they turned slightly and made a bee line for the very tree I was sitting in, passing right below me in water so clear that they might as well have been floating above it for all the difference it made to the visibility. Black Jack was at the front, with the two big round females flanking him, all three looked big but the women were practically waddling due to their rotund spring figures. From the corner of my eye I spied another fish appear from behind the island but I was so engrossed with the bigguns I only really gave it a good look over as the larger fished passed from view, and I still regret that today.

From what I could make out it was comparable in size/weight to the others although longer and leaner in appearance and, I couldn't be sure but something made me think it may well be a common, I'd left it too late to be sure as it slipped from view and I never saw it again.

Unfortunately for me, another angler, one who usually only fishes there in the winter, had decided to take a year off work and fish the lake all summer, doing at least four nights a week. Now, two anglers on a massive lake like this may not seem many but, take into account that it only holds about twenty five carp and they would soon be shoaling up before spawning, and you can see that there would often only be one area that held carp at any one time. I knew the guy as well and he had fished waters like Wraysbury in the past, therefore he was very accomplished at big water carping and was sure to find the fish as often as I would, but I only had two nights a week and he had the whole summer.

On only my second trip I came up against this exact problem, having waded across the gaps I found a few fish in the largest of the small lakes, unbeknown to me Mr Whippy (a nickname given to him because of his job as an ice cream man) had also seen them and was making his way around the lake from the other direction with his tackle. We ended up bumping into each other on the path behind the swim, both loaded up with gear and rushing for the same spot!

As it turned out we fished side-by-side and only succeeded in spooking the fish off to another area.

Over the next few weeks I managed to get on the fish quite a few times but, never once did I see them feed and any bait I introduced just stayed there until it rotted. It was very frustrating and I don't think I have ever come up against fish of this sort before. They obviously must feed somewhere but I had no idea where that area might be and I could only assume that they saved their major feeding for the time that they spent out in the larger section of the lake.

I had tried in previous seasons to bait areas in the big lake in an attempt to create a feeding situation but that had never worked either and, over the years, I had come to the conclusion that stalking with a single bait such as a tiger nut probably offered the very best chance of all. After all, I had only ever had two bites from the lake in the past and both of those had fallen to this method so that would be my main approach.

About five weeks into my campaign I had arranged a guest session for my old mate Phil Thompson, we hadn't fished together for a while as he has just bought a lake in France and spends a lot of his time out there nowadays.

I spent the day before his arrival walking the banks of the small lakes,

*Looking across to the stalking reeds*

taking in the outstanding beauty and remoteness of the whole scene, obviously the main idea was to locate a few carp and, as such, most of the time was spent hanging from trees or peering in through thick reed beds. After hours of trying, and just as I was about to give it up as a lost cause, I found two big fish in the bottom of Shingle Bay, so I rushed back to the car for my tackle and set up on the end of dead tree point.

I had found from experiences in past years that actually fishing for the carp in Shingle Bay was the wrong way to approach them, as they were only ever in there to sunbathe but, as they left in the evenings, they always did a couple of circuits of a small island at the mouth of the bay so I decided to fish for them there.

Later on in the afternoon Phil arrived, armed as always with just a bed, brolly and two lightweight rods. I've never seen Phil with more than just one tiny rucksack full of gear and that includes his sleeping bag as well, and I thought I travelled lightly.

He set up in a little swim that faced out into the bigger of the small lakes, considerately keeping the bottom of Shingle Bay nice and quiet for me.

The evening passed by without any carp action and, once again, the fish ignored my offerings but the social scene was excellent. We ordered up a big Indian take away from a local restaurant and Mickey, the bailiff's son, went and collected it for us, along with plenty of cold lager of course.

By lunchtime the next day it was obvious that the fish had no intention of returning to the bay so I bid farewell to Phil, stashed my gear, and set off for another days searching for fish.

Unusually, and luckily, I found them in the very first place that I looked, sunbathing on the shallow sand in the bottom of the spawning bay. The only way to see into this area (other than wading) was to climb a particularly tall tree at the back of the dense reed bed and look down on them from a great height; consequently it was always extremely hard to make out what fish were there and how big they might be. This particular day I had convinced myself that they were all only the small male fish, getting in there early to get the best spots before the big females arrived at some time in the coming weeks for spawning.

Having not had a fish for ages I decided to try and stalk one of these smaller fish by wading through the dense reeds, which were at least eight feet high and ten yards thick at this time of year.

Although the water in front of the reeds, where the fish were, was only about knee deep and the lake bed firm and sandy, the reeds grew out of a much softer bottom and it was hard to wade through without sinking up to my waist. Keeping quiet as I approached the area where the fish were was a nightmare and I couldn't even see for sure if I was headed in the right direction, as the reeds were so high and thick. Suddenly, I came to the outskirts of the reed bed and, as I parted the curtain of stems to peer through, I could see that I was right on top of the fish, which were no more than a few feet in front of me!

I pushed the rod tip through the reeds and un-clipped the baited rig from the butt ring. To drop even a small lead on top of them in such mega-shallow water would definitely send them all rushing for cover but I had to get the rig down there somehow so I leant back into the reeds, out of sight, and flicked the rig out beyond the fish, landing ten yards behind them. Keeping the line high and out of their way, I slowly brought the rig back towards them, praying that I didn't pick up any weed on the way. Luckily, it all went to plan and the single tiger nut was soon resting on the sand in the centre of the group of six fish.

Although I had brought bank sticks out there with me I couldn't risk the disturbance of pushing them into the ground, so I opted to hold the butt of the rod and let the tip rest on the sandy lakebed. As I peered through the reed stems at the fish I suddenly became aware that they weren't quite as small as I'd originally thought and I could have sworn I could make out a light brown circle on the flank of the biggest one, in the same place as the 'Round Brown' fish had a patch. I looked back at the bait, which had been clearly visible in clear shallow water, and noticed that the second biggest fish had drifted right over it, he looked very dark indeed and, just as I started to realise that it was indeed Black Jack himself, he twisted in the water and spooked off suddenly. Before I realised what had happened, the rod kicked around in my hand and line was ripped from the clutch as it became clear why he'd spooked; I'd actually hooked him at last!

Leaping from my refuge in the reeds, I bent the rod into him as he powered off across the shallow bay, sending a big plume of water up from his shoulders as he went. It was imperative that I didn't let him get through the gap between the island and the reeds as, if I did, he would be in a different section of the lake and all sorts of things could go wrong then. I was reluctant to let him have any line at all so I threw the net out into the lake ahead of me and followed him out onto the shallows, with him thrashing around on a short line and me hanging on for all I was worth. The battle was mercifully short but incredibly frantic and, at one stage, he was upright on his head with three quarters of his body sticking out from the water!

If there had been anybody around to watch as he finally went into the net they would have run off and called the police, convinced there was an

*Black Jack Shellack*

escaped lunatic at large. I was soaking wet, standing out in the middle of the lake; laughing my head off and shouting into the net "You're not so bloody clever now, are you?"

The feelings of relief and joy at catching him after all that time were overwhelming, I felt like I was going to burst into flames!

Rather than wade back through the reeds with him in the net I took a short cut across the corner of the bay and ended up sinking down in some stinking thick black ooze, I sunk down until I was up to my armpits in the stuff and methane gas was bubbling out of the lake bed, smelling like a thousand rotten eggs but I didn't care a bit, I'd caught Black Jack!

On the mat he looked huge and I was genuinely amazed when he only weighed thirty three and a half pounds, it didn't matter of course what he weighed, he could have weighed ten pounds or fifty it made no difference to me, he was what he was, and I'd spent four years tying to catch the bugger.

It was hard to believe just how black he really was, I'd never seen a fish so dark before in my life, even his lips were jet black, he truly was an amazing beast. I called up Mickey on the phone, as I wanted some good photo's of this one for certain, I also called the small band of friends who would appreciate this capture for what it really was rather than just treat it as another thirty pound carp. Everybody was overjoyed for me, and I even sent a text to Keith who was on holiday in the middle of the Indian Ocean.

It was a massive turning point for me, catching that fish, and although the others were still in there (especially the considerably bigger Round Brown one) I felt that I'd achieved what I'd wanted, for one year at least.

I may return again and try and hunt down one of the other jewels that live there or I may let them swim in peace and be thankful for what I've already had, after all life is short and a challenge like that is immense, only time will tell I suppose.

For now, though, I have the picture of Jack and I in the water set up as my desk top wallpaper on my computer and I get to see him every time I sit down to write, so he is a constant source of inspiration and one of my favourite ever captures.

I did return for a session the next week, just to see if they were still in the bay, which they were, in fact there were even more of them this time but they had other things on their minds.

The temperatures had shot up since the previous week and with the water temperature finally reaching the required level, the fish started their once a year spawning ritual.

I knew that once they had finished they would be off into their own respective parts of the lakes and it was likely that they would not shoal up in any numbers again until the following spring.

Quietly, so as not to disturb them, I made my way back out through the reeds to the spot from where I had caught Black Jack, this time I was armed only with a camera. For about three hours I stayed and watched, taking a few good photos before setting off to look at another lake in the same valley, another unknown quantity and, who knows, maybe it would have its very own 'Black Jack'.

# Chapter 19

# Going Home

"*It was just turning light as I threw the gear over the fence; I'd briefly pulled up at the side of the road and pushed it all out of the back of the car and into the cover of the ditch, before parking up in the lay-by*".

It's always a twitchy moment when I have to load up the Mere with all the kit, no matter how well I plan it there has to be a brief period when I am blatantly on view from any passing cars. It's pretty hard to look nonchalant and innocent when you are standing next to a no fishing sign surrounded by a big heap of fishing tackle, an inflatable boat, water bottles, bait and a big pile of camouflage netting.

I struggled up the little path, across the grass, and into the trees three or four times, with various green bags, green bottles and green everything else until, finally safe in the undergrowth, I collapsed in the damp grass, sweating from head to toe under the Gortex suit and already cursing the place before I could even see the lake!

After stashing all the kit under a massive set of bushes I clambered over the big fallen tree and waded through the marsh until I picked up the old walkers path at the point where it just ended in the middle of nowhere, ever since the day the Mere had decided to reclaim itself by dropping a bloody great oak tree across the entrance to its domain.

Since then the path had disappeared under a spread of head high bulrushes and the marshland had extended back from the lake, turning the ground into peaty mush.

It amazes me really how the people who claim to look after the Mere can kick up such a fuss about the odd angler fishing there at all. Basically, if it wasn't for us, the entire place would have become an impenetrable jungle years ago and it's only the odd camo clad fisherman that ever gets to even see the Mere for what it really is anyway!

Stepping back onto the banks again was like going back in time, the place seems to be held in an eternal loop, as if it just repeats itself constantly from the moment I leave and picks up the script once more as I duck under the first familiar branch and draw blood on the first of many thorns.

I made my way along the footpath side, peering in to the crystal depths whenever I could get close enough to the edge, the lake was in terrific condition and not the slightest stain of algae tinted the water.

After a few hundred yards I started to notice signs of recent angler presence, little paths into gaps, where trees had shiny surfaces worn onto the lower boughs from the regular attention of heavy boots. On the lakebed beneath some of these trees were spotless and shiny little cleared areas, the like of which I hadn't seen before at the Mere.

The fish had always cleaned off their feeding spots but these were different, polished and shined in a way that only the attention of hungry, smaller fish like Tench and smaller carp could achieve.

Obviously, the extra fish that the lake had received in the floods were changing the game plan somewhat and creating actual feeding areas, further evidence that I should have continued my efforts the previous two years after I'd caught the thirty-pound common and then the twenty eight the following year.

I still felt like a fool for walking away from a potential situation like that, even though I had caught those wonderful fish from Dinton and St Ives as a result, I knew I'd potentially missed out on a chance of something special.

The new carp in the Mere were mainly commons around the low twenty mark, not 'stockies' as such as they'd made their own way into the lake, more like 'Tourists' really, I suppose.

The one thing they had done is feed well and helped to create more obvious spots. I should have capitalised on this a lot more and used them to get at the bigger fish, but you learn by your mistakes and at least I was now back for another crack at it.

I was determined this time, though. I'd caught 'Black Jack' and, in doing so, closed all the accounts that I'd held open, and now there was just this one left to deal with, the ultimate goal, I was completely resolute, this time it was shit or bust!

Moving up to the Reedy point, I shinned up a familiar spindly willow and looked down at the spot where I'd had old 'twisted mouth' the previous year, it certainly looked well visited but there were no sightings down there for me on this occasion. Looking out across the lake I could see weed everywhere, the top most tendrils peppering the surface all through the middle section of the lake.

Stretching across from the little bar below me to the margins of the 'Rat Hole' on the opposite bank and tapering away to the left as far as the 'Beach' at the other end, was a carpet of thick weed. Viewed from this angle, and with the light reflecting from its stems, I could see at a glance that the lake was probably as choked as I'd ever seen it before, obviously the water had been clear all spring and the penetrating sunlight had done a good job of cultivating the weed to its thickest level for years.

From the corner of my eye I spied movement on the far bank as a carp rolled on the surface near to the 'Long Run' and, as I watched, I saw it crease the surface once again.

That was good enough for a starting point, I knew the area well and, as long as the path was manageable, I could walk around there with a rod and have a little 'pull about'.

I loaded up with the rods and rucksack and made my way around to the far side, stopping off for a look in all the old spots along the way.

Somebody had obviously been putting in a bit of time this year, keeping the brambles trimmed back and the nettles trodden down, so as to make the actual task of manoeuvring around the lake a viable option.

Don't get me wrong here, it was hardly a straightforward stroll about in the sunshine but, compared to the jungle warfare of previous years, it made a pleasant change and before long I was in position and looking out at a couple of dorsal fins creasing the surface in the weed.

I say 'in position' but there was no way that I could actually fish from this spot as, apart from being totally exposed from the other bank, I was also ten feet above the water and separated from the edge by a wall of bramble and bank side bushes that extended like a tall hedge in either direction. I couldn't actually see the margins as a result but, luckily, this meant that nobody else could see the two totally hidden swims that I knew existed below the bramble hedge, dug into the bank beneath me. Both of these 'Rat Holes' were actually hollowed out behind trees that grew from the bank and hung out over the lake, the perfect camouflage really.

The wall of bramble behind them meant that they were only accessible

by boat and, in one of them, an old bivvy had been left to actually 'grow' into the surroundings and was now totally integrated into the undergrowth, hidden from view from all sides!

I decided that I'd start my new campaign by picking a couple of spots in this area and baiting them heavily.

As casting from the Rat Holes was almost impossible, I decided to have a cast about from where I was, looking for clear spots that I could mark up with anchored corks for the coming weeks.

Most of the area was solid weed but I had a bit of prior knowledge on my side and, on the fourth cast, I landed the lead down with a nice thump on the bottom. I clipped up the rod as a marker (it had an old rig on the end with a bit of plastic corn on the hook at the time) the plan was to swap the rig for a float, cast to the clip and mark up the area. Then, having boated all my gear into the swim, I could row out with a cork and mark it up properly before rowing back to shore and retrieving the marker rod.

Obviously, then I'd have to get back into the swim, bait up and repeat the whole process for the next rod, before stashing the boat and setting up my gear in a space the size of a small cupboard!

All in all, I expected the whole task of setting up to take about four or five hours, and involve plenty of accidental soakings, tangles, splinters and definitely a plethora of bites and stings.

What I wasn't expecting was what happened next.

I lifted the rod tip and felt the lead slide off the clear section of bottom and then, suddenly and violently, the tip was wrenched back down towards the surface of the lake, as a pike shot out from the weed and grabbed the plastic corn.

Normally this wouldn't be too much of a drama but I was ten feet above, and six feet back, from the lake with absolutely no way whatsoever of getting anywhere near the margins to unhook him.

I couldn't walk left or right as it was a jungle in both directions, the margins were ten feet deep and I couldn't even see them due to the position I was in, now I was really up against it.

I tried leaving him on a slack line, to shake the hook, but it wasn't happening so the only option left available was to swing him in!

I suppose the pike probably weighed somewhere in the region of five pounds, which was about two pounds more than the test curve of the rod and a hell of a weight to try and lift ten feet straight up in the air, but I had no other choice but to try. Luckily, I had decided to bring my new rods with me this year as the old camo things I had used in the past would have just exploded. Somehow, with the butt creaking and groaning, I managed to lift him up into the air, swinging him pendulum like slowly towards me. The next thing I knew I was on my arse in the brambles, the rod and rig were all tangled up in the trees behind me and I had stars twittering around my head.

It turned out that the hook had straightened under the immense strain and a thrashing noise in the bushes below me gave away the location of one very surprised pike! I couldn't see him, but he sounded like he was a fair way into the thicket and getting lower with each frantic rustle so, I grabbed the top of the branches and shook the hedge as hard as I could, which seemed to do the trick as a loud 'plop' signalled his sudden return to the lake, the poor bugger.

An hour or so later, as I boated my gear into the swim, I passed the spot where he had gone back in, and there he was, laying in the margins looking very confused, a bit dishevelled, but very much alive and, as soon as he set eyes on me again he shot off into the depths like a torpedo, which I can understand really.

There was a bivvy already set up in the Rat hole and had been for some years, it was totally encased in brambles and I had to pull the inflatable up to it really carefully in case of a puncture. The front was concealed behind a curtain of prickly fronds that hung down into the water like a curtain.

By the state of it I guessed that it probably hadn't been occupied at all in at least a year or more. I tied the boat up under the tree and climbed overboard into the lake, making sure I was high enough up the slope to actually touch bottom, before I waded gingerly up to the entrance.

Behind the brambles I pulled aside the army netting, that was full of spider's webs and half eaten mosquitoes, then tentatively unzipped the door praying that there wouldn't be a half decomposed angler festering inside.

What was inside, though, looked like a national abseiling convention as about fifty spiders all fell from the bivvy roof on gossamer threads and scurried away from the light that I'd allowed in for the first time in months.

On the floor were five enormous bumble bees, perfect in every detail, apart from the fact that they were dead of course, and an army of ants seemed to be patrolling the entrance from the outside, reluctant to cross the threshold-maybe they knew something that I didn't?

Oh well, it was home of a sort, and a good spring clean would soon have the place habitable once again, although there was a bloody great hole in the roof that would need sorting out.

The worst things about fishing like this, apart from not being in a position to see much of the lake, or any real daylight, and the fact that you can't stand upright without first putting on waders and getting into the lake, and of course the heat and the insects, apart from all that- the worse thing is the weeing into a plastic bottle!

As there is no ground, apart from the bit under the tiny kids size bivvy, and the water comes right up to the door, the two alternatives are to either wee in the lake right in front of your door and risk choking on ammonia fumes by the end of the session, or cut a water bottle in half, wee in that and then wade along the edge as far as possible and empty it into the bushes, nice eh?

By dusk on the first day I had found two half decent spots to fish, marked them up with corks attached to four pound line, baited up and dropped the rigs. I'd even managed to fix the roof and de-bug the bivvy, although the ants were proving a bit more troublesome. Every time I swept them all away and flooded the holes, they'd just re-route and appear somewhere else but, all in all, the place looked a bit more acceptable.

However, after three sessions totalling five nights I had, unsurprisingly, had more than I could handle of living life like a mole.

I was beginning to fear for my sanity a bit, as well, as I sat it out in that little Hell Hole, chatting away to any ant that would listen.

I'd had no action on the rods whatsoever, and I'd seen no real signs of

anymore fish in the area either so, on the final afternoon of that third week, I came to a decision; I was going to fish it my way. Sod the consequences, I was going to travel light, move about, and fish for the carp wherever I found them and, further more, I was going to start straight away.

The 'rat hole' could serve as a base and a tackle stash, although I would keep the bait going in just in case the fish turned up there later in the year, as they often did.

I moved the rods, net and all the bits needed for stalking into a more accessible part of the lake, and one that I wouldn't need the boat to reach, I then set about baiting a few margin areas and working out various ambush spots and hidey holes, plan two was coming into operation.

I knew I'd made the right decision straight away as, before that afternoon was even up, I'd found a nice mirror skulking about under a tree in the reedy corner, I'd even watched him feed for a bit on the marginal shelf, albeit in a very strange and 'twitchy' way.

In fact, I would have had a go for him but a pike came in to the swim and spooked him off as I tried to get a closer look, I could have sworn it was that bugger I'd tried to swing over the bushes, oh well, we were sort of even now I suppose.

I couldn't wait to get down to the lake on my next session and all the lethargy of looking forward to two days in a cave had gone. I was confident again, even more so when I arrived to find the same 'Twitchy mirror' was still under the same spindly little tree.

I suppose he was about thirty pounds and I didn't recognise him at all from previous seasons, he definitely wasn't one of the original crew, but he was a lovely looking fish all the same and well worth fishing for.

He seemed to be quite happy under the tree, feeding confidently for a few minutes at a time before setting off on little circuits of the area and then returning to his meal. I crept back down the tree and went off in search of some tackle.

The rods were easy, as I'd marked the route to their hidey hole with some carefully placed twigs, but it took me ages to find the other bits, the bushes were so thick and they all looked the same after a while but, eventually, I had all I needed to fish with.

Shinning up the tree for another look, I saw that another fish had joined him; a bigger darker shape was moving about further down the slope, I could see a white mark near his tail where a loose scale showed the skin beneath. As the bigger fish glided in beside the twitchy mirror I could see him clearly, one of the Mere's original commons, almost black in colour and easily thirty five or thirty six pounds in weight, an absolute corker.

I hardly dared breathe, as I know how in tune these fish are with everything in their world and just one sight or sound of me and he'd be gone.

I watched him for a while and then crept back down to get the rod. Pushing the tip silently through the branches, I tried to get a bait into position but it was futile in the given situation and, as one clumsy movement caught their eye, they both just melted away.

I wasn't overly disheartened, though, as they obviously liked it under the tree so, while they were gone, I quickly waded a bait into position and then located another classic looking gravel patch at the bottom of the marginal drop off, for the other rod.

A small hump rose from the bottom a bit further out in the swim, I could see shiny stones on the very apex of it, where the fish had stripped back the silkweed that covered the gravel. This was actually the very spot I'd caught the twisted mouth common from the previous year and an ideal spot for the third rod. I had to fish all the lines very slack, though, as three lines made it a bit busy in such a small area.

A large tree branch that had half fallen in the last big winds had cut off the normal swim that this area would be fished from. It stuck out over the water, just a few feet above the surface, and really needed removing so I could get the rods at a better angle, but there was no way of chopping it down without it falling into the lake and spooking anything in the area.

With the rods in their new position, just under the marginal bushes, I made a clearing in the undergrowth for myself, just out of sight of the lake and the path; I set up a hanging mosquito net by tying it off to the trees and bushes.

I put the bed chair underneath the net and threw a handful of branches and leaves over the top making the perfect little open-air shelter in which to sit and wait for the return of the fish, as long as it didn't rain of course.

In this sort of situation it's almost impossible not to keep climbing the tree and checking to see if the fish have returned, I literally had to sit on my hands and force myself not to look. I suppose during the next four or five hours leading up to nightfall, I only relented and climbed up the willow about twenty times but there was still no sign of them.

The corner I was fishing was near to some overhanging trees and a couple of snags and, as such, it would need an instant reaction if I got a bite. I had already worked out that I'd have to jump straight in the margins and hold the fish away from the trees, and then wade along the edge in order to be able to lift the rod up straight because of the overhead branches. My waders were set up next to the bed, in a way that I could step straight into them in the night, any pointy sticks at eye level were removed from the trees and, eventually, I settled into bed, trying to ignore the many weird nocturnal sounds that surrounded me. There really are plenty of screechy, snuffley, and always unseen beasties crawling around that place after dark but at least I was safely protected by a piece of green net curtain draped over me!

The next thing I remember I was thrashing to get through the net, the sounder box by my bed was howling a shrill single note that only panicked me more and how I managed to get the boots on so quickly I'll never know. A run at the Mere is an exciting but, somehow, terrifying experience, they are so rare and the possibilities so incredible, that they always frighten me senseless.

With my heart pounding I leapt the few yards through the dark trees, trusting my future eye sight to the meticulous pruning of the previous evening, and jumped straight into the lake-landing neatly beside the rods.

The fish had picked up the rod on the hump and made off into open water, it was going at an alarming rate of knots and nothing I could do seemed to be able to stop it. The rod twisted and bucked in my hand, I could feel every surge from its powerful tail and then, with a sickening finality that defied belief, the rod sprang straight as the line parted like cotton. Eighteen pound breaking strain line flapping in the breeze, hopelessly ineffective against the fury and outrage of a hooked Mere carp!

I sat on the bank trembling, I wanted to cry, it's unforgivable to lose them in the Mere, and they come at such a price that to lose one is criminal, I was truly gutted.

After two cups of tea, and with dawn creeping up over the distant horizon, I forced myself to recover the rod from the bushes, where I'd hurled it in temper, and slowly and carefully I retackled it for a future battle , although god knows when that might come.

As the light increased to the first blue black of a new day I climbed the tree to look out over the hump and see if it was light enough for a cast.  I could only just make out the differing shades of the bottom in the gloom but, as I checked below my feet on the margin spot, I saw a movement down there on the gravel. It was a real strain to see anything in the gloom but, as I looked, I could just make out the outline of a fish at the bottom of the spot, slowly working his way toward my bait.

Sure enough, the twitchy mirror came ponderously into view and I suddenly realised that there was a massive chance that I was just about to hook him.  I decided to stay up the tree until the last second, as to climb down then would probably spook him anyway.

As he got closer I could make out the outline of his gills as they rose and fell and, even in the half-light, I could clearly see the flash of colour as his top lip extended as he sucked at the stones and sand of the clear spot.

With only a foot to go before he reached the hookbait, I turned to pick my footing for a stealthy decent when the alarm burst into life, the other alarm!

Something had crept in at the bottom of the shelf, while I'd been concentrating on twitchy, and taken the other bait, unfortunately, due to the proximity of the overhanging branches, there was nothing else for it but to leap out of the tree into the lake and grab the rod as quickly as possible.

The only bad thing about this, apart from the inevitable soaking, was that I'd have to land right next to the twitchy mirror, which was still feeding confidently, and continued to do, right up until the moment that I smashed through surface of the water and frightened the life out of him. If he was twitchy before that, then he was a nervous bloody wreck afterwards, in fact that was the last time I ever saw him on that spot!

I was determined not to lose this one on the end though, as a second chance was a rarity beyond belief and I hung on for dear life. Just like the first fish he made away from the branches and out into open water, just like the first fish, he also stripped line from the tight clutch and then, just like the first fish, he was gone!

Once again the eighteen pound line was left fluttering from the rod, cut clean on an unseen obstacle in the same area as before. I was furious, hurling the rod as far as I could into the bushes I stormed away from the lake and stomped up and down the path, swearing and cursing at everything and anything.

After a while I calmed down a bit, not much but enough to go back to the swim and think about what to do next. Obviously I'd lost all confidence in the line I was using at this stage so I wound in the remaining rods and went for a walk in the woods to find the hidden inflatable dingy. It was a bit of a risk boating over to the rat hole in broad daylight but I just had to change the line on my reels and I knew that, had another reel over there, one that was loaded up with enough new fifteen pound line to split between all three rods.

Ignoring the risk of capture, I pumped up the boat and pushed off from the margins, keeping well clear of my actual swim, although I strongly suspected that I'd already ruined that by losing two fish and jumping on another!

Even rowing as fast as was humanly possible across the three hundred yards of water seemed to take forever, especially as I was trying to make myself inconspicuous by keeping my head down and not looking around me, like a kid who thinks he can't be seen if he's got his eyes closed.

Rowing into the wind didn't help matters, it had been strengthening all morning and dark clouds were starting to pile up on the horizon, spreading slowly over the sky like a blanket but, luckily, I also had a brolly stashed in the rat hole.

I didn't fancy another night under the mosquito net if it was going to chuck it down. I was miserable enough as it was, having lost two fish and thrown myself in the lake twice, not to mention now being totally soaked, once again, from the leaking floor of the boat; to sleep out in the rain as well would have been the last straw.

Getting the brolly out proved trickier than I thought and I managed to rip a big gash in my hand on the brambles that had entwined themselves throughout the swim, but that was becoming so common place at the Mere that I couldn't even be bothered to swear. I just washed it in the lake, gathered up my new supplies and pushed the boat (that now resembled a paddling pool) out into the lake, striking out with the oar for the far bank and a much needed cup of tea.

After tea and the re-spooling of all three reels, I decided to pop out to the shops for some supplies as I hadn't eaten all day, and I really fancied a drop of wine as well. Also, I just wanted to get out in the open for a while and try and stop fretting about the two lost carp, although, as it turned out, the trip only made things worse.

On the way back in, after polishing off a whole pizza on the drive back from the local take away, I paused at the entrance to the lake, near to the Beach Swim, and I saw a fish behaving very strangely on the surface in a small hole in the weed. Before I'd even got up the tree to investigate further I'd pretty much figured it out but, from up the tree, it was all made even clearer.

The fish was the big black common that I'd seen in my swim the previous day, I could clearly see the white mark near his tail, and he was pushing his head into the weed and then charging across the hole to repeat the motion in the weed on the other side. I couldn't see any sign of a rig, so I suppose he had already shed the hook and was just rubbing his face to

make sure he was rid of every last aspect of his strange ordeal, he looked really annoyed about the whole thing, and, to be honest so was I.

With the rods re-cast and a new camp dug deeper into the bushes, I sat back on the bed and opened a nice bottle of red wine and, when I thought about everything that I'd been through that day, I reckoned I bloody well deserved it.

Half a bottle later and just as the first drizzle started to pitter-patter through the canopy above and fall rhythmically onto the brolly roof, I drifted off into a deep sleep.

Something in the bushes by the path woke me from my slumbers around four in the morning, probably the foxes as they seem to love feasting on the hoards of blackberries at the Mere, leaving a trail of little black turds everywhere, just so as you know that they've been. At times, the entire lake can just stink of over-ripe fruit and your trousers get stained purple as you try and push through the berry-laden branches of the bramble bushes. It can be quite handy if you're thirsty, and miles from a drink, as they start out to be quite refreshing, but they do tend to get a bit sickly after a while, and just the thought of the smell of them tends to turn my stomach a bit nowadays.

By five o'clock in the morning I was back up the spindly tree hoping and praying that there may be at least one fish that hadn't heard all the commotion of the previous days disasters when, low and behold, there was! Looking down onto 'Twitchy's spot' I saw the familiar outline of a carp starting his way up the slope from the gloomy depths, I really hadn't expected to see him back again but I had a bait already in position, just in case. Of course, I couldn't be sure that it was definitely him as there was next to no light this early in the morning, but it was his spot so I figured that it probably was.

I clambered down as quietly as possible and decided on a cup of tea while I waited, but I never even made it as far as the kettle before two beeps on the alarm signalled his mistake, and I jumped in again and bent into him before he could get up any steam. No way was this one getting away and I heaved the rod round giving him no quarter whatsoever, he boiled angrily under the tree before I forced him around in front of me into the clear margin where he rolled on the surface and, somehow, turned from the expected twitchy mirror into a long and angry looking common of about twenty three pounds!

I was just glad to actually land him really, and gain a bit of confidence back again, and as for him not being the 'Twitchy Mirror' well, it's not surprising really as I doubt he'll ever swim under that tree again!

The fish still refused to spook from the swim, even though I'd already hooked three of them, and I saw two more commons drift in from the weed-beds during the morning. They milled about near the gravel spots for a while and then sank from view so it came as no real surprise when the rod at the bottom of the shelf burst into life and another twenty-three pound common graced my net.

This was totally unbelievable fishing for the Mere, even taking into account that the two fish landed were tourists, to have four runs of any description in two days angling was unheard of. I baited up the spots heavily before I left and vowed to remove the big branch before the next session, so I wouldn't have to keep jumping in the margins every time anything occurred.

My next session started at 10.30 in the evening on a Sunday, I wanted to get rid of that branch before setting up and that meant a bit of after dark pruning so I stayed at home until late, feasting in the garden on roast chicken and salad with the family.

It was a bit strange watching other people drinking wine but not joining in, I was nearly tempted a few times but I really wanted to be rid of that branch, I could see that lost black common in my minds eye and I dearly wanted to redress the balance.

Turning up at the lake at that time should have meant that there was nobody about but unfortunately that wasn't the case. The lake next door had been holding a water skiing regatta and there were people everywhere, three cars drove out of the gate right past me as I tried to unload the car at the roadside and, in the end, I had to lift the bonnet and pretend I'd broken down.

It was hilarious, really, as I tinkered with the engine until the next car passed and then quickly vaulted the gate with the saw or a bag of bait or food, until all my items were safely stashed, before parking up the car in the lay-by up the road.

It took about an hour just to get everything from the car to the swim and, under the Gortex clothing, I was soaked to the skin with sweat by the time I arrived.

Peering through the bushes at the clubhouse on the ski lake I could see that there were still revellers milling about on the lawn, drinking and chatting and I could even hear snippets of conversation as they drifted across the calm water. It was going to be next to impossible to saw through a bloody great tree limb without being heard as it was one of those still nights where even the slightest of noises carries for miles.

Being right on the flight path, I decided to wait for a plane to fly over, and then saw like a madman under the cover of engine noise as it passed, and keep repeating that until the bough broke.

If I was hot beforehand, then I was almost melting as I sat there, straddled around the branch, hanging in space above the lake with my arm going back and forth like a fiddlers elbow as the jumbo jets roared overhead. Just as it became obvious that I'd be there all bloody night at such a slow rate, my prayers were answered as somebody put the first match to a massive firework display in the village. That was more like it, the noise was far louder than the sawing and I hurtled through the dry timber in no time at all, unfortunately the end of the limb had to fall into the lake but it didn't make too much of a splash really.

By about half past midnight I had finally managed to drag the twenty foot limb from the lake and paddle across the lake, in the moonlight, to collect the gear from its hiding place on the far bank, wondering all the time about my own sanity and, whether all this effort would ever actually be rewarded in full. After all, I hadn't seen the 'Black Mirror' for a while now and he'd certainly not visited the corner swim so far. I started to wonder if he ever would, especially with the commotion caused by catching the tourists, he wasn't going to just blunder into an obvious trap and give himself up, was he?

The more I though about it, as I set up all the gear in the swim, the more I began to doubt what I was doing, particularly as all but one fish I'd seen in that area had been new ones.

By midday the next day I had seen no fish at all and, in the back of my mind, I'd already convinced myself that this wasn't the area that I'd catch the Black Mirror from anyway, so it was back in the boat and risk another look about for signs of feeding activity or cleared areas elsewhere in the lake.

The sun was beating down on the surface of the lake and the glare was hard to deal with, even with a cap and dark polarized glasses I was struggling to see very far into the water. I spent an hour or so looking about in the weed and on the shallows but I couldn't see any fish, or any inspiration, so I packed up all the gear and rowed it into the rat hole to stash it away before drifting up to the canopy tree for a look about at that end instead.

Half way along the west bank, just as I came level with the snaggy point, I thought I saw a movement, a shadow just below the surface and I flicked the oar once more to send me cruising into the area. Just in time, I saw them there, laying just below the surface only a few yards from seeing me as I drifted ever closer. Slowly and quietly I pushed the oar into the surface, acting as a brake and, somehow, I managed to will the boat out of the area without making a ripple.

I had seen at least four fish lying in the sun above the exposed gravel on top of the shallow bar and I wanted to dock the boat as far away as possible and silently creep along the bank for a closer look.

I was determined not to spook them this time, crawling the last few yards to the tree as quietly as I knew how. Eventually, I pulled myself up into the branches of the viewing tree above the bar and they were still there, totally unaware of my presence.

There were five fish visible at first glance and only three of them were tourists, one mirror of about twenty pounds and two commons a little bit bigger. The other two looked huge by comparison, both were commons and the smaller of the two was the black common with the lifted scale that I'd lost the previous week. The exciting thing was just 'how much' smaller he was, as the other one was bloody massive!

I had no idea what to do next as my tackle was all stashed away two hundred yards further up the lake and, like a prat, I'd put it in a boat-only swim, and the last thing I wanted to do now was start splashing about in the lake again. As I stood there at the top of the tree pondering the situation in my head, I saw another two fish moving in from further up the lake to my left and I could tell, even from thirty yards away, that the one on the left was the ultimate prize; the Black Mirror was on his way.

As he passed beneath me over the clear yellow sand on the bar he looked truly awe-inspiring, massive beyond belief, and I suddenly felt incredibly unprepared and insignificant. My first gut reaction was that if I were ever lucky enough to hook such an outstanding creature as this, then I'd never land him in a million years. He was colossal and every square inch of him looked muscular and dynamic, without a trace of body fat anywhere, I just shook my head slowly in disbelief, humbled by the inconceivable notion that I could actually beat him in a fair fight.

If somebody had told me at that point that he weighed sixty-five pounds, then I would have believed them without question as I watched him drift through the shallow water, casting a ridiculously long shadow over the polished stones beneath him as he went.

All thoughts of going home were abandoned as I tried to silently paddle the little boat out into the middle of the lake in order to give the area the widest berth possible. Had there been any other way to get my gear without going afloat, then I'd have taken it, regardless of the brambles. Unfortunately, short of hacking a path through thirty yards of thicket into the back of the hidden swim with my bare hands, I could see no other option.

Just as I thought I was clear of the swim I risked a peek over the side and there, not ten yards away and staring straight at me, was the small mirror. He just watched for a moment, deliberating his next move and then spooked back towards the swim to tell the others, hopefully the rest of the pack wouldn't take him too seriously.

Half an hour later I arrived back in the swim, having parked the boat and walked half the way to avoid any further disturbance, but I could tell at a single glance the damage had already been done.

That little mirror must have been more convincing than I thought as there was not a single fish to be seen anywhere, another perfectly good chance blown by the sheer nature of the lake. I stayed the night, as you would have to do in the given circumstances, but the only other fish I saw was at dawn the next day when a small common decided to play at being a dolphin for an hour or so, just a few yards out from my rod tips.

I was still very encouraged by what I'd seen and I drove home full of plans for my next session. Which, as it happened, would not be for two weeks, as the annual kids fish-in over at Oxford was planned for the following Monday, Tuesday and Wednesday.

All my life I have driven around in a succession of battered up old heaps of metal, that very loosely could be termed as cars or vans but, realistically, are more liable to be listed under the general heading of 'Scrap'.

Now, after years of tying bits back on with string, using screwdrivers to turn the ignition, and always parking on a downwards slope, I had invested in a decent motor and what happened, I smashed the bloody thing up, that's what!

On the way to the kids fish-in I had been over for a look at a private Estate Lake in Oxford, one that I'd gained permission for the odd visit to.

I'd been following Dave, who had shown me the way there and given me a quick, guided tour, of the place. On the way back we came to a busy junction, where we had to pull out onto a fast stretch of road, and I ended up following just a little too closely. He pulled out into a gap in the traffic and I, still looking out the side window into the flow, floored the accelerator to follow him. Unbeknown to me, he'd changed his mind at the last minute and stopped, as I found out by smashing straight into the back of him! The result was me turning up at the kids do with a completely mangled up motor. The bonnet, wings, bumper, light and grill were totally destroyed and Dave's little Vauxhall Corsa wasn't exactly looking too happy either. Luckily, I know a man who can fix these things and the resulting mess was sorted out for the bargain price of £1,000!

I don't know which was worse, coughing up a big wad of hard earned readies, or not being able to return to the Mere for another week while it was fixed.

By the time I got back, the fish had left the snags area and I eventually found them again right up at the far end where the lake narrows down to a point. It's here that the weed gathers throughout the autumn to create a great big raft where the fish can hide in safety for days, and sometimes weeks, on end.

I saw one of the better commons lying tight to a snag tree, surrounded by floating weed and, from the vantage point of an overhanging branch, I watched as it was joined by three more fish. Two of the group were commons, both original fish and well over thirty pounds each, another fish was a small mirror of low twenties and the final one was my old mate, the twitchy mirror.

It was good to see that he hadn't died of a heart attack after our last meeting and he actually looked quite relaxed for a change as he drifted in and out of the raft.

I spent a few hours looking about and eventually, deep down on the bottom near the tree line that leads into the corner, I glimpsed the unmistakable form of the Black Mirror himself. I could clearly see the top tail lobe, with the tell tale scoop out of it's profile as he lay there motionless on the bottom, gills slowly pumping as he contemplated the meaning of life.

Within minutes my own gills were pumping as well, only not so slowly, as I raced off to uncover the gear and drag it right around the lake to the far side where I could cast back over towards the trees.

It was a bugger of a place to fish to, as the weed was really thick and the spots were tiny. I could have flicked the baits out from the path side but I'd be right on top of the fish and right out in the open if anyone came along. Also, there was no real way of getting a rod down to the water without hacking a big hole in the undergrowth so I opted for the other side of the bay and a forty-yard lob.

It took the standard half a day to get everything into position, rods out, bivvy hidden and the boat stashed nearby just in case. I had wanted to just try and stalk the fish to start with but it wasn't really a viable option and I knew that, by now, the carp would know I was there and trying to catch them. I was encouraged to see a couple of fish still around as I crouched down by the rods, constructing a 'natural' hide to conceal the shiny carbon from view from the opposite bank. The only position for the rods was totally out in the open (which is a rarity in itself at the Mere) and I needed to hide them, well but still be able to leap on them if I had a take.

After a bit of thought I came up with a perfect plan. I took my coat, unhooking mat and a small piece of groundsheet material and taped my

spare landing net handle all along one side of them, forming a great big green flag. I laid this over the entire set up and then covered it with nettles and old bits of bush and long grasses until the whole lot was indistinguishable from the surroundings. I left just the grip at the end of the landing net visible and, by lifting it up and across, I could uncover all three rods in one swift movement. By the time I had finished it was about ten in the evening and I celebrated my achievements with a cup of tea and a jumbo sized pack of Cheese Doritos, which I ate in my little secluded camp in the bushes.

As hard as I try, I can't ever remember a night as hot or oppressive as the one that followed, sleep was not really an option and the mosquitoes were lethal and extremely determined.

It was far too hot to cover up with anything but mosquito mesh and most of that was being used to keep the gear hidden from view. By two in the morning my eyes were stinging from the sweat dripping into them and the insects were attacking me from all angles so, eventually, I dug out a clean carp sack and wrapped my head in it before drifting off into a troubled doze on top of the sleeping bag.

Sometimes I'd love to be sitting outside my own bivvy, as a casual observer, when the alarm bursts into action and the pantomime begins!

To see myself blindly staggering around with a black nylon turban wrapped around my face and head must have been worth its weight in gold, not only did I have to first free myself from the blindfold but then I had to identify the correct piece of undergrowth to rip up in order to find the rods, somehow I succeeded and I was soon bent into a lively, but obviously not very large, carp.

Once again my carefully laid trap had been sprung by an invader and another twenty something common splashed its way to the net, letting the Black Mirror know that it was time to move on again as it did so.

I wasn't overly bothered, really, as I would have struggled to stay hidden for long in the thin bushes so near to the path, although, if the right fish would have picked up the bait, I could have been packing up for the very last time.

It seemed that I was doomed to be pestered to death by these new tourists, and it was a bit of a job to see a way around it. They were so well integrated into the Mere carp community that it was odds on one of them would be first to pick up the bait every time.

Unless I could actually stalk the Black Mirror visually, it was going to be a mission impossible to single him out from the pack.

The one good thing that did come out that day, however, occurred on the way home. I had decided to find a new stash spot for the gear and, as I was not far from the canopy tree swim, I thought I'd start by having a look around that area first.

In the back of the boat I always have the glass-bottomed bucket and, usually, a couple of cork markers already tied up, just in case. I had learnt from my old days on Wraysbury that you always tend to find the best spots when you have nothing to mark them with and, inevitably, by the time you have rowed to shore and sorted out a marker, then you can't find the bloody spot again.

As I drifted into the area I knew that it was one of those special days when the visibility is at its absolute best, they are rare days indeed but, every so often, the water in a lake will clear completely for a short period and everything becomes, quite literally, crystal clear.

I could almost see the bottom in sixteen feet of water without the aid of the bucket but, through the glass, I could see every leaf, stone and stem of weed as if I were looking through the side of a fish tank.

I was fascinated, as I'd never, in seven years, seen the bottom of the very deepest parts of the lake before and it was obvious straight away that the fish had, and quite recently at that!

There were small scuffed up areas where the stones were exposed and polished, totally impossible to cast to and probably not regular areas but still evidence of a single visit from a hungry carp, determined to unearth a crop of bloodworm or caddis.

I marked up the biggest of these, as I knew it would soon be lost forever when the water coloured up once more. I could see all the ridges in the bottom and variations in depth that I knew so well from a marker float but now, for the first time, I was seeing them for real, weed-beds clung to the contours and, over towards the swim, just at the edge of vision, I could make out a diffused yellow glow from a much larger area of cleared bottom.

I paddled over with my head still under the water in the bucket the whole way, transfixed by the sheer volume of information I was receiving with every passing yard.

As I reached the yellow area I knew I'd struck gold, it was a definite feeding area and within half an hour I'd found another one to match.

The first was a long trough that ran from a small gravel hump and curled away towards some over hanging trees just along from the canopy swim. The second was very exciting, situated only ten yards from the bottom bank, a large hump had been stripped clean down one side while the other side lay untouched and coated in silkweed and wisps of milfoil.

By the white colouration of the stones, and the lack of settled silt on top of them, I could tell straight away that this area had been recently visited, as I only had two cork markers in the boat with me and I wanted to earmark three spots, I left this last hump un-marked, it would be the easiest to find again anyway, due to the fact that it was only ten yards out from the bottom bank and right in front of a large overhanging tree.

My plan was to keep this area baited up but not to actually fish it until the right weather conditions came along, conditions that would guarantee the presence of those majestic monsters of the Mere.

Being at the extreme Southerly end of the lake, the Canopy tree swim would only be affected by a Northerly wind, the one wind that had been noticeable by its absence the entire summer. The previous year there had been North winds aplenty but the summer of 2004 had been dominated by Southerlies and I decided to bide my time and just keep the bait going in.

I'd chosen to use a blend of pellets and boilies, mainly because I had four dustbins full of mixed Mainline pellets in my garage that needed using up, and it was easier to leave pellets in the car in air tight buckets, and even to stash them at the lake until I needed them.

As often as I could, I made the trip up the hideous M25 to bait up, using the leaky old inflatable.

The Mere had really taken its toll on my regular old boat by now and I'd started trying to resurrect my old Butlins Boat at home, although the mouse hole in the side was, a problem and all the camo paint wasn't helping the patch to stick down either.

In the end, I resorted to four coats of marine glue onto two home made patches, one inside and one outside the hole. I then got a couple of bits of plywood to sandwich the repaired section and clamped the whole lot down with a massive pair of G-clamps that I'd nicked off a building site, way back in my old steel fixing days.

Looking back on it all now, I must have been soft in the head to entrust my life to any of those pathetic little dinghies and I certainly wouldn't do it again. Too many anglers have perished over the years by pushing the limits, purely in an attempt to catch a fish, and it's such a waste of life.

At the time, though, I was obsessed and as long as the patch stayed in place when the clamps came off then that would be good enough for me!

The plan of action for baiting was simple; I would mix up a great big green nylon bag full of the four different pellets and two sizes of boilies and slide this into a big rucksack. After driving thirty five miles down the M25 I'd pull over at the side of the road, near the entrance, and casually jettison the rucksack out into the bushes, and then I'd carry on and park in the lay-by.

Trying to look inconspicuous in my full camo outfit, I'd walk back along the road, wait for a break in the pre-dawn commuter traffic and leap into the bushes alongside the rucksack.

When I was sure I wasn't being watched, I'd load up and lug it off through the bushes to the lake.

I had an old pair of waders wrapped in a bin bag and stashed in the crook of a tree on the lake next door, where nobody ever walked, so I'd change into these and wade along the brambly margins of the Mere until I reached the hidden platform that served as a boat park.

It was always a total nightmare to pump up the boat on the platform, as there wasn't room for it on the tiny piece of timber decking, so I had to float it in the water while I sat on the boards and pumped the little pump by hand, like one of those toy monkeys on the side of a wind up music box.

By the time the boat was inflated it was inevitably full of water and need emptying in a space barely big enough to turn it over in, it was futile anyway as the floor leaked and I always got soaked to the skin no matter how hard I tried to avoid it.

The inner sleeve of bait was then lifted out of the rucksack and placed in the front, where it immediately started soaking up some of the surplus water.

By the time I reached the first cork the contents of the bag were like lumpy porridge and I just scooped about ten kilos of slop over the side before hastily paddling over to the second mark. If I took too long, or it was too windy, I'd have to beat a hasty retreat to shore for a half time break to decant about eight inches of soup from the bottom of the boat.

Luckily, the actual tubes that kept me afloat were quite sound and I always ensured that I put my lifejacket on under my coat, no matter how sodden it had become since my previous visit.

With the two corks and the visible short range mark baited, it was time to reverse the entire process, stash the boat waders and lifejacket and squelch back to the car, emptying my pockets of mashed up pellets along the way.

See, I told you it was simple!

To be honest, my original plan of driving there three times a week didn't last long and I usually managed once, just for baiting, and the same ritual on the last day of a session.

When I did fish I stuck to the plan and tried different areas, leaving the baited spots for the first Northerlies.

I knew fish would be feeding on them but I didn't want to spring another trap with a tourist, so I did a horrible wet session in the snags, writing off three sets of clothes in twenty four hours, followed by a return to the South Westerly corner where I managed to spook a good common.

When the wind did eventually come I nearly missed out on my opportunity altogether, in fact there were so many events conspiring to keep me away that I wondered if the Mere really did have magical powers to protect itself with.

An untimely trip to France meant one week missed, although this wasn't too much of a problem, but on my return I saw the first signs of change on the long range weather forecast and decided that an immediate baiting trip was needed.

The normal result of a soaking was guaranteed of course but this time, as I returned dripping and stinking to the motor, I found a new disaster waiting in the wings.

The immobiliser decided that it much preferred immobile to mobile, so much so that it wouldn't even let me in the bloody car at first. After much persuasion I managed to get the door open but the engine was having none of it. I'd had the odd warning sign in the past but I'd managed to bodge my way out of it by a torturous method of turning the ignition on and off and pushing the little dibber on the key until the interior light flashed three times, apparently this re-sets the whole alarm system.

Because this had always worked before I hadn't even thought of getting it checked out; compared to the normal list of peculiarities that each of my previous chariots had had, a tiny thing like this didn't even warrant a second thought.

Two hours later, and with a very perplexed AA man scratching his head with a greasy rubber glove, it was getting a third and fourth thought, the fourth being burning the bloody thing!

In the end I had to be towed to the nearest Vauxhall dealership where I left the car to be fixed over night while I, still caked in mud, bait, and clad in camouflage clothing, had to take a tube to Victoria and then a mainline train back to Three Bridges. Mind you, that was one journey where I didn't have to push, shove or share a seat, I had my own pungent little oasis of space that I wore like a force field all the way back to my bathroom.

The Car ended up being more of a nightmare than I anticipated and it was a full week before I was reacquainted with the old beast, this also meant no baiting up as the missus wasn't up for lending me her motor, I can't imagine why!

I managed to cadge a lift back to the garage, so a big sack of pellet and boilies went with me, bound for a certain pair of tethered corks.

It seemed like an eternity since I'd last waded along the margins with the smelly rucksack on my back, even though it had only been eight days in reality. The water had started to take on a green tinge since my last visit and as I peered over the edge at the usually visible close mark I could only just make out a faint yellow glow where the sand stretched down the side of the hump.

I know how quickly the algae can take hold on the Mere so I rowed back to the shore and tied up another wine cork marker, just to be on the safe side. I had to empty and re-inflate the boat a bit before setting back out into the lake, and I was wringing wet from the holes in the floor, so I vowed to myself to bring the recently restored Butlins boat from home on my next visit.

The weather man told me that the time was near, a big depression in the North was working its way towards Britain and the first of the big winds were on their way.

The Mere also knew what was coming and somehow managed to wave its magic wand and create yet another disaster out of thin air. I was due to fish on Monday morning, the wind was due to start later in the week but I had three nights free so I might just get the start of it. All I had to get through, before Monday, was a dinner party for Sues sisters family and a few friends, it was always going to be a bit messy but I figured I had Sunday to recover.

Unfortunately, things didn't go quite as planned. I somehow managed to knock over a whole table full of wine glasses and bottles and Sue somehow managed to tread bare foot on half a wine glass!

The result was a trip to Crawley hospital, half the night in accident and emergency, eight stitches and no fishing trip.

The poor girl couldn't walk a step and, with two kids and an invalided wife to look after, the Mere would unfortunately have to wait for a while. Obviously, I couldn't moan about it (not out loud anyway) as it was my own stupid fault, although I'm sure the Mere had a hand in it somehow!

The one good thing was that the first wave of Northerlies didn't amount to anything and the next was forecast for the following week.

A week is not long enough to heal a gashed foot, and Sue still couldn't walk properly but I think she was so sick of me pacing up and down to the window, looking wistfully at the sky, that she discharged me early and I was soon hurtling down the M25 with the freshly painted Butlins boat and another sack of bait.

I arrived just before dawn on the Monday morning and the Mere looked fantastic, even though the water had coloured up with the algae, the first breath of a new wind trickled into the little hidden boat park and I could just make out the closest cork rising and falling gently in the breeze.

I unwrapped the old leaky tub and found the pump. After gently floating the pristine, camouflaged and far more robust Butlins boat on the surface, I set to work with the little pump.

Pathetic is a good word to describe the results, although it wasn't the word I chose at the time, as the lovingly prepared and adhered patch wafted slowly to the bottom of the lake and the air all rushed out like a popped balloon, somewhere in the distance a duck started laughing!

I was understandably furious as I knew the old boat was on its last rowlocks, so to speak, but there was no way I was not fishing, not after everything I'd been through to get there.

Resigned to another soaking, I pumped her up anyway and lowered the supplies into the two inches of water that had already covered the floor. Making the most of the time I had, I'd retrieved one rod from its hiding place before setting off, this way I could drop the rig as I passed the close cork and make one less trip before I had all three in position.

The left hand mark was the easiest to hit and, by standing on the edge of the marginal shelf in three feet of water, I could swing the bait around the tree and land by the cork.

The other two were boat only as the sheer nature of the swim and the trees meant that there was physically nowhere to swing the rod.

By the time I had sorted the rods and dragged all my kit from its various hiding places I was knackered, bitten, scratched and soaked right through so I treated myself to one of the two sets of dry clothes and a nice cup of tea.

The wind was even better than I had expected, not only was it from the North but it had a bit of Easterly mixed with it, this swung it around and directed it straight into the Canopy tree swim, absolutely ideal!

I strapped the camera around my neck and battled my way to the top of the tree to take a few aerial shots of the lake, as the view from the upper branches is terrific. The canopy is the tallest tree in the area and, on a clear day, you can see for miles in every direction.

It was one of those perfect days when you just know you are going to catch one, the wind just kept getting stronger and the leaves in the swim were rustling all around me as I sat by the rods, propped in the crook of the small willow that grew from the waters edge. There was no choice of where to sit as the only other spot had been taken over by a colony of wasps and the main entrance into their domain was right in the centre of the bank, directly in front of my brolly.

It would have been a bit hairy sharing such an enclosed space with a thousand potential disasters so I opted to cram in next to the rods, on a tiny spot that was barely big enough for the unhooking mat I was using as a chair. I managed to wriggle into a fairly comfortable position and I spent the evening sitting there with the wind blowing in my face, drinking some wine and listening to tunes on the Ipod.

I was so comfortable that I actually drifted off for a bit but an incoming text woke me back up.

In was the third text that evening, all from different mates and all wishing me luck in the new wind, I obviously wasn't the only one that knew something was in the air. Martin had sent one saying that tonight was Black Mirror night and he knew the moods of the Mere that year, as well as anyone.

Lee Jackson, who knew how long I'd been waiting, for these conditions, sent me one saying 'crack open a bottle of red, the Black Mirrors on its way' although he was a bit late as I'd almost finished the bottle by then.

It wasn't the Black Mirror that was on my mind as I finally climbed into my little camouflaged bed, it was just a crack at one of the better Mere carp, and anyone would do.

I'd been quite unlucky, really, over the years I'd fished there, most of the fish I'd captured had been the smaller originals or tourists, in fact I'd only ever had one thirty plus common, which was not a good average considering the stock.

I was still a bit sick about the loss of the dark common on that fateful night when I ruined two consecutive chances in the south westerly corner, and I was desperate to make amends.

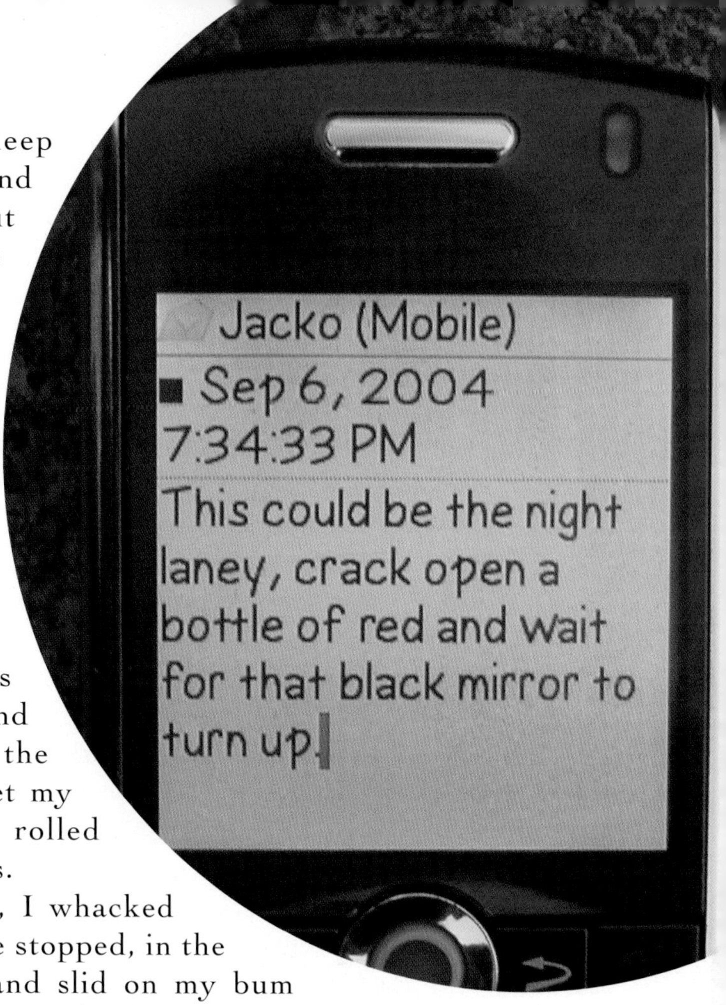

I suppose I got to sleep about midnight in the end and it must have only been about three hours later when the sounder box erupted in a constant wail as I threw myself out from the bed.

It was imperative to put the waders on before attempting the death defying run across the sloping bank under the tree to the rods. I'd practised it in my mind so many times but the sounder box was screaming for my attention and I was panicking badly in the dark, fumbling to try and get my feet in the holes while I rolled around in the dust and leaves.

The solution was simple, I whacked the sounder box and the noise stopped, in the sudden calm I 'booted up' and slid on my bum down to the rods, splashing neatly down in the water between the three rods and the landing net.

The red light of the right hand rod was glowing through the cover netting and I could hear the spool still spinning furiously. I ripped the camo cover from the rods and leant forward as far as I could from the undergrowth before striking as hard as I dared. The rod tip clattered momentarily into the branches above and then it was wrenched back down towards the dark surface of the water.

Any bite at the Mere is a nerve racking experience but all alone, in the dead of night, it takes on an almost scary feel as you battle with the unknown. This was to be no exception as the fish found the sanctuary of a weed bed and everything ground to a stuttering halt.

It was the bait on the close hump that had been picked up which meant that seventy or eighty yards of line must have been out by now, the fish appeared to have run parallel to the bank, past the boat hide and up along the margins somewhere to sulk.

I piled on pressure and the line started to creak as the weed stems slowly gave way, then suddenly, and with a great lunge, he was free from

Jacko (Mobile)

Sep 6, 2004
7:34:33 PM

This could be the night laney, crack open a bottle of red and wait for that black mirror to turn up.

the weed and kiting around into the deep water out in the middle of the lake.

I was praying for an original Mere monster to be on the end and by the way he shot off it certainly didn't feel like another small one.

I remember standing there in the margins, with the wind piling into the branches draped behind me and the rod hooped over, just thinking over and over please don't fall off.

I had an over riding image in my mind of the dark common and the harder the fish fought the more convinced I became that I was in the process of righting a wrong, and it was a battle I was determined to win.

The line was cutting through the waves as the fish headed left, I figured it must be getting perilously close to the middle rod so I locked everything down and gave it as much welly as I could, the result was instant.

Whatever was on the other end exploded on the surface, somewhere out there in the darkness all hell broke loose. I kept the pressure on as hard as I thought the line would take and two more loud eruptions convinced me that this one was worth all the grief that the Mere had ever thrown at me.

It was one of those fights that I look back on and shiver at just how much stick I gave that fish, and how easily I could have over done it and never had known just what was on the end.

Even in the margins, I never gave him an inch and the rod bucked and kicked in protest as the unseen monster tried in vain to wrap me around the marginal snags.

The landing net was always going to be a problem, as the swim wasn't big enough to manoeuvre it out from its hiding place in the bushes and actually get it into the water. Somehow I must have managed it because the next thing I remember is another massive explosion, only this time it was within the magic triangle of the landing net arms, so I scooped the front of the cord up and dropped the rod so I could get a better grip.

Lifting the whole lot out onto the bank wasn't an immediate option as there wasn't a bit of bank big enough, and the mat was still in the bushes.

It was obviously still pitch black, as it usually is at half three in the morning, but my eyes had adjusted to the gloom well enough to allow me to see within the folds of the net.

I was still expecting to see a mid-thirty pound common staring back at me but, when I realised the entire tail section was still sticking out from the top of the net, the penny started to drop.

It was blatantly the wrist of a mirror that the tail was attached to, and obviously a great big one at that. The check for the missing section on the top lobe was just a formality and an amazing realisation started to wash over me like a warm tidal wave.

I'd actually caught him, the infamous Black Mirror; I'd finally, incredibly and unbelievably caught the bloody thing!

I didn't know what to do so I just started laughing, laughing seemed a better option than crying and either could have been possible at that exact moment in time, seven years of coming and going, seven years of being beaten back by the Mere and failing totally in my quest and now, suddenly, it was all over.

Getting back out of the lake with the added weight of over fifty pounds of mirror carp was a nightmare, and finding a spot big enough to lay the mat down on was even harder, but pure adrenalin kicked in as I hoisted him safely ashore, although I'd seen him on the bank once before, it was still a totally awesome experience and I was glad that I'd had the foresight to lay an extra large sack under the bottom of the tree, just in case.

After wrestling him into the folds I tried, like a fool, to hoist him up on the scales; as if I even cared what he weighed! With the sack and the mat I settled for somewhere between fifty two and fifty eight pounds, which is not really that accurate and the ridiculousness of the situation must have suddenly hit me as I gave up trying and set about securing the cord to the tree I'd been using as a sofa back the previous evening, all the time checking and re-checking the knots to ensure that he couldn't escape.

It was about four in the morning by the time I sat back on the bed and tried to take it all in, the enormity of it all was overwhelming and I just had to share the moment with someone so I grabbed the phone and made three quick calls.

Each call I let ring for three rings and then hung up again, finally putting the phone on the bed next to me while I awaited the response.

Two seconds later the phone rang and Keith was there, knowing full well who and why he'd been dragged out of bed, he hadn't even checked the number! Its fantastic to have mates who really understand the moment like that and we whooped and hollered together for a while before I hung up to accept the next call from Chilly, and then the same again from Martin. The strange thing was they had all been expecting it and, in a strange sort of way, I suppose that I had as well.

After the last call I dug around in the leaves next to the bed and found the Ipod laying where it had dropped the previous night, as I'd fallen asleep to Pink Floyd, but what tune could fit the bill now?

After a quick scan I decided on Bob Dylan's 'It's All Over Now Baby Blue' followed by some U2 at full volume, as I stood in the margins next to my prize like a modern day conquistador!

373

Chilly had promised to be down at first light but half an hour later, as I sat back on my Bedchair brewing a tea, his head popped around the side of the brolly, unable to sleep with excitement he had come straight over as soon as we'd got off the phone.

Somehow he'd picked up a stray along the way, a young lad who had ventured down to the Mere for his very first look.

Chilly reckoned he'd taken pity on him and tagged him along for a look at the great beast, but I reckon it was more down to the fact that the poor fool had turned up in shorts.

I mean, walking around the place in a suit of armour would be dangerous enough but even those mad Japanese endurance shows wouldn't have gone as far as the Mere with bare legs, the midges must have thought that it was a national festival!.

Martin wasn't far behind Chilly, either, and he'd brought a mate as well, only this one was a bit better dressed and had a video camera slung about his neck.

We all crammed into the little swim under the canopy tree, sipping tea and waiting for the dim blanket of dawn to be fully pulled back across the sky. Suddenly, Chilly let out a yelp of pain and started hopping about like a man possessed and it was about that exact moment that I remembered the wasps, in all the excitement I'd clean forgotten to mention them!

Chilly had actually been standing with one foot in the front door of hell and his leg was encased in a yellow and black striped sock of very angry wasps.

I think he suffered a good half a dozen stings before he shook them all off and the air suddenly filled with the little buggers. Talk about mayhem, we all fell over each other in a mad panic to be first out of the swim. There were only five of us present but we made enough noise for ten times that number as we all shrieked and swatted like a bunch of girl guides whose picnic had just been swarmed by bees!

Now picture the scene...now think about a forest of brambles, dog rose and stinging nettles, add a thousand enraged wasps...now imagine wearing shorts!

It took at least an hour before the swim returned to normal and even then the odd marauder would still buzz in like a kamikaze pilot, delivering a well aimed sting, luckily for the rest of us there was an obvious target.

I zipped the fish up in a big padded mat to keep him safe on his journey up through the bushes and nettles to the back of the swim, which was the only spot we could find with some decent light for the photos.

The ground there was covered in high nettle beds but, luckily I had a big piece of tarpaulin, about ten feet square, which I threw over the

nettles and we all jumped up and down on it to flatten a 'safe area' to take the pictures and video.

It's rare at the Mere to find any space big enough to fit five blokes and over fifty pound of fish into, but somehow we managed.

If it wasn't for the video footage I don't suppose I'd ever be able to recall the events of the following half hour, but the memories are there on celluloid for eternity. The sack cord was the first stumbling block as there must have been about twenty knots in the short length around the top of the sack, it took me forever to actually get the neck open and peer inside. I must have been so paranoid about the fish getting away again that I'd just tied knot after knot after knot to make extra sure he was staying attached to the tree.

The fish was the star of the show and the air turned blue with descriptive nouns as soon as I peeled back the black mesh of the sack and exposed the majesty that lay within.

Later on when Chilly heard the video soundtrack he apologised profusely "That's another bloody video I've ruined" he said "I can't help it, I just swear a lot when I get excited"!

I think we were all totally blown away to be fair and none of really knew what to say so we clicked away, smiled and joked and, of course, swore a lot. Holding up a carp of that size for any length of time would normally be bloody hard work but I was so full of adrenalin that I hardly noticed it at all, I was in my element.

I've caught the odd big carp in my time, of that I'm sure there is no doubt but never, not even once, has anything held a candle even close to the glow that radiated from that fish, at that time, in such a hostile yet magical place.

The strange reality is that I don't imagine that anything ever will again.

I'd dreamt about it for years and, when I'd felt brave enough, I'd day dreamed about it as well, tempting fate by imagining myself all alone in the dark battling it out with such an incredible fish. If I think back to the time

I saw him off the snags point in the sun, magnified over the shallow gravel and looking totally unattainable, it makes me wonder how the hell I ever landed him. All those times I'd been so close, so very, very close that I'd watched his eyes move over my bait, watched him ignore the little snail I'd dangled through the weed to try and tempt him, watched him watching me and known that he was thinking "you'll have to try harder than that sunshine", and now I had. Now I had eventually closed that final gap and the uncatchable had been caught, the myth a reality, the dream laid before me on the wet mat in the sun, beaten but still looking proud and strong.

Between us we manhandled him up onto the scales, as my own attempt a few hours earlier had been pathetic and totally ineffective. I didn't really care what he weighed and although a lot of people say that after a momentous capture, I really mean it, he was the Black Mirror and that was always going to be good enough for me.

We settled on a weight of fifty three pounds and a few ounces in the end, most of it made up of muscle and sinew coated in deep red and black flesh. A truly awesome beast.

I carefully zipped him back up in the mat and, with the help of everyone present, passed him back down the treacherous slope to the waters edge. Holding him there in the margins as he regained his composure was an amazing moment, he grew stronger and stronger until, with a little kiss on the head I finally released him and, with a flick of the tail he was gone.

Looking back at the video I cannot believe that I didn't stay at the Mere another night as I was almost guaranteed to catch something in those conditions, after all, the elusive monster common couldn't have been far away, but something made me leave.

Maybe it was the fact that four able bodied lads had offered to help me de-robe the Mere of year's worth of stashed tackle and finally draw a line under the whole saga.

Maybe it was the romantic notion that the final episode had to involve the ultimate prize, and anything less would be an anti-climax that would dint the memory.

Maybe it was the pub!

Whatever the reason, I loaded them all up like pack horses in front of me and I trudged through the bushes, pushed through the brambles, endured the stings of the nettles for the very last time.

It was a walk that I'd started to believe I'd never actually make, I had a grin like a drunken Cheshire cat and my feet were so light of step that I barely broke a blade of grass, it was over, I was going home